LEARNING ITALIAN
in ITALY

To complement this book Simon and Louise Read have created
their own website www.learningitalianinitaly.org.

It will provide you with updated information and also give you
the chance to give feedback on the book and comments about
your own experiences of your chosen school.

Thank you for buying one of our books. We hope you'll enjoy it and that you'll have as good a time Learning Italian in Italy as our authors have done.

We always try to ensure our books are up to date, but contact details seem to change so quickly that it can be very hard to keep up with them. If you do have any problems contacting any of the organisations listed in the book please get in touch, and either we or the authors will do what we can to help. And if you do find correct contact details that differ from those in the book, please let us know so that we can put it right when we reprint.

Please do also give us your feedback so we can go on making books that you want to read. If there's anything you particularly liked about this book – or you have suggestions about how it could be improved in the future – email us on info@howtobooks.co.uk

Good luck with Learning Italian.

The Publishers
www.howtobooks.co.uk

Please send for a free copy of the latest catalogue:

How To Books
3 Newtec Place, Magdalen Road,
Oxford OX4 1RE, United Kingdom
email: info@howtobooks.co.uk
http://www.howtobooks.co.uk

LEARNING ITALIAN *in* ITALY

LOUISE & SIMON READ

howtobooks

Published by How To Books Ltd,
3 Newtec Place, Magdalen Road,
Oxford OX4 1RE. United Kingdom.
Tel: (01865) 793806. Fax: (01865) 248780
Email: info@howtobooks.co.uk

First edition 2004

British Library Cataloguing in Publication Data.
A catalogue record for this book is available from the British Library

Illustrations by Nickie Averill

Produced for How To Books by Deer Park Productions, Tavistock
Typeset and design by Pantek Arts Ltd, Maidstone, Kent
Cover design by Baseline Arts Ltd., Oxford
Backcover photograph, Gian-Paul Tracey
Printed and bound by Bell & Bain Ltd, Glasgow

NOTE: The material contained in this book is set out in good faith for general
guidance and no liability can be accepted for loss or expense incurred as a result
of relying in particular circumstances on statements made in this book. Laws and
regulations are complex and liable to change, and readers should check the current
positions with the relevant authorities before making personal arrangements.

Contents

Preface

We had the idea to go to Italy when working as junior doctors in London. We were spending long nights on-call in dimly lit wards and eating hospital food in airless canteens. It was enough to drive anyone *pazzo*. We started to scheme our escape. We spoke to our Italian friends and patients about Italy, we cooked Italian food, we dreamt of olive trees, we saved and we tweaked our jobs. An Italian friend recommended Perugia and seemingly quite suddenly, we left.

While many were wondering what had happened, we were speeding off in our Mini; first through France to Liguria and then to live in Perugia, Umbria. We rented a tiny *monolocale* in the heart of the old town and signed up at the *Università per Stranieri*. In the morning we learnt Italian with views of the green Umbrian hills and Assisi. In the afternoons we sipped *espressi* on the *Corso Vanucci*, pondered over our *compiti* and went home to cook.

We spent a year in search of the best language school for this book. During our research we often found that the quality of the brochure and Internet sites bore no relation to the quality of the schools.

Learning Italian at home had been boring and difficult. In Italy it was easy and exciting. Our six-month trip turned into a year. We drove 18,000 miles, visited language schools in every region and fell head over heels in love with the country, people, food and language. It was the best year of our lives.

Louise and Simon Read

Acknowledgements

Thank you to Silvana Ferrini, the *bravissima* teacher from the *Università per Stranieri* in Perugia for help with writing and correcting the Italian for this book, for making Italian lessons fun, for her friendship and our evenings of cooking together in our fourteenth century *monolocale*.

Thank you to Franco and Franziska Passalacqua for their friendship and generosity, dinners by *il brace*, pizza lessons with views of Assisi, the first *nouvello* olive oil and the painting of the Umbrian trees in autumn.

Thank you to everyone who helped and gave advice, Susan Armstrong, Edward du Cann, Andrea and Patrick Cooke, Joe and Scott Drummond, Peter Paice, Norma and Peter Read and Sophie Scott.

Finally, thank you to Nikki Read and Giles Lewis at How To Books for their help and enthusiasm.

Disclaimer

The authors have visited all the schools listed and meticulously checked all the information in the text but accept no responsibility for any loss, injury or inconvenience sustained by anyone using this book. All prices are correct at the time of going to press. However these are subject to change so we advise you to contact the school of your choice to confirm the fees.

Introduction
Introduzione

This book is a fun, comprehensive guide to all aspects of learning Italian in an Italian language school or university. It is essential reading for anyone planning or daydreaming about speaking Italian. This includes those wanting weekend breaks or short holidays as well as gap year students and professionals wanting longer courses with qualifications. We have visited schools all over Italy to find the best. Learning Italian does not have to be expensive, courses start at €105 per month and the cost of living is cheaper in Italy. Speaking another language will enhance your CV and can provide extra qualifications.

The guide is packed with practical information on planning and organising your own trip. It gives clear advice about developing the initial idea and then choosing the right course in the right area of Italy. There is detailed information on budgeting, arranging accommodation, enrolling and settling into Italian life. The guide makes this kind of trip a realistic prospect for everyone and ensures the reader gets excellent value for money.

Chapters 1 to 3 cover the practical aspects of organising and planning a trip. The rest of the book includes chapters on living and studying in the university towns and the private language schools all over Italy. Every area of Italy has been given a summary paragraph highlighting the exceptional features of that area. Each university chapter includes an 'insider's guide' to all aspects of living and studying in the town. We have devised a unique city walk for each of the towns to quickly acquaint you with the essential amenities, the best food shops, markets, cafés, restaurants and unusual sights. Throughout the book we have included useful colloquial Italian phrases.

Myths about studying a language abroad

I'm hopeless at languages!
In Italy it is easy. You will be speaking Italian molto presto.

I'm too old!
Our class ranged from 18–80.

It will be too expensive.
One of the best courses in Italy costs just €233 per month and the cost of living is less than in the UK.

I can't take time off work or my career will be ruined.
Courses range from a weekend to a year and if two doctors can do it, so can you.

I would rather lie on a beach/play golf/cook/dive/paint/ski/just relax.
Why not do both? We have listed schools that combine all of these.

I can't go on my own!
You will be surrounded by people of all ages and backgrounds in the same position.

I need a car.
Italy has one of the cheapest train and bus networks in Europe.

Where is Italian spoken?
Dove è parlata la lingua italiana?

Over 120 million people worldwide, half of whom live outside Italy, speak Italian. This includes Switzerland, the Alps, the Côte d'Azur and communities in America, Slovenia, Croatia, Brazil, Argentina and Somalia. It is also the official language of good coffee bars the world over.

Who is learning Italian?
Chi impara l'Italiano?

The Italian language is having a boom. Between 1995 and 2000 the number of people learning Italian rose by almost 40%. In the same period the number of courses rose by 60% (Tullio de Mauro et al, *Università La*

Sapienza, Roma, 2000). Italian is currently one of the most studied foreign languages in Eastern Europe. In the Ukraine it is at the top of the list, in Hungry it is second only to English and in Russia it is equal in popularity with French and German.

It is not surprising the numbers are escalating. According to UNESCO Italy contains 50% of the world's art treasures. It is the birthplace of opera, Slow Food and the Fiat 500. In the last 50 years the country has become one of the world's major industrial powers, setting the standard for family based industry, fashion and design.

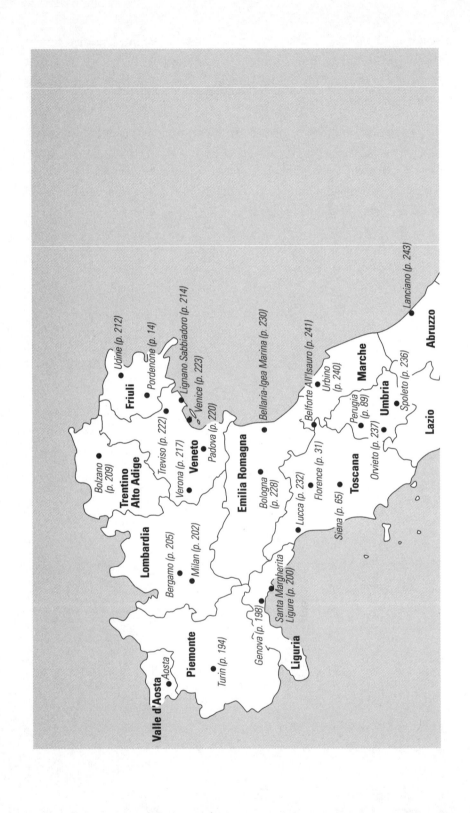

Udine (p. 212)
Pordenone (p. 14)
Lignano Sabbiadoro (p. 214)
Friuli
Venice (p. 223)
Padova (p. 220)
Treviso (p. 222)
Verona (p. 217)
Veneto
Bolzano (p. 209)
Trentino Alto Adige
Bellaria-Igea Marina (p. 230)
Belforte All'Isauro (p. 241)
Lanciano (p. 243)
Abruzzo
Marche
Urbino (p. 240)
Perugia (p. 89)
Umbria
Spoleto (p. 236)
Lazio
Florence (p. 31)
Toscana
Orvieto (p. 237)
Emilia Romagna
Bologna (p. 228)
Lucca (p. 232)
Siena (p. 65)
Lombardia
Bergamo (p. 205)
Milan (p. 202)
Santa Margherita Ligure (p. 200)
Genova (p. 198)
Liguria
Piemonte
Turin (p. 194)
Valle d'Aosta
Aosta

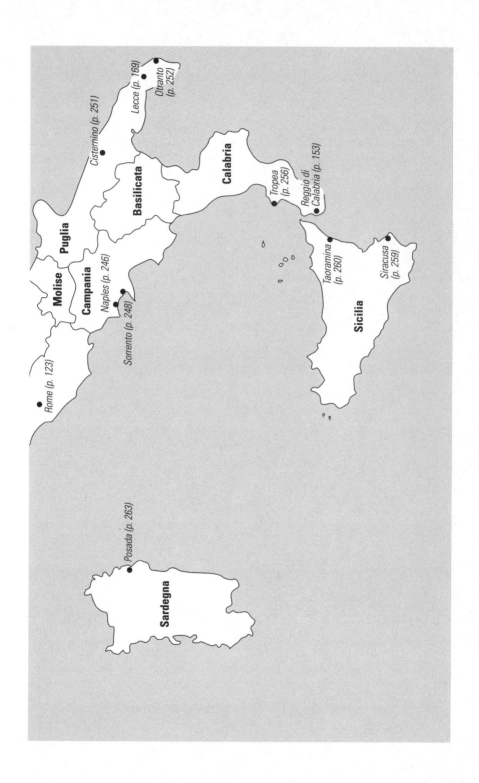

Lecce (p. 169)

Otranto (p. 252)

Cisternino (p. 251)

Basilicata

Puglia

Molise

Campania

Naples (p. 246)

Sorrento (p. 248)

Rome (p. 123)

Calabria

Tropea (p. 256)

Reggio di Calabria (p. 153)

Taormina (p. 260)

Siracusa (p. 259)

Sicilia

Posada (p. 263)

Sardegna

Choosing Your Course

Scegliendo il Tuo Corso

There are Italian language courses to suit everyone: short, long, intensive, cheap, by the beach, up a mountain, in a village or on a lake. There are courses for children and even courses combined with diving, golf, sailing, skiing or cooking. There are over 200 schools. We have done all of the hard work by visiting them and selecting the best for this book.

Universities for Foreigners and the
private language schools

The main distinction in language school is between the **Universities for Foreigners** (*Università per Stranieri*) and the **private language schools**. Throughout the year Universities for Foreigners offer high quality, good value courses at all levels of Italian. The length of the courses ranges from one to three months or longer but it is possible to attend for shorter periods. There are Universities for Foreigners in Perugia, Siena, Florence, Lecce and Reggio di Calabria. If you are considering a course of a month or more then one of these universities should be at the top of your list regardless of your age or educational background. Perugia is our favourite and has the most flexible range of courses starting every month of the year. The number of students per class can be high particularly in Perugia, Florence and Siena.

We have included chapters for each of these university towns (Chapters 4–9). These include everything you need to know about studying and *living* there. There are backgrounds to the towns, city highlights and full write-ups of the universities and the private language schools. Each chapter has a unique 'city walk' which has been designed to quickly orientate you to the best amenities, bars, shops, sights and other top tips.

In addition to the *Università per Stranieri* many other Italian universities run intensive summer courses in Italian language and culture. These are usually an all-inclusive package of lessons, accommodation and excursions. There is a list of these university courses on page 11.

The **private language schools** offer a more personal and supportive service than the universities. They are often small local businesses and it is in their interests to please their customers. They run flexible courses ranging from a weekend to several months for all levels of Italian. They are, however, much more expensive. If, however, you are considering a short course of a week or two then a private language school is the best bet. We have visited language schools all over Italy and included only the best. The private language schools are listed by area in Chapter 10, along with regional summaries and highlights. Throughout the book there are summary tables to make it easy to compare prices and facilities of the schools. The private language schools tend to overcharge for their accommodation, even if they claim to run a 'free' service. Booked locally accommodation will cost around half that booked through a private school (see page 24). Most of the private language schools charge an enrolment fee (*iscrizione*) in addition to the cost of the course. This is a one-off payment ranging from €20 to €100.

The *Società Dante Alighieri* is halfway between a private language school and a university. It is the oldest Italian association to teach Italian to foreigners. It was founded in 1889 following the initiative of some of the great cultural figures of the time. There are 500 committees worldwide and language schools throughout Italy. The schools have a similar atmosphere to the private language schools but are cheaper. They sometimes, however have classes of 20 or more students. The schools are usually housed in beautiful, historic buildings. We have included the schools in Florence (page 34), Siena (page 74), Rome (page 132), Bologna (page 229) and Milan (page 202). The schools award the PLIDA diploma (Progetto Lingua Italiana Dante Alighieri), which is an internationally recognised qualification (see page 16). There are many schools in Italy using the *Dante Alighieri* name but only the *Società Dante Alighieri* schools are part of this society.

In summary

The private language schools are good for short holiday courses but nothing beats the value and quality of teaching in the universities for courses of a month or more. For the more adventurous person, there are many regions still relatively unknown to tourists such as Lecce in Puglia and Reggio in Calabria.

For those who do not know Italy, begin by looking at the regional summaries and highlights in Chapter 10 along with the map at the front of the book. Then decide whether you are interested in going to one of the excellent university courses for a summer course or longer period or to one of our hand-picked private language schools. Decide on the type of location: small and intimate, larger and more professional, big or small town, near the sea or near the mountains, food and wine regions or combined with other interests. The following lists may help.

Categories of Language Schools

The following language schools have special features for different requirements. These include language schools for children, weekend courses, schools with access for everyone, the cheapest individual lessons, schools offering evening classes, schools with spectacular locations, courses combined with other interests, Italian for professional use and free courses.

Language by the beach (or on the coast)

▶ A Door to Italy in Genova (Liguria) (page 199): on the coast

▶ Athena School in Lanciano (Abbruzzo) (page 243)

▶ Babilonia in Taormina (Sicily) (page 261): on the coast

▶ Caffè Italiano Club in Tropea (page 256)

▶ Centro Italiano in Naples (page 247)

▶ Demischool near Rimini (Emilia-Romagna) (page 230):

▶ Istituto Venezia in Venice (page 223)

▶ Linguaviva Summer School for Juniors in Lignano, near Venice (page 214)

▶ Mediterranean Centre for Arts and Sciences in Siracusa (page 259)

▶ Scuola Porta d'Oriente in Otranto (page 253)

▶ Sun Studies in Posada (Sardinia) (page 263)

▶ University of Genova's course in Santa Margherita Ligure (page 199): one of the best!

▶ University for Foreigners in Reggio di Calabria (page 154).

Language on a budget

▶ Arco di Dusco in Rome (Lazio) (page 126)

▶ Demischool near Rimini (Emilia-Romagna) (page 230)

▶ Il Globo in Florence (Tuscany) (page 42)

▶ Società Dante Alighieri in Rome (Lazio) (page 132), Siena (Tuscany) (page 74), Florence (Tuscany) (page 43), Milan (Lombardia) (page 202) and Bolgna (Emilia-Romagna) (page 229)

▶ University for Foreigners in Perugia (Umbria) (page 91)

▶ University for Foreigners in Reggio di Calabria (Calabria) (page 154).

Cheapest individual lessons *Le lezioni più economiche*

▶ ABC in Florence (Tuscany) from €15 per hour (page 37)

▶ ABC in Perugia (Umbria) one or two people from €11 per person (page 99)

▶ Ardo di Drusco in Rome (Lazio) from €18 per hour (page 126)

▶ CSH Hodegitria in Cisternino (Puglia) from €13 (page 252)

▶ Centro 'Giacomo Leopardi' in Belforte all'Isauro (Marche) (page 241)

▶ Demischool near Rimini (Emilia-Romagna) from €16 per hour (page 230)

▶ Instituto Europeo in Spoletto (Umbria) from €12 per hour (page 236).

Schools for children *Scuole di lingua per bambini*

Many of the private language schools will offer individual lessons for children on request. The following schools have specific courses for children.

▶ Accademia Italiana in Florence (Tuscany): courses are open to children (page 38)

▶ Athena in Lanciano (Abruzzo): courses for children and families on request (page 243)

▶ Centro Linguistico Italiano Dante Alighieri (CLIDA) in Florence (Tuscany): for children over the age of 14 (page 41)

▶ Cultura Italiana in Bologna (Emilia-Romagna): childcare facilities with Italian children (page 228)

▶ Demischool near Rimini (Emilia-Romagna): courses for children of all ages (page 230)

▶ Linguaviva Summer School for juniors in Lignano (near Venice): residential summer courses for 10–16 year olds (page 214)

▶ Marco Polo in Treviso (Veneto): residential summer course for 14–18 and 6–13 year olds in July (page 222)

▶ Scuola Porta D'Oriente in Otranto (Puglia): language courses for children (page 253)

▶ Scuola Dí Italiano in Lecce (Puglia): courses for children and childcare facilities (page 175). The tennis club in Lecce also has lessons for children.

▶ Società Dante Alighieri in Florence (Tuscany) has courses for children over 6 whose parents are attending the school (page 43).

Language courses combined with other interests

▶ Language and cinema: Scuola Porta d'Oriente (page 253)

▶ Language and cooking: most of the private schools offer regional cookery lessons. These have dedicated cooking courses:

– Babilonia in Taormina (Sicily) (page 261)

– Centro Italiano in Naples (Campania) (page 247)

– Sun Studies in Posada (Sardinia) (page 263)

▶ Language and diving/sailing: Sun Studies in Posada (Sardinia) (page 263)

▶ Language and fashion design:

– Accademia Italiana in Florence (Tuscany) (page 38)

– Scuola Porta d' Oriente (page 253)

▶ Language and golf: Babilonia, Sicily (page 261)

▶ Language and jewellery: ABC school in Florence (Tuscany) (page 37)

▶ Language and lace-making: Istituto Venezia (page 223)

▶ Language and mask-making: Istituto Venezia (page 223)

▶ Language on Capri or Ischia: Centro Italiano (Campania) (page 247)

▶ Language and opera: British Institute in Florence (Tuscany) (page 39), Verona (Veneto) (page 218), Spoleto (Umbria) (page 236), or during the excellent opera seasons in Lecce (Puglia) (page 169), Naples (Campania) (page 246) and Bologna (Emilia-Romagna) (page 228).

▶ Language and practical art classes:

– British Institute in Florence (Tuscany) (page 39)

– Istituto Venezia (page 223)

▶ Language and skiing: Turin University (Piemonte) (page 194) and Linguaviva (page 214)

▶ Language and theatre: Scuola Porta d'Oriente (page 253)

▶ Language and walking around the sites of Rome: ItaliaIdea (page 130).

Evening courses *Corsi serali*

▶ A Door to Italy in Genova (Liguria) (page 199)

▶ Arco di Drusco in Rome (Lazio) (page 126)

▶ British Institute in Florence (Tuscany) (page 39)

▶ Ciao Italia in Rome (Lazio) (page 128)

▶ Cultura Italiana in Bologna (Emilia-Romagna) (page 228)

▶ International House in Milan (Lombardia) (page 203)

▶ Istituto Linguistico Europeo in Spoleto (Umbria) (page 236)

▶ ItaliaIdea in Rome (Lazio) (page 130)

▶ Società Dante Alighieri in Rome (Lazio) (page 132).

Free courses *Corsi gratis*

▶ Centro Caritas, S. Luigi Gonzaga, Scuola per Stranieri in Lecce (Puglia) (page 176)

▶ Scuola Media Statale Aosta in Verona (Veneto) (page 218) (September only).

Language laboratories

The *laboratorio linguistico* (language laboratory) is a good way of supplementing learning with practical computer based exercises. These include listening to conversations and music as well as grammar. The answers are replayed and compared with the correct response, which helps to improve pronunciation as well as understanding. Most of the Universities for Foreigners and a few private language schools have this facility. These schools have very good *laboratorios*:

▶ Eurocentre in Florence (Tuscany) (page 41)

▶ Prolingua in Rome (Lazio) (page 126)

▶ University of Bergamo (Lombardia) (page 205)

▶ University for Foreigners in Siena (Tuscany) (page 68)

▶ University of Venice (Veneto) (page 225).

Over 50s Club

▶ Lingua Si in Orvieto (Umbria) (page 237)

▶ Società Dante Alighieri in Siena (Tuscany) (page 74)

▶ Torre di Babele in Rome Lazio (page 134).

Italian for professional use

Perugia and Siena Universities for Foreigners offer intensive one-month courses in August each year in Italian for medicine and natural sciences, architecture and history of art, law, economics and business. All of the schools listed can arrange individual lessons focusing on Italian for business use. The following schools have special courses.

▶ A door to Italy in Genova (Liguria) (page 199)

▶ Centro Italiano in Naples (Campania) (page 247)

▶ DILIT International House in Rome (Lazio) (page 129)

▶ Il Globo in Florence (Tuscany) (page 42)

▶ Italia Idea in Rome (Lazio) (page 130)

▶ LinguaIt in Verona (Veneto) (page 217)

▶ Lingua Sì in Orvieto (Umbria) (page 237)

▶ Saena Iulia Scuola in Siena (Tuscany) (page 75)

▶ University of Bergamo (Lombardia) (page 205)

▶ University for Foreigners Lecce (Puglia) (page 170)

▶ University for Foreigners Perugia (Umbria) (page 91)

▶ University for Foreigners Siena (Tuscany) (page 68).

Part-time courses

▶ Alpha Beta in Bolzano (Trentino-Alto Adige) (page 210)

▶ Centro Italiano in Naples (Campania) (page 247)

▶ Ciao Italia in Rome (Lazio) (page 128)

▶ Istituto Linguistico Europeo Turin (page 197)

▶ Società Dante Alighieri in Bologna (Emilia-Romagna) (page 229)

▶ University of Bergamo (Lombardia) (page 205)

▶ University of Udine (Friuli-Venezia Giulia) (page 212)

▶ University of Venice (Veneto) (page 225).

Schools with spectacular locations *Posizioni spettacolari*

We have selected our favourites for people who want a language school with flare, such as location of the school, design of the building or view from its classrooms.

▶ Accademia Italiana in Florence: a 'penthouse suite' classroom over-looking Piazza de'Pitti (page 38)

▶ Babilonia language school in Sicily: a five-star terrace overlooking Mount Etna (page 261)

▶ Italia Idea in Rome: has a design award for its modern language school near the Spanish steps (page 130)

▶ University of Florence course has large historic villa on a Florentine hill-side overlooking the city (page 34)

▶ University of Genova's Summer Course in Santa Margherita Ligure: a spectacular hillside villa on the dramatic Riviera di Levante (page 199)

▶ University of Milan's Summer Course on Lake Garda: a splendid nineteenth century Palazzo on the shores of Lake Garda (page 207)

▶ Univeristy at Perugia: views across the Vale of Umbria to Assisi and Monte Subasio (page 91).

Schools for people with visual impairment

▶ Demischool near Rimini (Emilia-Romagna) teaches Italian in brail (page 230).

Schools with wheelchair access *Le scuole per i personi con disabilità*

Italy is behind Britain with wheelchair access. Schools that said they had access often did not when we checked. Fortunately there are some excellent language schools and universities with good access for everyone. Students should, however, phone the schools listed to check on individual requirements.

▶ Accademia Italiana in Florence has facilities for wheelchair users and spacious classrooms (page 38).

▶ Prolingua in Rome has a chair lift and bathroom for wheelchair users (page 126).

▶ University for Foreigners in Lecce has good access and the town is flat with ramped pavements (page 170).

▶ University for Foreigners in Siena has wheelchair access and facilities in the *Sede Didattica at Piazzetta Grassi* (the location of classes, the *laboratorio linguistico* and *aula multimediale*) (page 68).

▶ University of Verona summer course has wheelchair access (as does the Roman Arena for the Opera Festival) (page 219).

Weekend courses *Corsi nei fine settimana*

▶ ABC Italiano in Florence offers intensive weekend courses (page 37)

▶ ABC in Perugia can organise weekend courses on request. They require a minimum of two people and cost €11 an hour (page 99)

▶ Ciao Italia in Rome offers weekend courses in May, September and October in Tuscany (page 128)

▶ LinguaIt in Verona (page 217)

▶ Scuola D´ Italiano in Lecce (page 175).

University summer courses *Corsi estivi universitari*

A number of Italian universities offer summer Italian language and culture courses, which are open to all regardless of educational background. These courses are good value packages including accommodation, meals and guided visits. Some of the universities listed also offer non-intensive courses at other times of the year.

▶ University for Foreigners in Perugia (Umbria) page 91)

▶ University for Foreigners in Reggio di Calabria (Calabria) page 154

▶ University for Foreigners in Siena (Tuscany) page 68

▶ University of Bergamo (Lombardy) page 205

▶ University of Florence (Tuscany) page 34

▶ University of Genoa (Liguria) page 199

▶ University of Lecce (Puglia) page 170

▶ University of Milan at Lake Garda (Lombardy) page 207

▶ University of Turin (Piedmont) page 194

▶ University of Udine (Friuli-Venezia-Giulia) page 212

▶ University of Urbino (Marche) page 240

▶ University of Venice (Veneto) page 225

▶ University of Verona (Veneto) page 219

Summary table of the Universities for Foreigners
Università per Stranieri

University	Perugia	Florence	Siena	Lecce	Reggio
Hours per month, standard course	80	48	60	64	80
Hours per month, intensive course	108	–	75	80	80 (teaching more rapid)
Cost per month, standard course	€233	€207	€300	€400	€103+€52 enrolment
Cost per month, intensive course	€310	–	€550	€650 or €400 without extracurricular activities	€103+€52 enrolment fee
Exams, cost and dates	CELI €78 June Nov.	End of course exam €6	CILS €60–€150 June Dec.	Lecce University exam currently in development	PLIDA May Nov.
Region	Umbria	Tuscany	Tuscany	Puglia	Calabria
Population	158,000	374,500	54,3000	97,500	187,000
Students	6,000	2,000	2,000	150	1,000
Founded	1921	1915	1920	1998	1984
Who can enrol?	Anyone over 16 years old	Must be eligible for University	Anyone for one month course	Anyone over 18 years old	Anyone over 16 years old
Where in the town or city	Centre	20 min bus ride from centre	Centre	Just outside city walls	Centre

Scholarships *Borse di studio*

There are a large number of scholarships that are well worth applying for. These cover part or all of the tuition fees and sometimes board and lodging. Applicants are judged on motivation, enthusiasm and commitment to putting the language skills to good use.

Availability of scholarships changes each year. Ask at the school, well in advance of the proposed course, for the latest information. Most language schools require a letter of support from a recognised institution or language teacher in the student's home country. Asking your own language teacher is the easiest way of applying for a scholarship. The applications usually require a short Italian CV, a covering letter and the letter of support.

Some schools insist that students apply for scholarships through the Italian Cultural Institutes. The Italian Cultural Institutes vary enormously in the quality of information provided about scholarships and in the fairness with which they are distributed. The Italian Cultural Institute of Scotland and Northern Ireland (based in Edinburgh), for example, offers the scholarships that are given to anyone living in Scotland or Northern Ireland. The Italian Cultural Institute of England (based in London), in contrast, only awards these scholarships to their own students! You may be better off asking elsewhere. We have included details about scholarships in each of the language school entries and some useful addresses below.

Italian Cultural Institute (Scotland and Northern Ireland)
82 Nicolson Street
Edinburgh EH8 9EW
Tel: (0131) 668 2232
Open Monday to Friday 09.00–13.00 and 14.00–17.00
Email info@italcult.org.uk Website www.italcult.org.uk

Italian Cultural Institute (England)
39 Belgrave Square
London SW1X 8NX
Tel: (0207) 235 1461
Open Monday to Friday 10.00–17.00
Email ici@italcultur.org.uk Website www.italcultur.org.uk

IRSE: Istituto Regionale di Studi Europei del Friuli Venezia Giulia

Via Concordia 7, I 33170 Pordenone

Tel: (0434) 365326/ 365387 Fax (0434) 364584

Email irse@culturacdspn.it

Website www.culturacdspn.it/corso_italiano03/corso_eng03.html

Open to 22–35 year olds with at least an intermediate level of Italian.

The IRSE (Regional Institute of European Studies in Friuli-Venezia-Giulia) runs an intensive three-week summer course in Italian language, culture and current affairs. This is open to young people who want to deepen their understanding of Italian and in particular the Friuli-Venezia-Giulia region for their future or current work, for example in tourism, trade, teaching, medicine, or youth exchange schemes. The scholarship covers all course fees (>100 hours), board and lodging, outings and tours. The course takes place in late August/September. Applications must be made several months in advance.

Professor John Winter

Association of the Friends of the University for Foreigners of Perugia

12B Elsee Road

Rugby

Warwickshire CV21 3BA

Tel: (01788) 561690

Open to every UK citizen, all levels of Italian. Professor Winter co-ordinates scholarship applications with the University for Foreigners in Perugia (Umbria). There is a scholarship of €620 to cover the cost of a one-month course and expenses. He also has a number of scholarships with private language schools. Apply in writing stating your education background and why you would like to learn Italian.

Professor E. O'Ceallachain

Department of Italian

University of Glasgow

Bute Gardens

Glasgow G12 8QQ

Tel: (0141) 3304135

Two scholarships are given each year to University of Glasgow students studying Italian. One scholarship for €620 is available for a month course at the University for Foreigners in Perugia and the other is for an intensive one-month course at the University of Siena for €500.

Qualifications *Qualificazione*

Qualifications range from certificates of attendance to diplomas, A-levels or degrees. Most of the private schools and universities can help you work towards one of the recognised diplomas and all give a certificate of attendance. The best known diplomas are listed below. These are official qualifications that denote the degree of linguistic competency of Italian as a foreign language and are internationally recognised.

CELI Certificato di Conoscenza della Lingua Italiana
Certificate of Knowledge of the Italian Language
Università per Stranieri di Perugia
Student Advisory Office
Tel: (075) 5746211
Email relstu@unistrapg.it Website www.unistrapg.it
This diploma is awarded by Perugia's University for Foreigners (page 91). There are five levels, the first corresponding to very basic Italian. Exams are held in June and November in Perugia and other authorised centres and cost €78. Perugia also awards the CIC Certificate of Knowledge of Italian for Business (intermediate and advanced), held once a year in June in authorised centres throughout Italy and abroad.

CILS (Certificato Italiano Lingua Seconda)
Certification of Italian as a Foreign Language
Università per Stranieri di Siena
Centro Certificazione CILS
Via Sallustio Bandini 35, Siena 53100
Tel: (0577) 240467
Email: cils@unistrasi.it Website www.unistrasi.it
This diploma is awarded by the University for Foreigners in Siena. There are four levels and two 'pre-CILS' levels for very basic Italian. The exam tests listening and reading comprehension as well as written and spoken Italian. They are held in December and June each year in Siena and other authorised centres and cost €60–€150.

IT and ele.IT
Certificato di ITaliano Come Lingua Straniera (L2)
Dipartimento di Linguistica dell'Università Roma Tre

Via Ostiense 236, third floor, 00146 Rome

Email certifL2@uniroma3.it

Website www.uniroma3.it (only in Italian): click on *'dipartimenti'* then *'linguistica'* then on the *'sito Web'* and finally on *'Italiano L2'*!

Tel: (06) 54577310 or (06) 54577343 Fax: (06) 54577344

These diplomas are awarded by the University of Rome Tre. The IT exam is for students with a very good level of Italian, equivalent to C2 on the Common European Framework (see below) and costs €160. The ele.IT (elementary IT) exam is for students with a more basic understanding, equivalent to B1 in the Common European Framework and costs €80. The exam tests listening and reading comprehension as well as written and spoken Italian. Exams are held once a year in Rome and authorised centres abroad.

PLIDA Progetto Lingua Italiana Dante Alighieri

Società Dante Alighieri Comitato di Firenze

Via Gino Capponi 4, 50124 Florence

Tel: (055) 2478981 Fax: (055) 2264682

Website www.dantealighieri.it

This diploma is awarded by the Società Dante Alighieri. Exams take place in May and November every year and cost €64 (see also page 2 *Società Dante Alighieri*)

Diploma 'Firenze'

This diploma is awarded by the Accademia Italiana di Lingua (AIL). AIL is a professional association of schools and institutions teaching foreign languages which have initiated a diploma of modern Italian. There are four levels. Exams are held four times a year at officially approved examination centres www.acad.it.

A-level

The British institute in Florence runs A-level courses and is an examination centre for the University of London and EDEXCEL A-level exams.

The Common European Framework (CEF)
for Language Assessment

The Council of Europe has developed a framework to standardise foreign language assessment. There are six levels of language user: Basic (A1 and A2), Independent (B1 and B2) and Proficient (C1 and C2). The framework makes it easy to compare the level of one exam with another and to make an assessment of your own level. The full text of the framework, including a useful self-assessment grid, can be downloaded from the website: www.coe.int click on 'education', 'languages' then 'language policy division' to see the full text. The self-assessment grid is on page 26–27 of their document.

Further information

When to go? *Quando andare in Italia?*

Italy has extremes of temperature. When we were there in 2002/2003 temperatures ranged from -7° C to 38° C. But every season is special in Italy and each has its advantages. In autumn the hills become a free fall of colour, *funghi* and truffles and the weather stays warm until the end of November. In winter hotels are cheap, bars are cosy and the sights and galleries deserted. There is also the prospect of weekend skiing and Italian Christmas shopping. In springtime the evenings are longer and there are wild flowers and asparagus. In the sizzling summers *caffè shakerati* are served in shady piazzas, Italians pose by the beaches and lakes or cool off in the mountains with the butterflies. July is peak season and hotels need to be booked well in advance. August is a holiday month in Italy. Many public services and family businesses are closed. It is the hottest, busiest and most expensive month of the year.

National and regional holidays *Periodi di vacanza*

Language schools close for national and regional holidays. Some reschedule classes or organise an outing instead but very few offer refunds. Check when booking your course, as you may be able to negotiate a discount.

The following dates are a guide:

▶ Christmas and New Year Holidays (*Natale e Capodanno*) from 23 December to around 7 January after Epiphany (*Epifania I talic*).

▶ Good Friday (*Venerdì Santo*) to Monday of Easter (Pasqua)

▶ 25 April Liberation Day (*Anniv. della Liberazione*)

▶ 1 May Labour Day (*Festa del Lavoro*)

▶ 1 June Feast of the Ascension (*Ascensione*)

▶ 2 June (*Festa della Repubblica*)

▶ a period in August for general holidays

▶ and 8 December (*Imm. Concezione*).

A note on the hours and course descriptions *Gli orari*

Language schools vary as to the length of each lesson. At the *Università per Stranieri* in Perugia the 'teaching hour' is 45 minutes teaching and 15 minutes coffee break. Others teach for a 'psychiatric' 50-minute hour, some for 60 minutes per hour. In our opinion it doesn't matter. Studies show that it is hard to concentrate for more than 40 minutes without a short break. Therefore when we have listed the number of hours of teaching it includes short breaks.

For easy comparison of prices we have quoted, wherever possible, a two and four week course of four hours teaching a day (20 hours per week). We have used these as our 'standard' courses. Language schools vary as to what they call these courses; some call them 'standard' courses, others 'intensive.' We have also included short descriptions of other courses on offer, including more intensive options, evening and weekend courses.

Going alone *Andare da soli*

Travelling anywhere alone can feel daunting particularly when you don't speak the language. The fact is you are not alone. When you arrive you will be surrounded by people in the same position. It is easy to meet people and to make friends and you will soon be speaking enough Italian to make

Italian friends. It is almost always possible to get around by a mixture of Italian, English, sign language and laughter. It is one of the most exciting, fun, rewarding and life enhancing experiences you can undertake.

For older people

You are never too old to learn a language. We were in classes with people aged between 18 and 80. Learning Italian is also a very good start to retirement. Schools with classes specifically for over 50s are listed on page 8.

Travelling with children *Andare con i bambini*

Italians love children. Doors open for parents wherever they go and children are welcomed everywhere. Service is perked up, ice cream brought out and pampering emerges from all corners. Surprisingly, however, there are very few facilities for babies: few baby changing areas and even fewer crèches. Fortunately, some language schools offer baby-sitting services and many run language courses for children. The only problem will be keeping up with the pace at which children learn a new language (page 5).

Before You Go

2

Prima di Partire

Learning some Italian before you go

Arriving in Italy is more fun if you already know some basic Italian. There are some brilliant language courses in England. The Italian Cultural Institutes in Edinburgh and London offer courses for all levels from intensive weekends to several months (addresses under 'scholarships' page 13).

There are many language courses with books, tapes and CDs. Our favourite is a series of ten CDs by Michel Thomas. He has a patented way of teaching where you are encouraged to relax, enjoy yourself and to try not to memorise anything. He also does not set any homework. The first eight CDs cost about £60 and can be bought from Amazon (www.amazon.co.uk). For computer boffins, the Learn Italian Now! 9.0 by Transparent Language (about £50 from Amazon) is a superb fully interactive package with videos, word games with a recording and playback option. The *Italian for Adults* paperback by C. Duff (Hodder and Stoughton Educational, 1974) is a small book that is easy and fun to work through.

Planning an exploratory trip

For courses of more than a month make an exploratory trip. Visiting the language schools, booking accommodation and being in the area will help clarify what you want and make planning and saving for the trip more exciting. It is cheaper to book accommodation locally than going through a private language school and there is the added advantage of seeing it before parting with any money. It is easier to enrol in person than sending an international bank transfer with all the associated *documenti*.

Planning the budget

Bills

Utilities (gas, water, electricity) are not usually included in the rent and are more expensive than in the UK. Check the cost of the end of stay cleaning, agency commission and deposits. Deposits can be difficult to extract from landlords so avoid paying the last month's rent (or two).

Books and maps

A course grammar book and dictionary can easily be bought in Italy for less than €30. Regional maps are widely available from *tabacchi*, bookshops and petrol stations and are cheaper than in Britain.

Eating out and food

Eating out is much cheaper in Italy. Pizza is fast, informal and very tasty and can cost well under €10 per pizza or €1 per slice for a take away. In most restaurants it is perfectly acceptable to share dishes between two or to ask for a half portion (*mezza porzione*). Even if you are not on a budget, this is a good way to try more dishes. Picnics are also a good way to cut costs. Buying food in local markets, with the local Italians, is cheap, fresh and good Italian practice. Standing at the bar for coffee is cheaper than sitting at the table – an espresso drunk at the bar is cheap just about everywhere.

For the ultimate cost cutting trick invest in a 'portable kitchen'. Ours consisted of a small rucksack with a portable hob, a pan for boiling pasta, a mat and oven glove (for insulation and safety), a small chopping board for salad, plastic plate, cutlery, a plastic box for a jar of pasta sauce and two glasses, salt, pepper, a heating element and a tin cup. In Italy it is easy to buy portable hobs as well as small heating elements for heating up water for drinks. With this kit it is possible to make a range of cheap meals (where allowed) including pasta and with different sauces, soups, eggs and salads.

Personal insurance

Backpackers' insurance offers competitive, flexible policies which include adventure sports. A search on the internet under 'backpackers insurance' will find the current cheapest deal. Insureandgo (Tel: (0870) 9013674, website www.insureandgo.com) were offering good deals at the time of writing. It is difficult to change an insurance policy once abroad so decide whether you need adventure sport cover before leaving. If you do not have an exact return date make sure you have in writing that the policy is valid without one.

Car insurance

You will need a green card, which insures your car in the UK and in Europe. We recommend Stuart Collins and Co. 114 Walter Road, Swansea SA1 5QQ. Tel: (01792) 655562.
Email mail@stuartcollins.com
Website www.stuartcollins.com

Mail redirection

Royal Mail Redirection Service. Tel: (0845) 7740 740, website www.royal-mail.com. Prices start from £12/month/named person. The Post Office is strict about the documents required which include a passport, two utility bills and a bank statement, both of which must be less than three months old. Signatures are required by everyone who is having their mail forwarded. Once the redirection has started no refunds are given but it can be extended over the telephone by credit card or by sending a cheque. Keep your reference number safely.

Car parking

There are numerous underground car parks in all the major cities but prices vary widely. A tourist pass in Perugia costs from €5 per day, in Rome €18 a day and in Florence closer to €30. There is free street parking outside the centre in virtually every town.

Pharmacies

Pharmacy items and toiletries are phenomenally expensive in Italy, at least three times the cost of the UK. Take a good supply with you. Examples include everyday medicines (paracetamol, antihistamines etc), toiletries, tampons, plasters, antiseptic creams, insect repellant and bandages.

Weekends away

Bed and breakfast costs about €30/night/person and youth hostels about €15/night/person. The Touring Club of Italy's *Italian Bed and Breakfasts* guide covers all regions of Italy (see Useful Books). Public transport is inexpensive (see city chapters for examples). Car hire between two or more people is cheap and convenient.

Sports *Sport*

Most Italian gyms and sports centres require a recent medical certificate, ideally written in Italian, stating that you are medically fit to play sport or work out with weights. The certificate should list the type of sport you want to play. A separate dermatology certificate is required for swimming, which should state that you are free from infectious skin conditions. These certificates can be obtained from your GP for a small fee.

Accommodation *Alloggio*

Booking accommodation locally is cheaper than going through a private language school or agency. It is possible to find accommodation even if you do not speak much Italian. Landlords advertise in shop windows: *in affitto* means 'for rent'. There are free property newspapers in most towns. The local tourist information centres can often put you in touch with land-lords (see www.enit.it for a list of the TIC offices in Italy). All towns have estate agents although they usually charge one month's rent in commission. Remember to bargain: *vorrei uno sconto* means 'I would like a discount.' *Vorrei qualcosa di più economico* means 'I would like something cheaper!' Think about what accommodation you want: a single or shared room, with an Italian family or in a private flat. Most Italian towns have a pretty historic centre (*centro storico*) and a cheaper, ugly periphery. Be specific in your questioning and requests.

▶ how far is it by foot from the school?

quanti minuti dista a piedi dalla scuola?

▶ With a nice view   *con una bella vista*

▶ With a balcony   *con un balcone*

▶ In the historic centre   *nel centro storico*

▶ A quiet room   *una camera tranquilla*

▶ Is the bathroom private?   *il bagno è privato?*

For those who want to cook, check there is a proper kitchen (*cucina*). Many offer a tiny *angolo cottura* (cooking corner) with an electric hob and a fridge. If you are a bread or cake chef you may want to ask for a proper oven *vorrei un fornello per cuocere pane e torte e per arrostire* (I would like an oven for cooking bread, cakes and roasting).

Leaving your accommodation in your home country *Lasciando il tuo alloggio nel tuo paese*

Make sure someone reliable has a set of keys, your contact details and knows what to do if there is a problem. Renting out your property could be a way of financing your trip. Most estate agents charge 15% of the rent collected for a full management service where they will be responsible for sorting out problems that arise. The expenses are taken out of the rent. Legally you must let your insurance company know about your plans otherwise if disaster does strike you may not be covered. Some mortgage companies do not allow you to rent out your property.

Your Health *La Tua Salute*

1 Check you are uptodate with your routine vaccines such as tetanus. No special vaccines are needed for Italy.

2 Check you are not missing health-screening appointments while you are away, such as cervical smears and mammograms.

3 Have your teeth checked to avoid Italian dental work.

4 Get that mole or lump that you have been worrying about checked before you leave.

5 If you take regular medication make sure you have enough for your trip or a prescription.

6 If you wear glasses take a spare pair and a copy of your prescription. Contact lenses can be bought over the counter in Italy and are cheaper than in England.

7 If you want to use an Italian gym or sports centre you need to take a recent medical certificate (see sports page 24).

8 Obtain an E111 form from the Post Office before leaving; it entitles you to free emergency health care in Italy. You will still need a separate health insurance policy (see planning the budget page 23).

Arriving in Italy

3

Arrivando in Italia

Documents *Documenti*

Documenti, along with football, are a national obsession. Have a folder for the following documents and photocopy correspondence about your trip.

▶ passport (and photocopy of it)

▶ driving licence

▶ car insurance and green card/vehicle registration document

▶ medical certificate/dermatology certificate (for sports)

▶ personal and health insurance policy/E111 form

▶ passport photos.

Student Card *Tessera*

The *tessera* is an official student card supplied by the universities after enrolling and paying for a course. It is used for accessing facilities and lessons and for student discounts. There are often spot checks so keep it on you at all times.

Permit of Stay *Permesso di Sioggorno*

Within eight days of arriving in Italy foreigners need to register with the police. The language schools will advise you on where to go and the latest rules concerning who needs a Permit of Stay. The following documents are required.

▶ passport and a passport photocopy

▶ proof of enrolment on the course (or a *tessera*)

▶ proof of your address in Italy

▶ four to six passport photos.

Non-EU citizens should check with the Italian consulate in their home country for the latest visa requirements.

Shopping *Fare la spesa*

Shopping in Italy is different. The service is more personal and on entering a shop you will often be asked what you would like to see. We have seen a shop full of people waiting to be served while a *signora* finished her discussion with the assistant about which of the seven gas lighters opened for her was the best.

Tobacconist *Tabacchi*

The *tabacchi* (marked by a 'T' sign) sells tobacco, lighters, stamps (*francobolli*), postcards (*cartoline*) and leather wallets. Newspapers and magazines are sold by the news stands (*edicole*).

Stationary and stamps *Cartolerie e francobolli*

Stamps (*francobolli*) can be bought from *tabacci* or post offices (*ufficio postale*). First class stamps are called *prioritria*.

Telephones *Telefoni*

International call centres have the cheapest rates. Public telephones use telephone cards which can be bought from news stands (*edicole*). SIM cards for mobile telephones are good value; you need identification to buy one. Handsets are more expensive than in the UK.

Working in Italy

Part-time work includes au-pairing, seasonal farm work, bar work (particularly in English or Irish pubs), seasonal work at tourist villages or ski resorts, working as a groom or at an *agriturismo* (farm holidays). Youth hostels may offer discounted lodging in exchange for work. Teaching English at a private school or by local advertisements in universities is possible particularly if you hold a TEFL certificate (Teaching English as a Foreign Language). Cooking in a ski chalet or a holiday home is well paid, particularly if you hold a recognised cooking certificate.

Au Pair Italy

Via Demetrio Martinelli 11/d
40133 Bologna, Italy
Tel: (051) 383466
Website www.aupairitaly.com

Leiths School of Food and Wine Ltd

21 St Alban's Grove
London W8 5BP
Tel: (0207) 2290177 Fax: (0207) 9375257
Email info@leiths.com Website www.leiths.com
Leiths run excellent cooking courses, including a one-month basic certificate in practical cookery for people wanting to work in holiday homes and ski chalets.

TEFL Teaching English as a Foreign Language

Website www.tefl.com

The site includes a good comparison of the TEFL courses as well as job adverts across the globe.

Florence

Firenze

4

Florence is one of the world's artistic capitals, a monument to the Renaissance and a thriving industrial centre. Writers and artists such as Dante, Machiavelli, Botticelli, Michelangelo and Donatello have found inspiration here. The majority of the famous sights can be easily explored on foot and there are a vast quantity of English services for tourists. The city has a population of 380,000, is 277km from Rome and 298km from Milan. It has the oldest art school in the world, the *Accademia di Belle Arti*, founded in 1563. This houses the famous statue of *David* that established Michelangelo's career at the tender age of 29. The Duomo is the fourth biggest in Europe and at 91m is the tallest building in Florence. Its dome was built without scaffolding in 1463. There are markets and restaurants for the keenest of cooks and the best designers for the shoppers. The prices, however, are double those of other towns and one hears as many English as Italian voices. Despite this, there are more language schools, beautiful monuments and museums than in almost any other city in Italy.

Florence and the Italian language

Firenze e la lingua Italiana

Florence is where the Italian language as we know it today was born. Dante was the first major writer to use the Florentine vernacular as opposed to Latin. His *Divine Comedy* helped establish the Florentine dialect as the 'Italian standard.'

Don't Miss *Da Non Perdere*

▶ views over Tuscany from the Boboli Gardens (page 61)

▶ window-shopping in Florence's most exclusive street, Via de'Tornabuoni

▶ the view of Florence's oldest bridge, Ponte Vecchio (1345) from Ponte Trinità

▶ the free weekly lectures and concerts at the Harold Acton Library (page 39)

▶ the Bargello museum (page 54) with Italy's finest collection of Renaissance sculpture

▶ climbing Giotto's 85m white, green and pink marble Campanile (1359)

▶ the Florentine food markets, some of the best in Italy (page 52)

▶ Donatello's *David* (1430) in the Bargello Musuem

▶ dipping *cantucci* (almond biscuits) into *vin santo* (sweet wine) at the end of a meal

▶ Michelangelo's *David* (1504) in the *Accademia di Belle Arti*

▶ a day trip to the isolated Camaldoli monastery in the Tuscan forests.

Table comparing Florence's language schools

School	University Of Florence	ABC	Acc. Italiana	British Institute	Cento Ling. It. D.A.	Euro Centre	Il Globo	Società Dante Alighieri
Two week course	–	€280	€250	€402	€420	€340	€255	€270
Four week course	€165.60*	€520	€400	€805	€620	€648	€440	€455
Enrolment fee	None	€20 text book	€80 or €160 for 1:1	None	€80	€85	€40	€50
Individual lessons per hour	–	€20 or €15/h 40 lessons	€22.5/ 20 lessons	€49.06	€46	€43	€30	€31
Single lodging two weeks	–	€223	€200	–	From €300	€410 (HB)**	€220	–
Single lodging four weeks	€400	€380	€400	€520	From €500	€820 (HB)	€395	€415– 465
Maximum group size	No max average =20	6	10	13	13	13	7	10
Laboratory	No	Yes	No	Yes	Yes	Yes	Tiny	No
Air conditioning	No	Yes	Yes	Yes	Yes	Yes	No	No
Cost of additional weeks	10 weeks costs €414	€120/ week	No Discounts	5% after four weeks	10% if course booked more than three months in advance	€170	€100 after eight weeks	Three-month saves €125 six-month saves €354
Scholarships	Yes	Yes	No	Yes	No	No	Yes	Yes

The courses refer to four hours teaching per day (20 hours a week) unless specified.
* Price of four weeks of a ten-week course.
** HB-halfboard

University of Florence: Centre for Foreigners

Villa *La Quiete alle Montalve*
Via di Boldrone 2
50141 Firenze
Italia
Tel: (055) 454016/31 Fax: (055) 454019
Email cecustra@unifi.it
Website www.unifi.it/unifi/ccs/ (in English and Italian).
Segreteria open Monday to Friday 09.00–12.00 (Italian only).

For those who have two months or more and want to study Italian in
Florence the University should be top of the list. The courses are good
value, have a fully inclusive cultural programme and a spectacular location. The *'La Quiete alle Montalve'* is a beautifully restored historic villa, on
a hill overlooking Florence and the Tuscan countryside. There are cool
marble floors, secluded inner courtyards with frescoed ceilings and a
walled garden with a fountain and box hedging. The classrooms (*aule*) are
spacious and well equipped. There is a *laboratorio linguistico* (page 36) for
intermediate and advanced classes. The villa is a 20-minute bus or cycle
ride from the centre.

The University is open to anyone over the age of 18, who is or was entitled to go to university in their own country. Proof is needed in the form
of a school certificate, a diploma, a degree, or letter confirming education
to the level required to enter university. You do not need to have a degree
or to have attended university before. There is a broad mix of students of
all ages and nationalities. The class size averages 20 but can be more.

Courses *Corsi*

There are four courses per year, which consist of language lessons in the
morning and an extensive programme of cultural sessions in the afternoon.
The language lessons are divided into four levels: preparatory, intermediate, advanced-intermediate and advanced. There is a test on the first day to
determine the student's levels. There is a wide choice of cultural lectures
and visits that are included in the price. The subjects include Italian literature, history, history of art and music, Etruscan civilization, Dante, Italian

film and contemporary Italy. They include visits to some of the main art centres in Tuscany, Florentine museums and other historic buildings.

Costs *Costi*

▶ Ten-week winter (*inverno*) course from January to mid-March, 120 hours of language lessons, €414.

▶ Ten-week spring (*primavera*) course from April to mid-June, 120 hours of language lessons, €414.

▶ Four-week summer (*estate*) course from the end of June to the beginning of August, 60 hours of language lessons, €284.

▶ The ten-week autumn (*autunno*) course runs from October to mid-December, has 120 hours of language lessons, €414.

Other expenses include a grammar book €19, museums entrance €6, excursions €12 and examinations fee €6.

Enrolment *Iscrizione*

Students must apply for their course at least 15 days before the start of the course. The staff at the *segreteria* do not speak English but their website has all the necessary information in English. The following *documenti* are required:

▶ application form (can be downloaded and submitted from the website)

▶ certificate (or copy) of educational qualifications

▶ two passport photographs

▶ receipt of payment.

To pay *Per pagare*

Italy is still in the dark ages concerning payments with credit cards. To pay from abroad either send a postal order (*vaglia postale*) to Centro di Cultura per Stranieri, via di Boldrone 2, 50141 Firenze or pay by bank order (*bonifico*) to the details outlined on the application form. Remember to include your name and the dates of the course. If you are in Florence you can pay in cash at the *segreteria*. Keep all documents and receipts relating to your application.

Accommodation *Alloggio*

The University provides a list of local Italian families who take paying guests. The student must contact the landlord directly and the University does not take any responsibility for problems arising with the landlord. Make sure you are happy with the accommodation before paying. The cost of a single room is about €400 per month depending on the season.

Facilities

There is a *laboratorio linguistico*, which is used for all levels except elementary. It is only available during lessons and not for independent study.
There are canteens (*mense*) and vending machines (*distributore automatico*) at Via S. Gallo, 25a and at Viale Morgagni 47/51.
The University sports centre is at Via V. della Rovere, 2.

How to get to the University *Come andare all'Università*

On a standard 1:12000 street map of Florence, the University Villa is marked near the Careggi Hospital (*Ospedale di Careggi*) in the La Quiete area. It can be reached on the following buses:

▶ From the train station (Piazza della Stazione): Bus 14B to the end of the line (Via Niccolo da Tolentino), a 10-minute walk from the University. Bus 28 to Via Reginaldo Giuliani at bus stop number 7.

▶ From Piazza San Marco: Bus 20 to the end of the line at Largo Caruso.

▶ From Piazza Dalmazia: Bus 43U to the University Villa is a shuttle bus which runs during term-time.

Starting a course *Inizio dei corsi*

On the first day go to the *segreteria*, which is on the ground floor of the Villa. Bring all *documenti* including a letter confirming enrolment and a passport photograph. There is a small test to determine the student's levels and classes start the following day.

Private Language Schools *Scuole Private di Lingua*

ABC Centro di Lingua e Cultura Italiana

Via de' Rustici 7

50122 Firenze

Tel: (055) 212001 Fax: (055) 212112

Email info@abcschool.com Website www.abcschool.com

This excellent language school is centrally located in a quiet street in the Santa Croce district. The entrance to the building is between the red numbers 21 and 23. The school is on the second floor, up the stairs to the right. It reminded us of a National Trust property with its cream and taupe walls and iron banisters. Next to the secretaries' desk is a large open space for studying, watching videos, playing games or relaxing. The school has eight airy classrooms with large windows and views over the rooftops. There is small *laboratorio linguistico*, a common room and library with videos, newspapers and games. Groups have a maximum of six students.

Courses and costs *Corsi e costi*

The **standard** course of four hours teaching per day (20 hours a week) is €280 for two weeks or €520 for four weeks. The school offers more **intensive** courses which have the same standard group course with individual lessons in addition. Individual lessons are good value at €20 per hour for single sessions or €15 per hour for a course of 40. **Weekend courses** have lessons on Saturdays and Sundays from 09.15 to 13.15 and 14.15 to 16.00. The courses cost €100 for ten hours or €130 for 14 hours. The groups have a maximum of 3 students for these weekend courses. The school also runs **specialised** courses in art, jewellery, history of art, cooking and wine. There is no **enrolment** fee but students must buy a €20 textbook.

Accommodation *Alloggio*

The school offers shared apartments with other students or rooms with Italian families. The Italian families live outside the city centre. A single room with use of the kitchen costs €233 for two weeks or €380 for four weeks (not including breakfast).

Accademia Italiana

International School

Piazza de' Pitti, 15

50125 Firenze

Tel: (055) 284616 or (055) 211619 Fax: (055)284486

Email modaita@tin.it Website www.accademiaitaliana.com

Accademia is a small international school offering professional and short courses in fashion, design, art and language. There is a mix of nationalities, disciplines and age groups. It is located on the second and third floors of the Temple-Leader Building on Piazza de'Pitti, near Ponte Vecchio. This is one of the nicest locations of any language school in Florence (see also the University page 34). The large classroom on the third floor has huge windows along three aspects, directly facing the Pitti Palace. There are two tiny classrooms used for small group teaching and a roof terrace with spectacular views across Florence and the surrounding hills. There is a small frescoed library with language textbooks and magazines. Computers are available with free Internet access. The school has excellent facilities for **wheelchair users**.

Courses and costs *Corsi e costi*

This is one of the cheapest private language schools in Florence (see also *Il Globo* page 42). Courses are in three levels: **basic**, **intermediate** and **advanced**. Each level takes one month to complete but courses from one week or more are available every month except December. A **standard** course of four hours teaching a day (20 hours a week) costs €200 for two weeks or €400 for a month. A **less intensive** course of two hours teaching a day (ten hours a week) costs €125 for two weeks or €250 for a month. The language courses are open to **children** as well as adults. There is an €85 **enrolment** fee.

Accommodation *Alloggio*

The school can advise on accommodation and has contact details of landlords or families. Apartments can be shared with students from the same or other disciplines.

The British Institute of Florence

Palazzo Strozzino
Piazza Strozzi 2
50123 Firenze
Email info@britishinstutute.it Website www.britishinstitute.it
Tel: (055) 2677 8200 Fax: (055) 2677 8222
Open Monday to Friday from 09.00–17.30 and Saturday 09.00–12.30

Harold Acton Library and cultural centre
Palazzo Lanfredini (first floor)
Lungarno Guicciardini 9
50125 Firenze
Open Monday to Friday from 10.00–18.30
Email library@britishinstitute.it
Tel: (055) 2677 8270 Fax: (055) 2677 8252

The British Institute was founded in 1917 to increase cultural understanding between Italy and Britain through the teaching of both languages. It has a public school atmosphere and a price to match. The Institute is on the fourth floor of a pretty palazzo in the historic centre with views over Florence's rooftops. It is in the same square as the Palazzo Strozzi art gallery and is in the same building as the Odeon cinema. Groups have a maximum of 13 students.

The British Institute also owns the impressive Harold Acton Library (page 51). This is in a sixteenth century palazzo and has over 50,000 volumes including hundreds of Italian grammar and exercise books. Membership of the library is free to students of the British Institute but they still have to pay €35 a month to use the library's multimedia resource centre.

The British Institute in Florence is not associated with the British Institute in Rome, which is not included in this guide.

Courses and costs *Corsi e costi*
There is a large range of courses including Italian language (and A-level), English, history of art, cooking, drawing, opera and teaching English as a foreign language.

There are two types of language course for **beginners**. The intensive beginner course has four hours teaching a day (20 hours a week) and costs €400 for two weeks or €805 for four weeks. The less intensive beginner course has two hours teaching a day (ten hours a week) costs €215 for two weeks or €430 for four weeks.

For students who already know some Italian there is a '**standard**' course of three hours per day (15 hours a week) which costs €315 for two weeks or €630 for four. **Individual** lessons can be arranged costing €49.08 per hour. The school also offers **evening classes**. These consist of two hours teaching twice a week for ten weeks (40 hours in total) and cost €430. There are also **A-level** Italian courses. The full A-level course is divided into three terms from late September to the exam in June and costs €3,520. There is a one-week A-level revision course in April which costs €270.

The Institute runs a range of **cultural courses** including courses on Dante, the great names of Florence and opera. These courses last ten hours over one week and cost €150 each. There are two-week practical **art courses** in life drawing or landscape watercolours which cost €250 and a new one-week **fresco painting** course costing €170.

In the first two weeks of **August** the British Institute moves to Massa Marittima. This is a small town 1,300m above sea level a few miles from the Tuscan coast. A two-week language course of four hours teaching a day (20 hours a week) costs €450 and can be combined with the town's **Opera Week**. The opera course consists of five afternoon sessions over one week. It focuses on the operas performed during the Massa Opera Week and costs €145 (not including tickets to performances). There is a €45 enrolment fee for the summer courses. The cheapest accommodation is in the converted old seminary building and starts at €20 per night per person.

Scholarships and discounts are available for one-month courses. Contact the Institute for the latest availability.

Accommodation *Alloggio*

There is an accommodation advisor who books accommodation but this is purely an intermediary service. Students are responsible for their own arrangements but the Institute monitors the accommodation to ensure a reasonable standard. A single room in a shared apartment costs €550 per month.

Centro Linguistico *Italiano Dante Alighieri* (CLIDA)

Piazza della Repubblica 5

Firenze 50123

Tel: (055) 210808 Fax: (055) 287828

Email study@clida.it Website www.clidante.com

This school has an excellent central location overlooking the Piazza della Repubblica. It is on the second floor of a beautiful palazzo next to the Caffè Cinema where Via Brunelleschi joins the square. The school was founded in 1966 by Alberto and Gabriella Materassi, a husband and wife team. Their son Stefano now helps run the school. The classrooms are bright and airy and have views over the piazza. There is a well-equipped computer room with multimedia and Internet access. There is also a small cinema for watching Italian videos. Classes have a maximum of 13 students but usually much less than this. **Children** over the age of 14 can attend the courses. The school is expensive but the facilities and quality of service are fantastic.

Courses and costs *Corsi e costi*

The **standard** course of four hours a day (20 hours a week) costs €420 for two weeks or €620 for a month. There are more **intensive** options with individual lessons in the afternoons. The individual lessons work out at €40 an hour. There is an €80 **enrolment** fee. A 10% discount is available if you book more than three months before the course starts. The school organises a full range of **extracurricular activities** which cost €150 per month.

Accommodation *Alloggio*

The school needs about two months' notice to find accommodation. A single room in a shared apartment with other students costs between €500 and €650 per month. There are also all-inclusive packages (language course and accommodation) which offer a small discount.

Eurocentres

Piazza S. Spirito 9

50125 Firenze

Tel: (055) 213030 Fax: (055) 216497

Email fir-info@eurocentres.com Website www.eurocentres.it

Open Monday to Friday 08.30–18.00

Multimedia Language Centre Monday to Friday 10.30–18.00

Eurocentres have language schools all over the world and are a high quality organisation. This school is on the second floor of a beautifully restored sixteenth century palazzo a two-minute walk from Piazza de'Pitti and Ponte Vecchio. Piazza S. Spirito is a peaceful tree-lined square with outdoor cafes and a fountain. It manages to escape the hordes of tourists despite being near to some of the major sites. The school is spacious and has excellent facilities. Some of the classrooms have frescoes and all have modern fittings and large windows overlooking the square. There is a small outdoor terrace, without views. The excellent free multimedia language centre has computers with language learning tools, audiotapes and a teacher available in the afternoons. There are also computers with free Internet access. Classes have a maximum of 13 students.

Courses and costs *Corsi e costi*

The **standard** course of four hours a day (20 hours a week) costs €340 for two weeks or €648 for a month. **Individual** lessons cost €43 an hour. There is an €85 **enrolment** fee.

Accommodation *Alloggio*

The school can arrange accommodation in a family home. A single room with breakfast costs €636 for two weeks or €750 half-board.

Il Globo

Piazza Santa Maria Novella 22

50123 Firenze

Tel/fax: (055) 2657883

Email info@ilglobo.it Website www.ilglobo.it

This tiny school is on the top floor of an eighteenth century palazzo overlooking Piazza Santa Maria Novella. This is a large grassy square near the train station and is a ten-minute walk from the Duomo. The prices are among the lowest in Florence and equal to the Accademia (page 38) when the enrolment fees are taken into account. Il Globo is a more personal, less trendy option than the Accademia. There are two small classrooms which overlook the square, a couple of computers with Internet access and CD-ROM, and a tape and video recorder which can be used after the lessons. The school includes a range of extracurricular activities of at least six hours per week. The classes are small with a maximum of seven students.

Courses and costs *Corsi e costi*

The **standard** course of four hours a day (20 hours a week) costs €255 for two weeks and €440 for four weeks. There is a more **intensive** option which has the addition of two hours of conversation class in the afternoon (total of 30 hours teaching a week). This combination is good value at €380 for two weeks or €660 for four weeks. The conversation classes can be taken on their own and cost €150 per week. The school runs **specialist** tailor-made courses in pronunciation for opera singers, business Italian, Italian literature, culture and society and history of art. These are priced according to the demand. **Individual** lessons cost €30 per hour. The **enrolment** fee is €40. **Scholarships** are available for 50% of the course fees. Students should apply with a letter of support from a recognised school, college, university or Italian cultural institute.

Accommodation *Alloggio*

Single and double rooms are available in shared apartments with other students. A single room costs €395 for four weeks and a double costs €330 (per person). A single room with an Italian family costs €23/day including breakfast or €29/day half-board. Independent apartments cost from €750 per month.

Società Dante Alighieri

Via Gino Capponi 4

50121 Firenze
Tel: (055) 2478981 Fax: (055) 2264682
Email info@dantealighieri.it Website www.dantealighieri.it
Open Monday to Friday 09.00–17.00
This is the only Dante Alighieri Society school in Florence (page 2, *Società Dante Alighieri*). It is just off the pretty Piazza S.S. Annunziata in the centre of Florence. The location is impressive but would not suit everyone. It is

in the beautiful fifteenth century church-like 'Cloister di S. Pierino.' It is easy to miss the entrance of the school as the two large wooden doors are unmarked. It is about 50 meters from the Piazza Annunzita, on the right, just next to a plaque giving information about the *Oratorio di San Pierino*. Above the doors is a glazed terracotta lunette depicting the Annunciation. Immediately inside there is a courtyard with sixteenth century frescoes and terracotta pots filled with plants. This leads through another set of doors to the offices. There are two small windowless classrooms on the ground floor and another two downstairs in the cloisters. There are regular concerts and lectures given in the great hall. The school organises a range of free extra curricular activities including a weekly film and a welcome buffet. The combined Italian language and culture courses are particularly good value.

Courses and costs *Corsi e costi*

A **standard** course of four hours teaching a day (20 hours a week) costs €270 for two weeks and €455 for four weeks. There is a **less intensive** course of three hours a day (15 hours a week) costing €362 for four weeks. The groups have a maximum of ten students.

For students with at least an intermediate level of Italian there is an excellent group course in **Italian language and culture**. This consists of four hours teaching a day (20 hours a week) and two afternoons a week (five hours per week) of cultural seminars. This costs €325 for two weeks (40 hours teaching plus ten hours of cultural seminars) or €570 for four weeks (80 hours of teaching plus 20 hours of cultural seminars). The school can arrange **mini-group** courses (three to four students) which cost €517 for four weeks (80 hours). **Individual** lessons can be arranged for €31 per lesson at any level. There are courses for **children** of students at the school over the age of 6 years old. Children learn Italian through games and playing. A one-month course of 80 hours costs €429.

The school runs **specialised** courses in history of art, contemporary Italy, history of Italian theatre, cinema and music and Italian literature. These consist of 16 hours of teaching over one month and cost €119.

There is an **enrolment** fee of €50 which includes museum visits and cultural activities.

Accommodation *Alloggio*

There is a free accommodation service but at least two months' notice is advised. A single room in a shared apartment costs between €415 and 465 per month.

Getting to and from Florence
Andare e Tornare da Firenze

Trains *Treni*

Stazione di S. Maria Novella

Piazza della stazione (a ten-minute walk from the centre)

Website www.fs-on-line.it

Florence's main train station has good facilities including a pharmacy (open daily from 07.00 to 23.00), left luggage, a few market stalls and a newspaper stand. The ticket office is open from 05.45 to 22.45. The best way to get information without having to queue is by using one of the automatic ticket machines. Those opposite the information office at the far end of the station tend to be less crowded. The information office is open daily from 07.00 to 22.00. The left luggage facility costs €3 for the first 12 hours and then €2 per 12 hours thereafter. Timetables cost €1 from the bookshop. There are connections across Italy and Europe from this station. Livorno and Bologna are approximately one-and-a-quarter hours away. Venice, Milan and Padova are three-and-a-half hours away. There are hourly trains to Pisa airport, which take an hour.

Airport *Aeroporto*

Florence airport is accessible by bus or car. The trip takes 30 minutes and buses leave every half-hour from 05.30 to 23.30 from the *Sita* coach station A, tel: (055) 214721.

Addresses for easy living in Florence

Florentine addresses

There is a rather confusing double system of numbering for addresses in Florence, one for businesses and the other for residential properties. The businesses have a red number and the address is followed by a letter r. The others have a black number. The two numbering systems bear no relation to each other so don't be surprised if you find yourself outside the wrong door!

Bakers *Panetterie*

Il Forno Pugi

Viale de Amicis

This small bakery teams with regulars at lunchtime. Their *focacce* and *pizza al taglio* (by the slice) are of local fame. Unless you are in the area however the trip is not for the fainthearted. It is a ten-minute walk from Piazza Alberti, heading towards the Campo di Marte. First you pass the tiny 'underpass market' on Via Lungo l'Affrico (see below, 'markets'). Then you walk up the busy Viale Edmondo de'Amicis to the bakery on your left.

Forno Pierguidi

Via San Niccolò 43r

08.00–13.00 and 17.00–20.00

Closed Saturday afternoons and Sundays

This excellent bakery is in the interesting southeast corner of town.

Bicycle, scooter and car Rental *Biciclette, vespe e macchine a noleggio*

Happy Rent

Via Borgo Ognissanti 153

Tel/Fax: (055) 2399696

Website www.happyrent.com

Open from 09.00 to 19.00 seven days a week

Happy Rent also have branches in Rome, Sorrento and Milan. Prices for a scooter start at €12 for an hour, €38 for a day and €170 for a week. Cars start at €65 for a day and €355 for a week. They have Smart cars from €75 per day.

Florence by Bike

Via San Zanobi 120/122r

Tel/Fax: (055) 488992

Email ecologica@dada.it Website www.florencebybike.it

This company has a good range of bikes including electric ones! A city bike costs €4 per hour, €12 for five hours, €20 per day or €195 per week. They have vespers costing €45 for five hours. They run daily **city tours** that last three hours as well as excursions into the Chianti hills (all advertised on their website).

Bookshops *Librerie*

The Paperback Exchange
Via Fiesolana 31
Tel: (055) 247 8154
Website www.papex.it
Open Monday to Fridays 09.00–09.30 Saturdays 10.00–13.00 and 15.30–19.00
This shop sells English books and language textbooks.

La Feltrinelli
Via Camillo Cavour 12/20r
Open Monday to Saturday from 09.00 to 19.30
This is the Florence branch of this excellent chain and is near the Duomo.

Butchers *Macellerie*

Rodolfo Mignani
Borgo S. Frediano 127–129
Tel: (055) 210 830
This is an old fashioned butcher with marble floors and walls, a wood ceiling, friendly service and high quality meats.

Car parks *Parcheggi*

Parking in Florence can cost as much as €3 per hour. There are strict traffic police with a tow-away penalty. The Oltrarno car park by the Porta Romana at the bottom of Via Roma is good value and is less than a ten-minute walk from Piazza Pitti. It costs €1.5 per hour, €15 per 24 hours or €52 per week.

Cinemas *Cinema*

Cinema Teatro Odeon
Via Degli Anselini 3
Tel: (055) 214068
Website www.cinehall.it
This cinema is in the same palazzo as the British Institute. It shows original language films on Mondays and Tuesdays.

Cinema Excelsior
Via Cerretani 4
Tel: (055) 212798

Cinema Piazza Beccaria
Tel: (055) 2343666
This cinema is conveniently situated next door to a very good *gelateria*.

Cinema Teatro Moderno
Viale Matteotti
Tel: (055) 8720058

Cobblers *Calzolai*

Clinica della Scarpa
Via Borgo la Croce 14r
Tel: (055) 245592
Open 08.00–12.30 and 15.30–19.30
Closed Saturday afternoon and Sundays (*sabato pomeriggio e domenica*)

Cooking courses *Corsi di Cucina*

Apicius
Office: Via Guelfa, 85,
50123 Florence
Tel: (055) 2658135, Fax (055) 2656689
Via Faenza 43
50123 Firenze
Tel: (055) 287143 or (055) 287360 Fax: (055) 2398920
Email info@apicius.it Website www.apicius.it

Many of the private language schools offer cooking classes. *Apicius* is an excellent private cooking school with a wide range of courses. These include **gastronomic walking tours** of the city and market walks. The school is based in new modern facilities in a quiet road near the Termini train station.

Delicatessen *Negozo di specialità gastronomiche*

Olio and Convivium
Via Santo Spirito 4
50123 Firenze
Tel: (055) 26 58 198
Email olio.convivium@conviviumfirenze.it Website www.convivium-firenze.it
This is a modern high-tech deli and restaurant. There is an excellent selection of cheese, breads and salamis including the rare *prosciutto di Cinta Senese* (a rare white collared pig). On the left of the entrance is a window looking into the tiny and immaculate kitchen. Cooking, wine and olive oil tasting can be arranged.

Department store *Grandi magazzini*

UPIM
Via Vincenzo Gioberti 70 (at the junction with Via Cimbue)
Tel: (055) 667689
Open 09.00–19.30 everyday except Monday

Home and kitchen shop *Negozo di casalinghi*

Dino Bartolini
Via dei Servi 30
Tel: (055) 21 18 95
Website www.dinobartolini.it
This multi-award winning kitchen shop is just behind the Duomo. Some of the prices are a little steep but the choice is huge and tempting.

Hotels and hostels *Alberghi e ostelli*

The Tourist House
Via della Scala 1
50123 Firenze
Tel: (055) 268675 Fax: (055) 282552
Email management@touristhouse.com Website www.touristhouse.com
This is the best economy option near the train station just off the lovely
Piazza S. Maria Novella. A double room with breakfast and a private bath-
room costs €75. It is spotlessly clean and many of the rooms are large with
a television. Ask for one of the rooms at the back, as they are quieter. You
can book online.

Santa Monica Hostel
Via Santa Monaca 6
50124 Firenze
Tel: (055) 268338 Fax: (055) 280185
Email info@ostello.it Website www.ostello.it
This hostel has cheap single-sex dormitory accommodation along with a
full set of rules. There are showers, a laundrette, a sitting room with a television, a kitchen, Internet and vending machine. The dormitories sleep
between four and 20 people in bunk beds and cost €16/person including
sheets. Check-in is between 09.30 and 13.00 and between 14.00 and 00.30.
Between 09.30 and 14.00 the rooms are closed for cleaning. There is a
curfew at 01.00. The office opens at 06.00 and the common room at 07.00 if
you are planning to arrive early. Reservations are only taken by email,
letter or fax.

L'Hotel Loggiato dei Servi
Piazza SS Annunziata 3
Tel: (055) 289592 or (055) 289593
This central three-star hotel has clean, basic rooms on a pretty piazza. A
single room costs €140 and a double costs €205 with breakfast in the high
season.

Ice cream shop *Gelaterie*

Vestri
Borgo Degli Albizi 11

Tel: (055) 2340374

Website www.cioccolateriavestri.com

This is the place for reasonably priced divine ice cream, chocolates and hot chocolate. There is also a shop in Arezzo, Via Romana, 161.

Internet *Internet*

There are lots of Internet cafes in Florence. These two are central, fast and good value.

Internet Pitti

Piazza Pitti 7/8r (opposite the Pitti Palace)

Tel: (055) 2728836

Open from 10.00–22.00

This Internet café has flat screens and fast connections. There are also vending machines with cold drinks.

Nettyweb

Via S. Spirito 42r

Tel: (055) 2654549

Monday–Friday 10.00–22.00

Saturday and Sunday 14.00–20.00

This is a modern Internet cafe in the *Oltrarno* district. Access costs €3 an hour.

Laundrettes *Lavanderie*

The Wash and Dry chain has eight branches in Florence. They are open from 08.00 to 22.00 every day including holidays. Washes of 8kg take 30 minutes and 25 minutes to dry. The addresses are: Via dei Servi 105, Via Del Sole 29, Via Della Scala 52/54, B.go S. Frediano 39, Via Dei Serragli 87, Via Nazionale 129, Via Ghibellina 143 and Via Dell'Agnolo 21.

Libraries *Biblioteche*

Harold Acton Library and Cultural Centre of the British Institute

Palazzo Lanfredini (first floor)

Lungarno Guicciardini 9 (near the South side of Ponte S. Trinità)

Open Monday to Friday from 10.00–18.30

Tel: (055) 2677 8270 Fax: (055) 2677 8252

Email library@britishinstitute.it

The Harold Acton Library is housed over four floors in an attractive six-teenth century palazzo overlooking the River Arno. Although it is owned by the British Institute membership is open to anyone. It has 50,000 volumes including British and Italian history, English literature, history of art and music and over 400 Italian grammar and textbooks. There are smaller sections covering film, travel, talking books, CDs, DVDs and videos. There is a sitting area with English newspapers and magazines and a study area. The library also has a small air-conditioned multimedia resource centre with Internet, DVD, videos, satellite television and language learning resources. There are free lectures and concerts on Wednesday evenings that are also open to non-members, with drinks served afterwards.

Full annual membership costs €56.50 or just €38.50 for students. A two-week 'consulting membership' costs €12.50 and allows you access to the library but not to borrow books. The multimedia resource centre costs €35 a month. Students at the British Institute (page 39) have free membership of the library but must still pay €35 per month to use the multimedia resource centre.

Biblioteca di Palagio di Parte Guelfa

Via di Capaccio 3 (near the Piazza del Mercato Nuovo)

Tel: (055) 2616029/30

Open Mondays, Tuesdays and Thursdays 08.30–22.30

Wednesdays and Fridays 08.30–18.30

Saturdays 08.30–13.30

This small public library is housed in a quiet eleventh century church in the heart of the historic centre. They have a selection of English newspapers and magazines and a small selection of English books.

Markets *Mercati*

Mercato di Sant'Ambrogio

Piazza Ghilberti

Open weekday mornings

This is an excellent covered food market on the east side of the city. It is near the daily flea market at Piazza Ciompi and is a lively, interesting part of town.

Mercato di San Lorenzo
Piazza San Lorenzo and Piazza del Mercato Centro (north of the Duomo)
Open Monday to Saturday mornings only
There is a huge eighteenth century covered food market in the Piazza del Mercato Centro.

Piazza San Lorenzo
Open Tuesday to Saturday
The whole area around this clothes and leather goods market is packed with stalls and gesticulating Italians.

Cascine market (Mercato delle Cascine)
Parco delle Cascine (west of the Termini train station)
Open every Tuesday morning
This is a large weekly market that sells everything from food, flowers, clothes and household goods to the occasional pet.

Underpass market
Open daily 07.30–14.00
There is a tiny but lively fruit and vegetable market on Via Lungo Africa in the east end of the city. It is under the flyover next to the railway line just beyond Piazza Alberti. On Tuesdays and Fridays there is also a small cheese and salami stall. This market is not far from the Forno Pugli bakery for stocking up of fresh bread at the same time.

Piazza Ciompi
Open daily from 09.00–13.00 and 15.30–19.30
There is a daily flea market in this pretty little square near the Sant'Ambrogio food market. It is run from wooden huts near the elegant Loggia del Pesce.

Piazza Santo Spirito
Open on the second Sunday of the month from 09.00–19.00
There is a lively antique market in this otherwise peaceful piazza a stone's throw from Piazza Pitti. Try the necci chestnut flour pancakes cooked by the elderly husband and wife team on their portable stove. They are served either plain (€1) or with fresh ricotta (2€).

Museums and galleries mentioned in the walk (page 59)
Musei e gallerie menzionati nella passeggiata

Bargello Museum
Via del Proconsolo 4
Tel: (055) 2388606
08.15–13.50 (or until 17.00 on holidays)

Uffizi Gallery
Loggiato degli Uffizi 6
Tel: (055) 294883
Open from 08.15–18.50 every day except Mondays
Unless it is the depth of winter it is worth booking your ticket in advance.
The queues can be horrendous.

Vasari Corridor
Entry via the Uffizi Gallery
Tel: (055) 2654321
The Vasari Corridor links Palazzo Pitti to Palazzo Vecchio via the Ponte
Vecchio (page 61). It is possible to book a visit on the above number and it
is usually open between June and December. The exact dates of opening
are at the discretion of the *sovrintendenza* (ministry of culture) who like to
keep everyone guessing.

Church of Santo Spirito
08.30–12.00 and 16.00–18.00
Saturdays 16.00–18.00
Closed Wednesday afternoons

Nail bar *Manicure*

Nails Shop
Via San Niccolò 35r
Tel: (055) 2340938
Open 10.00–19.00 Monday to Friday (*lunedì a venerdì*)
This is a small nail bar in an interesting part of Florence, south of the river.

Fresh pasta *Pasta fresca*

La Bolognese
Via dei Serragli 24
Tel: (055) 283 318
This shop has a good range of fresh pasta. There is the chance to see the huge sheets being made in the back.

Post offices *Poste*

The main post office is at Via Pellicceria 3. It is open Monday to Saturday from 08.15 to 19.00. The philatelic service for special stamps is open Monday to Friday from 08.15 to 13.30 and on Saturdays from 08.15 to 12.00.

There are several smaller branches in Florence including the post office in Via Pietra Piana 53r. This is open Monday to Friday from 08.30–19.00 and Saturdays from 08.15–13.30.

Restaurants and bars *Ristoranti e bar*

Café Coquinarius
Via delle Oche 15
Tel: (055) 23 02 153
Email coquinarius@tin.it
Closed Sundays (*Domenica*)
Open daily 09.00–23.00
This centrally located bar provides a comforting coffee and a cake or a tasty lunch or dinner. The artichoke (*carciofi*) pie deserves its Slow Food award.

Le volpe e l'uva Enoteca
Piazza de'Rossi 1r
50125 Firenze
Tel/Fax: (055) 2398132
Open 10.00–22.00
Closed Sundays (*Domenica*)
This small *enoteca* is in a secluded square close to the Ponte Veccio (south side). They serve an excellent range of wines and a tasty selection of local salami and cheese. There are English wine magazines to browse and seating outside or at the bar.

Senzanome Pizzeria

Via Doni 43

Tel: (055) 350696

Open every evening (*aperto ogni sera*)

This pizzeria is in the northwest of town. It has a wood-burning oven, as any good pizza restaurant should, friendly service and good prices.

Trattoria Nella

Via delle Terme 19r

Tel: (055) 2398222

Lunch (*pranzo*) 12.00–15.00, dinner (*cena*) 19.00–22.30

Closed Sundays (*Domenica*)

This is a small, popular *trattoria* in the centre of Florence.

Trattoria Ruggero

Via Senese 89r

Tel: (055) 220542.

Closed Tuesday and Wednesday (*Chiuso Martedì e Mercoledì*)

This is our favourite restaurant in Florence. If you like traditional cooking of fresh ingredients surrounded by local people then this is the place for you. It is an unpleasant ten-minute walk from Porta Romana (southwest of the centre), up the noisy, traffic-filled exit pipe of Via Senese. But once you step inside you are whisked away into a warm place full of cooking smells. Booking is essential.

Vecchia Bettola

Viale L. Ariosto 32–34r

Tel: (055) 224158

Closed Sundays and Mondays (*Domenica e Lunedì*)

This is a small restaurant serving typical Florentine fare in the 'foodies' quarter of town. Its food is delicious and the tables are nearly always packed with locals. It is on the corner of Via Ariosto where it meets the big main road Viale Aleardi. Booking is advised.

Sport and yoga Sport e yoga

The Yoga and Movement centre

Via dei Benci 20 (on the corner of Piazza S. Croce), first floor

Tel: (055) 2638808

Website www.clip2000.it (some information in English)
This centre has a variety of yoga and dance classes.

Stationery and printing *Cartolerie e tipografie*

Tipografia Arno
Via Guelfa 38
Tel: (055) 287878
This is more like a working museum, printing marbled papers, cards and items for the chain Il Papio. They still use the antique printers and will show you around.

Il Papagallo
Via Degli Alfani 61
Tel: (055) 2382664
Open 09.00–13.00 and 15.30–19.00 Monday to Friday (*Lunedì a Vernerdì*)
This is a stationers and print shop.

Supermarkets *Supermercati*

COOP
Via Cimbue 47
Open Monday to Friday from 08.00–21.00 and Saturday from 07.30–20.00. This large supermarket is in the east end of town, just off Via Vincenzo near Piazza Beccari. It is opposite an equally large UPIM department store.

Il Centro SRL
Via dei Ginori 41r
Tel: (055) 210354
Open Monday to Saturday from 08.00–20.00 and Sunday from 08.00–19.00. This supermarket sells fresh bread, cleaning products, groceries, pots and pans and toiletries. It is near the San Lorenzo market, just north of the Duomo.

Pegna
Via Belso Studo 7
This centrally located supermarket has been open since 1860 and has everything needed for stocking up your larder. It is open every day (*ogni giorno*) from 09.00–13.00 and 15.30–19.30.

Standa

Via Pietrapiana 44 (opposite the post office)

Tel: (055) 234 78 56

Open Monday to Saturday from 08.00 to 21.00 and Sunday from 09.00 to 20.00. This is a cheaper alternative to the above.

Swimming *Piscine*

Costoli

Viale Pasquale Paoli

Tel: (055) 236027/6236027

This is a large public swimming pool by the stadium. The *segreteria* is open Monday to Friday from 09.00–13.00 and also 14.30–17.30 on Wednesday and Thursdays. It costs €3.60 an hour and the sessions run from 12.50–14.50 and 19.30–21.30. To get there take a bus (numbers 3,6,10,11,17) to the stadium on Viale Paoli.

Tourist information *Pro loco*

Piazza della Stazione 4 (opposite the train station)

This is open Monday to Saturday from 8.30–19.00 and Sundays from 08.30 to 14.00.

Via Cavour 1r (next to Palazzo Medici)

This is a less busy tourist information centre. It is open from Monday to Saturday from 08.30 to 18.30 and on Sundays from 08.30 to 13.30.

Florence Concierge is a regular small English magazine with up-to-date information, articles and telephone numbers.

Towed away cars and scooters

These can be claimed and paid for at Via Circondaria 19, Tel: (055) 308 249.

Florence City Walk *La Passeggiata*

Finding the best shops, bars, restaurants, amenities and other secrets

The historic centre of Florence is compact, traffic free and easy to navigate. For this reason our walk starts and finishes in the centre but focuses on the beautiful but less visited outer quarters. It has been carefully designed to quickly orientate you to the best amenities, shops, bars, sights and monuments. Like all of our walks it includes viewing points, coffee and ice cream stops, restaurants and food markets. The walk takes about three hours including the stunning viewing point at Piazzale Michelangelo.

The walk begins in Piazza della Signoria, Florence's main civic square. Centre stage is the fortress-like town hall, Palazzo Vecchio (fourteenth century). Facing the Palazzo, to your right is the elegant Loggia dei Lanzi filled with statues. In one corner of the Loggia is the bronze *Perseus* by Cellini, holding Medusa's severed head. In the other corner is Giambologna's *The Rape of the Sabine Woman*. The Uffizi gallery is between the town hall and the River Arno. In the centre of the piazza is the equestrian statue of Cosimo I, next to Neptune's fountain.

Leave the piazza via the narrow street Calimaruzza. This street is straight ahead of you if you stand in front of the Cosimo statue facing the same way as the horse. This leads to the sixteenth century *loggia* in Piazza del Mercato. Cross the road and walk over to the bronze statue of the wild boar *Il Porcellino* on your right. Sliding a coin down its shiny tongue is thought to bring good luck. Continue past this statue and down the narrow Vicolo della Seta, which is unmarked at this end. There is a small **public library** (*Biblioteca di Palagio di Parte Guelfa*) housed in a quiet eleventh century church at the end of the road on the left. The library has a selection of English books, magazines and newspapers.

Turn left out of the library. At the T-junction with Via di Terme turn right, soon passing the popular **Trattoria Nella** at number 19r. The road ends at Piazza di Santa Trinità with its tall Column of Justice. The road to your right is Via Tornabuoni which has Florence's exclusive **designer shops**. Cross over the road to the Chiesa di Santa Trinità which has interesting fifteenth century frescoes.

Turn right out of the church and cross over Ponte Santa Trinità into the old Oltrarno district. Oltrarno refers to the districts of Florence on the south side (*other=altro*) of the river.

The Ponte Santa Trinità was rebuilt after being blown up in the Second World War. It has sixteenth Century statues of the four seasons on its corners and one of the best views of the Ponte Vecchio in Florence. There are also views of the tower of Piazza della Signoria and, on the other side of the river, the pretty seventeenth century bell tower of Chiesa di San Jacopo Sopr'Arno. If you want to visit the British Institute Library (via L. Guicciardini 9r, page 39) turn immediately right on the other side of the bridge. Otherwise take the next right into Via S. Spirito, opposite a corner mask fountain of an old man with bushy eyebrows and matching beard.

The high-tech **delicatessen** and restaurant Olio and Convivium is at number 4r. This sells a good selection of cheese and prosciutto including the excellent *Cinta Senese* (a rare white collared pig). There is a **print** shop L'Ippgrifo at number 5 which specialises in hand-made prints from engraved copperplates. At the end of the road at number 42r there is an **Internet** cafe. Unless you wish to visit any of these shops take the first left into Via D. Prestodi S. Martino. This leads into the pretty Piazza S. Spirito.

Piazza S. Spirito is a peaceful, tree-lined square with outdoor cafes, a fountain and a lively **antique market** on the second Sunday of the month (09.00–19.00). When the market it open try the *necci*, a chestnut flour pancake served with fresh ricotta and made by an elderly husband and wife team on a portable stove. The excellent Eurocentres language school is at number 9. If you walk to the far end of the Piazza by the statue of Cosimo and turn left into Via Mazzetta, there is another tiny **public library** (*biblioteca pubblica*) at number 10. Walk back to the church.

The big fifteenth century church of Santo Spirito looks rather plain from the outside with its eighteenth century plastered façade. Inside, however, it has 38 side altars decorated with fifteenth century paintings and sculptures and a colonnaded aisle. Turn left out of the church. There is a bespoke men's **shoe maker** (Roberto Ugolini) at number 17r. Walk straight into Via dei Michelozzi, cross the busy Via Maggio and continue into the sloping forecourt of **Piazza dei Pitti**.

Palazzo Pitti is the largest Palazzo in Florence and was started in the fifteenth century for the banker Luca Pitti in a failed attempt to top the Medici family. It houses several museums and an excellent art collection. Behind the Palazzo is the Giardino di Boboli, a large formal hillside garden. There are views across Florence from its shady avenues and it is a good place to bring a picnic. The ticket office is on the right as you face the palazzo. Entrance is free to EU citizens under 18 or over 65 and there are discounts for those 18–25 and teachers (proof is required). The excellent Accademia language school is at number 15r and the **Internet cafe** Internet Pitti is at number 7.

Coming out of the Palazzo Pitti turn right and walk along Via de'Guicciardini towards Ponte Vecchio, passing tourist shops which smell of leather. Before reaching the Ponte Vecchio turn right into Piazza Santa Felicita. Pass under the **Vasari Corridor** (*Corridoio Vasariano*) which here runs from the Chiesa di Santa Felicità to Ponte Vecchio.

The Vasari Corridor links the Palazzo Pitti with Palazzo Vecchio. It was built by Vasari in the sixteenth century to allow the Medici family to move about without mixing with the public. The corridor also gave access to the Chiesa di Santa Felicita, via a grate at the back of the church, enabling them to attend mass. It is possible to access the corridor via the Uffizi Gallery but this should be booked in advance (page 54). The exact opening dates are at the discretion of the *sovrintendenza* (part of the Ministry of Culture) who keep everyone guessing. Coming up with a good reason to visit can increase your chances of getting in. It is usually open from June–December.

On the other side of the corridor is the secluded Piazza dei Rossi. The Le Volpi e L'Uva **enoteca** has a good selection of wines by the glass and plates of local cheese and salami. Turn left out of the enoteca and walk up Via Stracciatella. Turn left at the end of the road into Costa del Pozza and first right into Vicolo del Canneto. This road bends around to the river with views across to the Ufizzi. Turn right and walk along the river on Lungarno Torrigiani. There are views through the arches of the Uffizi to the copy of Michelangelo's *David* in the Piazza della Signori where the walk started. To the left there are views of the Ponte Vecchio.

Just before the first bridge, Ponte alle Grazie, you pass a small shaded piazza on the right which overlooks the river. This has a pretty church, Chiesa Evangelica Luterana (1901) which was founded by the first German speaking Lutheran community in Florence. About 20 metres beyond the bridge on the right-hand side of the road there is a bus stop from which the number 13 goes to the viewing point, Piazzale Michelangelo. If you are walking (worth the effort) turn right at the bridge into Piazza de Mozzi and then first left into Via de'Renai. Just beyond the tree-lined park turn right into Via dell'Olmo and walk alongside the church of San Niccolò Oltrarno. At the bottom of the road turn left into Via S. Niccolò. On the wall of the church above the small wooden door on the left is a plaque showing the water level from the devastating 1966 flood. Continue along Via S. Niccolò, which has a number of interesting shops. At number 60r is the award winning **osteria** *Antica Mescita San Niccolò*, there is a **butcher** at number 56r, a dry cleaners at number 50r, a **baker** at number 43r and a **nail bar** at number 35r. At the far end of the road is Piazza Poggi with its fortified tower. From here bear right and walk up the hill. Follow this road which becomes a path and zigzags through a shady park to Piazzale Michelangelo. This is the best **viewpoint** of Florence.

Retrace your steps to the Ponte alle Grazie Bridge, cross over and turn right to walk along the river on the other side. There are views up to Piazzale Michaelangelo on the hill. Take the second left into Piazza dei Cavalleggeri and turn left again to walk around the **National Library**, *Biblioteca Nazionale*, with its carved white marble faces. Take the first right into Via Antonio Magliabech which soon leads into Piazza Santa Croce. Here, the heated **football match** *Gioco del Calcio Storico* is played in the last week in June (St Johns week). Teams representing the four quartieri of Florence dress up in medieval costume. The church of **Santa Croce** contains frescoes by Giotto and the tombs of many famous Florentines including Galileo and Michaelangelo.

Turn right out of the church and right again past the statue of Dante Alighieri into Largo Bargellini which merges with Via Giuseppe. Passing the Baldovino **Trattoria** and enoteca (22r and 18r), turn left when you reach the church of San Giuseppe into Via delle Conce. Walk right to the end of this long narrow road, over several crossroads. Although it is rather gloomy there is a pretty **garden** (*giardino*) on the right just before the

T-junction, *Giardino del Palazzo Vivarelli Colonna*. This is open Tuesdays and Thursdays from 10.00–18.00 from 1 April to 30 September. Turn left at the T-junction into Via dell'Agnolo and before reaching the Wash and Dry **laundrette** at number 21r, take the first right into Via de'Macci. Take the first right into Via Mino, which takes you into Piazza Lorenzo Ghiberti and the excellent daily **covered food market** of *Sant'Ambrogio*. On the left is the **teashop**, La Via del Tè, which has a selection of teas and fresh cakes.

Turn left out of the teashop, walk to the end of the Piazza and turn left again into Via Andrea del Verrocchio. At the end of this short road turn right into Via de' Macci, passing the expensive *Il Cibreo* restaurant. The road comes out to Piazza S. Ambrogio. If you turned right here, along Borgo la Croce, you would pass the wood burning (*forno a legna*) pizza restaurant Le Campane at 85r, Dr Vranje's shop at 44r selling handmade **perfumes** and fragrances, a **cobblers** at 14r and then the large Piazza C. Beccaria with its cinema and ice cream shop (*gelateria*). There is a large COOP supermarket and UPIM department store on the other side of the Piazza Beccaria, in Via Vincenzo. Unless you want to walk to any of these shops, turn left into Borgo la Croce and walk straight into Via Pietra Piana and then into Piazza Ciompi.

This piazza has a daily **flea market** and an elegant Loggia del Pesce, with fish (*pesce*) carved above the arches. Continue along Via Pietra Piana, passing a **post office** on your left at number 53r and a Standa **supermarket** opposite at number 94r. Walk into Piazza Gaetano Salvemini and then down Borgo degli Albizi in the far left-hand corner. The Vestri *gelateria* sells reasonably priced delicious ice creams and hot chocolate. Turn left out of the *gelateria* and continue along Borgo degli Albizi for several minutes. After passing Piazza Maggiore take the third left turn into Canto del Proconsolo. The **Bargello Museum**, housed in an old prison, is on the left at number 4r. This museum contains Italy's best collection of Renaissance sculpture, including Donatello's *David*.

Turn right out of the museum onto Canto del Proconsolo and take the first left into the unmarked, narrow Via Dante Alighieri. Continue past the tenth century Badia Fiorentina abbey on your left and turn right into Via Margherita to visit the tiny church of Santa Margherita. This is where **Dante** first met Beatrice Portinari who inspired his poetry. Despite the piped music the church and the street have a timeless quality. After visiting the church walk back to Via Alighieri and turn right soon passing Dante's birthplace, the Casa di Dante on the left. Via Dante Alighieri becomes Via dei Tavolini. Walk straight on until you come out into the wide Via dei Calzaiuoli, turn right to walk up to the **Duomo** and the end of the walk.

If you still have energy it is worth walking a couple of streets north of the Duomo to the San Lorenzo district and the Mercato centrale. This is a large **covered food market** (open Monday to Saturday mornings). Surrounding the covered market is a bustling **street market** selling clothes and leather good. Try the bars around the market for a cheap coffee or lunch with the Florentines.

Siena

5

Siena is a walled mediaeval hill town in the heart of Tuscany 68 miles south of Florence (*Firenze*). It sits on the southern border of the *Monte di Chianti*, the famous wine and olive oil region. It was built in the thirteenth century by the successful bankers and wool traders. For several centuries Siena was in fierce competition with *Firenze* who at one point stooped as low as catapulting faeces over their walls in a failed attempt to start a plague. There are 55,000 residents and 20,000 students making it a lively place to live.

The pedestrianised *centro storico* is built around one of the *più bella* piazzas in Italy. This shell-shaped *Piazza del Campo* slopes gently down to the fourteenth century bell tower *Torre del Mangia*. From the top there are views over Tuscany, Siena and the humbug-striped *Duomo* (1136–1382). The University for Foreigners *Università per Stranieri di Siena* offers high quality language courses in the centre of the old town. Siena has excellent public transport links across Italy so it is a good place to be based.

Don't Miss *Da Non Perdere*

▶ the view from the 102m *Torre del Mangia*, Italy's second tallest medieval tower

▶ *Il Palio*: Siena goes crazy during this biannual horse race on 2 July and 16 August

▶ a *siesta* on the warm bricks of the Piazza del Campo

▶ sunset over Tuscany from the quiet walls of the *Fortezza Medicea* (The Fort)

▶ eating *panforte* in the town where it was invented

▶ Tuscany's famous *ribollita* (vegetable and bean soup) drizzled with *novello* olive oil

▶ Siena Jazz Festival: for a fortnight from the end of July (www.siena-jazz.it)

▶ the *Settimana dei Vini* (wine week) in the first ten days of June

▶ vineyard hopping across Chianti

▶ weekends walking in Chianti and the Tuscan forests

▶ the striped marble Duomo – *è squisito!* (it's exquisite!).

Table comparing Siena and Lucca's Language Schools

Le Scuole di Lingua

School	University	Società Dante Alighieri	Saena Iulia Scuola	Centro Koinè (see page 233)
Town	Siena	Siena	Siena	Lucca
Two-week course	–	€360	€320	€360
Four-week course	€300	€610	€640	€586
Individual lessons per hour	–	€40	€30	€31
Enrolment fee	None	€60	€30	None
Single room two weeks	–	€300	€240	€260
Single room four weeks	€316	€425	€400	€410
Maximum group size	No max	12	8	12
Laboratory	Yes	Yes	No	No
Air conditioning	Yes	No	No	No
Scholarships	Yes	Yes	No	No

University for Foreigners of Siena
Università per Stranieri di Siena

Via Pantaneto 45
53100 Siena
Tel: (0577) 240115 Fax: (0577)281030
Email info@unistrasi.it Website www.unistrasi.it

▶ Porters *Portineria* (left of the main entrance)
Open Monday to Friday 07.30–20.00 Saturday 07.30–13.45

▶ Secretariat *segreteria* (through to the right after the *Portineria*)
Open Monday to Friday 10.30–13.00

▶ Student Assistance Office *Assistenza Studenti* (through to the left after the *Portineria*)
Tel: (0577) 240 104 Fax: (0577) 283 163
Open Monday to Friday 08.15–13.30 and Saturday 08.15–13.00

▶ Multi Media Room *Aula Multimediale* (marked 'Univerità per Stranieri')
Piazzetta Virgilio Grassi 2, first floor (turn right out of the University and take the first right into Via di Follonica which leads into the Piazzetta).
Open Mondays and Wednesdays 13.00–18.00, Tuesdays and Thursdays 09.00–12.00 and 13.00–18.00, Fridays 09.00–12.00 and 13.00–16.00. Sessions must be booked the day before at the *Portineria*.

▶ University Library *Biblioteca* Via di Pantaneto 109 (turning left out of the University it is on the left next to the Chiesa di San Giorgio)
Tel: (0577) 240453
Email biblio@unistrasi.it
Open Monday to Friday 08.30–18.30 and Saturday 08.30–13.30.

The University for Foreigners is one of our top choices if you have three or more weeks and can fit in with the dates of the courses. The main building is a beautiful *palazzo* with a shady garden in the historic centre of the town. As with all Italian universities there is no limit on the number of students enrolling so the class size can be large. The average is around 15–20 students which is smaller than at the *Università per Stranieri* in Perugia. The courses offer good value for money and include standard ten-week language courses, intensive three-week courses, cultural courses, diplomas, degrees and teaching Italian as a foreign language. To enrol on the three-month course at the University you need to be eligible to attend university in your home country (A-levels or equivalent). Anyone, regardless of educational background, can attend the one-month courses. Information in English is easier to find on the University website than by telephone.

Types of courses and costs *Tipo di corsi e costi*

1 **First level diploma courses** in Italian language. This is the standard ten-week language course with 15 hours of Italian language lessons a week. There are four levels: beginners, elementary, intermediate and advanced. For the beginners and elementary levels the University offers 20 hours of free lessons for those who fall behind in their group. The University will also organise free cultural courses depending on demand. These last ten hours and include Italian song, theatre, cinema, mass media and the figurative arts. The courses start at the beginning of October, January, and April, and in mid–July and cost €750.

2 **Second level diploma course** in Italian language and culture. This ten-week course is for students who already speak Italian well. The entry requirement for this three-month course is either a pass in the advanced level of the above course, or a CILS 3 certificate (see page 15) or a certificate of intermediate level in Italian language or a placement test. There are 15 hours of Italian language lessons a week and nine hours of cultural courses a week. Students choose three cultural subjects out of art, education, history, Italian language, literature, philosophy and sociology. Courses start at the beginning of October, the second week of January, April and in mid–July. The cost is €900.

3 **Intensive Italian language courses**. These courses consist of 75 hours of Italian language lessons over three or four weeks (i.e. 25 hours a week for the three-week course and about 19 hours a week for the four-week course). There are four levels: beginners, elementary, intermediate and advanced. The courses are only run when a minimum of eight students are enrolled. There are four courses a year. In January and September they last three weeks and in June and August they last four weeks. The

cost is €550. This is expensive when compared to the *Università per Stranieri* in Perugia where a similar course costs just €233 (see page 91).

Specialist courses and costs *Corsi speciali e costi*

1 **Courses for specific professions**. These courses last 20 hours and run every August. They cover four areas: architecture and art, history, medicine and natural sciences and law, business and commerce. They can be taken in conjunction with other courses and cost €300. There is a 50% discount for students enrolled on one of the other courses.

2 **Courses in drama, songs, conversation, writing, literature of translation**. These courses are available if a minimum of eight students apply. The courses are taken in conjunction with another course and last ten hours. They are available throughout the year and cost €25.

3 **Tailor-made courses for small groups by special request**. These include cuisine, wine, language and communication skills for business, music, history of art and literature.

4 **Preparation courses for the Certification of Italian as a Foreign Language (CILS)**. This is an internationally recognised Italian language qualification (see page 15). The exams are held in December and June each year. There are two one-month courses available, an 80 hour intensive course or a 20-hour course for students already on another language course. They are held in May and November each year and cost €500 for 80 hours or €250 for 20 hours.

5 **Preparation course for the Certificate of Teaching Italian to Foreigners (DITALS)**. This is an internationally recognised qualification for people who want to teach Italian to foreigners. It is a five-day course and there are strict entry criteria. You need to have an excellent knowledge of the Italian language including an A-level in Italian or equivalent, a degree in humanities or 150 hours of teaching Italian as a foreign language and a certificate of attendance in a DITALS preparation course of at least 30 hours. Courses are held in March and August and last 30 hours over five days. The cost is €400.

6 **Specialist courses** for teachers such as didactics, Italian literature, art history and refresher courses in linguistics and language.

7 **University degree programme** in teaching Italian as a foreign language. This is a three-year degree course in teaching Italian as a foreign language. The cost is €800 per year. For further information email corsiuni@unistrasi.it

Facilities

The university has good facilities and is on a quiet road full of useful shops. There is a self-access multimedia room (*aula multimediale*) on the first floor of *Dell'edificio della Sede Didattica at Piazzetta* Grassi 2. There are CD-ROMs for learning independently. See above for directions and opening times.

The university library *Biblioteca dell'Università per Stranieri* is at Via di Pantaneto 109. It is good place to study and has a notice board with local events and accommodation. There are also newspapers and magazines in Italian and English, computers and a photocopier. See above for directions and opening times.

There are two canteens (*mense*) one at Via Sallustio Bandini 47 and the other at Via St. Agatha. Both serve meals for €3 and need proof of enrolment at the University such as a student card (*tessera*). To find Via Sallustio Bandini turn right out of the University and right in Via di Follonica and take the first left uphill. The canteen is in the first right turning. Via St. Agatha is in the Siena City Walk (page 83).

Sports *Sport*

DSU Sportello Servizi Studenti
Email infostudenti@dsu.siena.it
This service has information on all sporting facilities in Siena, which give discounts (*sconti*) to students. The office is in the process of moving so ask at the *portineria* for the new address and opening times. Students at the *Università per Stranieri* can use the main University's sports centre *Centro Universitario* from October to the end of May. To enrol, go to the DSU with your academic *tessera* (student enrolment card) and a medical certificate. This is to certify that you are fit to do the type of sport that you want for the whole period of your stay in Siena (even if it's ping-pong!). The *Centro*

Universitario is a ten-minute ride on the number 11 bus from Piazza
Gramsci Antonio near the Stadium *Stadio Comunale*.

Accommodation *Alloggio*

Assistenza studenti will fax or email a copy in English of their accommodation options. There are central university halls of residence in Via San
Martino 14, and Via del Porrione 70. The 22 twin rooms with private bathrooms in Via San Martino are much nicer. The best rooms are numbers 24,
25, 26, 34, 35 and 36 which have stunning views over Tuscany. There is a
fridge on each floor and a windowless communal kitchen and television
room in the basement. The cost is €775 for the ten-week courses starting in
January or April per person. For the four-week intensive course in June
and September the cost is €316. There is a €50 per course reduction for
bunk beds. The prices include water, gas, electricity, heating, sheets and
weekly cleaning but not towels.

To reserve a place ask the *Assistenza Studenti* for a booking form for *San
Martino* and pay a €200 deposit by bank transfer. The details of the bank
account are on the application form. Fax the form with a copy of the bank
transfer to the *Assistenza* and they will confirm your place again by fax.
You must pay the full balance in cash when you arrive in Siena.

Assistenza Studenti also has a list of accommodation for privately owned
rooms and apartments. They do *not* take any responsibility for any problems that arise between the landlords and students (see accommodation
page 24). Rooms for rent (*in affitto*) are advertised on the notice boards
near the *portineria*, in the library and in the canteens.

Bed and Breakfast *Palazzo Landi Bruchi*
Via Pantaneto 105
53100 Siena
Tel/Fax: (0577) 287342
Email masignani@hotmail.com Website www.ilgiardino-masignani.it
This bed and breakfast is centrally located next to the University
Biblioteca. There are nine rooms for rent for a month or more from October

to Easter. There is a small communal kitchen with electric hobs. Room numbers one to four have large windows and good views. From October to Easter a single room costs €300 per month with a shared bathroom or €390 with a private bathroom. During the summer season a double room costs €65 a night including breakfast. Car parking is available around Porta Romana.

Enrolment *Iscrizione*

The application form is on the back of the *Università per Stranieri's* brochure and on their website. It is best to enrol at least 20 days in advance. The application requires two passport photos, a photocopy of your passport and a copy of the receipt for the deposit. The deposit for the course can be paid with a bank draft to the *Università per Stranieri di Siena*; details of the account are on the application form. Include your name, the course name and the course dates on the bank draft and photocopy everything before sending it off (see *documenti* page 27). If you are a European Union (EU) citizen you can confirm that you are entitled to attend university in your home country simply by signing the application form and listing your qualifications. If you are a non-EU citizen you also need to include a photocopy of the qualifications. The University will send you a pre-enrolment certificate confirming your booking.

What to expect when starting your course *Inizio dei corsi*

There is a short test at 9 o'clock on the first day to determine your level. The Student Assistance office (*Assistenza Studenti*) will tell you where to go for this. A list is posted on the notice board opposite the *portineria* the next day with your group's details. If you would like to be in the same class as someone else then ask on the first day. After the test you need to pay and enrol at the *segreteria*, which is on your right as you pass the *portineria*. You will need your pre-enrolment certificate, your receipt of payment of your deposit, your passport, passport photos and cash or a credit card. There is often a long queue on the first day so get there early or go a day later.

Private Language Schools

Società Dante Alighieri Comitato di Siena

Via Tommaso Pendola 37
53100 Siena
Tel: (0577) 49533 Fax: (0577) 270646
Email info@dantealighieri.com Website www.dantealighieri.com
The Siena branch of the *Societá Dante Alighieri* (see page 2 *Società Dante Alighieri*) was founded in 1979 and currently has over 1,200 students a year (250 per month in July and August). It is on the top floor of a spacious, frescoed seventeenth century palazzo at the far end of Via Tommaso Pendola at its junction with Via di San Quirico. This is a good location, only five minutes walk from the *Piazza del Campo* but away from the tourist groups. The palazzo's terracotta coloured brick and dark yellow exterior is easily recognised. There is a large library room with a selection of Italian audiotapes, videos, books and laminated Italian exercise sheets. The library is a quiet area for studying and there are views of the Tuscan countryside. There is a cosy sitting room, which has a guitar and piano. Internet access costs €2 per hour. The groups have a maximum size of 12 students. There are extracurricular activities in the afternoons, including lectures, seminars, film visits, excursions and trips to restaurants.

Courses and costs *Corsi e costi*
The standard language course is 20 hours per week and costs €360 for two weeks and €610 for four weeks. The school has a Club 50+ for over 50s, evening cookery classes and courses for opera singers. There are preparatory courses for the *Progetto Lingua* certificate of the *Società Dante Alighieri* and for the CILS certificate (Certificate in Italian as a Second Language) from the *Università per Stranieri* in Siena (see qualifications page 15). A certificate of attendance is awarded to all students. There is an enrolment fee of €60 for the accommodation or pick-up service.

Accommodation *Alloggio*
Single room half-board accommodation with an Italian family costs €390 for two weeks and €660 for four weeks. Mini apartments for two people cost €215–270 for two weeks per person or €290–350 for four weeks per person.

Saena Iulia Scuola di Lingua e Cultura Italiana

Via Monna Agnese 20
53100 Siena
Tel: (0577) 44 155 Fax: (0577) 28 3162
Email info@saenaiulia.it Website www.saenaiulia.it

This tiny language school could not be more welcoming. It is in the six-teenth century Palazzo del Magnifico next to the Duomo. To find it face the back of the Duomo from Piazza S. Giovanni and walk up the steps on the left. The school is in the building on the left as you climb. Go through an iron-gated courtyard and follow the signs to the dance school down through a cool stone passageway before the steps up to the school. You may be welcomed by the friendly English speaking Georgia who can tell you all about the courses and how the school is run. The school has a per-sonal atmosphere where students get to know each other and their teachers. Unlimited Internet access is paid for on a weekly rate.

Courses and costs *Corsi e costi*

The standard language course is 20 hours per week and runs from one week to several months. A two week course costs €320 and a four-week course costs €640. Groups are small, as few as two to a maximum of eight There is a strong focus on conversational Italian. The lessons are held in the mornings leaving the afternoons free for organised outings. There is a free weekly seminar on a cultural theme and an excursion every Thursday, which is paid for separately. They run a range of specialised courses includ-ing commercial Italian, Italian for tour operators, language of Italian opera and preparation for the CILS exams. There is an €80 enrolment fee which lasts for one year. This includes all study materials and access to the mem-bers' website where you can keep learning Italian at home.

Accommodation *Alloggio*

The school encourages students to stay with an Italian family. Furnished apartments are also available. It is best to book at least a month in advance. Georgia will try to find the place of your dreams even if 'you are allergic to cats, vegetarian and must have your own bathroom…'. A single room including half-board accommodation with an Italian family costs €436 for two weeks and €792 for four weeks. There is a 20% reduction for a double room. Mini apartments cost €480 for two weeks and €1,060 for four weeks.

Getting To and From Siena *Andare e Tornare da Siena*

Coach *Pulman*

The main bus station is in Piazza Gramsci. There is an underground ticket office where you can obtain free timetables and information in English. There is also a left luggage service with a full set of rules on what can be left, when and how. Luggage must be less than 15kg, can be left for one day only between the hours of 07.00 and 19.45 for a cash payment of €3.50. There are public telephones and toilets. The bus routes are divided into *urbani* (local) and *estraurbani* (long distance). The company running them is called *Tran*. The central information line is (0577) 204111 or look on their excellent website www.sena.it. Tickets can be reserved on the telephone (in Italian) or booked in person at the bus station.

The bus for Rome takes a little less than three hours and costs €16 for a single. Buses leave at least every two hours from 05.00–20.00. The bus for Bologna takes little over two hours and costs €10 for a single. They leave at least twice daily.

Trains *Treni*

The train station is in Piazzale Carlo Rosselli. There is a newsagent and a bar. The ticket office (*biglietteria*) is open from 05.50 to 20.00 every day. Siena is well served for trains throughout Italy. There are 12 trains per day to *Firenze* and 16 to *Roma*. The journey times are an hour-and-three quarters or three hours respectively. The excellent website www.fs-on-line.com has timetables and it is possible to book on line. There is a ticket office for buses, *biglietteria autobus*, in the same building, open Monday to Saturdays 05.50–20.00 and Sundays 07.20–12.40 and 15.40–19.30. The bus stop next to the station has bus numbers 3, 4, 7, 8, 9, 10, 14 17 and 77 for the centre. Tickets cost €0.77 and can be bought from the vending machine or at the ticket office.

Addresses for Easy Living in Siena

Bicycle and scooter rental *Biciclette e scooter a noleggio*

D.F. Moto Noleggi

Via dei Gazzani 16/18

Tel: (0577) 288387 Mobile: (347) 4058829

Open from May to September from 09.00–19.30 (including Sunday)

This shop rents bicycles from €10 a day, or €50 a week and scooters from €26 a day.

Bookshops *Librerie*

Liberia Universitaria Senese (LUS) Via Sallustio Bandini 17

Open Monday to Friday 09.00–13.00 and 15.00–19.00 and Saturdays 09.00–13.00 This shop offers a 10% discount on books and 20% discounts on dictionaries to students.

Feltrinelli

Banchi di Sopra 52 and 64

Website www.lafeltrinelli.it (Italian only)

These two book shops stock Italian grammar books and a full range of other subjects.

Car parking *Parccheggi*

There are several undercover car parks around the city walls. The main underground car park is in Via Pier Andrea Mattioli near Porta Tufi at the southern end of the town. There is free parking near Viali Vittorio Veneto near the Fort indicated by white lines. To park within the blue lines, buy a ticket from one of the machines.

Cinemas *Cinema*

Impero

Via Benso di Cavour 14 (outside the city walls, just beyond Porta Camollia)

Moderno
Piazza Tolomei
Tel: (0577) 289201 (recorded information in Italian)

Nuova Pendola
Via San Quirico 13
Tel: (0577) 43012 (recorded information in Italian)
Closed in July and August
This cinema has a stair lift, but no disabled toilet.

Odeon
Banci di Sopra 31 (through a stone arch and down the stairs on the left)

Cobbler *Calzolaio*

Il Ciabattino
Via Di Pantaneto 91
Open 08.00–12.30, 15.30–19.30, closed Monday morning and Saturday afternoon

Department store *Grando magazzino*

UPIM
Piazza Matteotti
Open Monday to Friday 09.00–19.50 and Saturday 08.30–19.50
This is a good value department store.

Electrical/kitchen/hardware shop *Elettrodomestici*

Apigas
Via dei Termini 75
Tel: (0577) 282259
This shop is run by a husband and wife team and sells useful things such as hairdryers, radios and coffee makers.

Gyms *Palestre*

There are several gyms within the city walls and lots of other sports opportunities. Tai Chi is available at *Palestra Salto*, Via Monna Agnese 29, tel: (0577) 288375 and there is a dance school on the same road.

Internet *Internet*

Internet Caffè
Via di Pantaneto 100/102
There are lots of Internet points; access here costs €2 an hour.

Laundrettes *Lavanderie*

Wash and Dry
Via Di Pantaneto 38 (opposite the *Università per Stranieri*)
Open daily from 08.00–22.00 with the last wash at 21.00. €3 wash and €3 dry.

Onda Blu
Casato di Sotto 19 (just off Piazza del Campo)
Open daily from 08.00–22.00

Music accademy *Accademia Musicale Chigiana*

Via di Citta 89
Tel: (0577) 22091
Website www.chigiana.it (only in Italian)
This academy holds regular concerts with reductions for students and people under 26. They also organise the *Settimana Musicale* (a week of concerts) in July.

Pharmacies *Farmacie*

The *farmacie* advertise who is doing the night service outside their shops. Those at numbers 2 and 77 Via di Citta are central.

Post office *Poste*

Piazza Matteotti
Open Monday to Friday 08.15 to 19.00 and Saturdays 08.15–18.00
This is Siena's main post office. Make sure you queue in the right place. The *prodotti postali queue* is for posting things and *prodotti banco-posta* for paying bills.

Via di Città, 142
Open Monday to Friday 08.15–13.30 and Saturdays 08.15–12.30

Restaurants and bars *Ristoranti e bar*

La Costarella
Via Di Città 31/33
Tel: (0577) 288076
This café has views of the Campo from upstairs and from its tiny balcony.

Osteria Castelvecchio
Via di Castelvecchio 65
Tel: (0577) 49586
Closed Tuesdays.

Osteria del Coro (Caffè New York)
Via Pantaneto 87
Tel: (0577) 222482
This small *osteria* is near the *Universitá per Stranieri* and serves simple but delicious pizza and pasta in a lively atmosphere.

Osteria Le Logge
Via del Porrione 33
Tel: (0577) 48013
This is one of Siena's most famous restaurants. The kitchen is visible from the street so you can watch the chefs at work.

Pizzeria Carla e Franca
Via Pantaneto 138
Tel: (0577) 284385
Sit upstairs with the other *ragazzi* and eat hot pizza fresh from the oven or take away a *mini calzone*.

Sports Pub/The Walkabout Pub
Via di Pantaneto 90
Open 12.00–02.00
This popular pub/bar shows all the matches.

Torrefazione Fiorella
Via di Citta 13
This is a great little coffee bar which also sells coffee beans, fresh cakes and *panini*.

Specialist food shops *Nogozi di specialitá gastronomiche*

Antica Pizzicheria al Palazzo della Chigiana

Via di Città 93/95

Tel: (0577) 289164 Fax: (0577) 279745

Open every day 08.00–20.00

This is one of the oldest food shops in Siena, founded in 1889. It is also one of the best speciality food shops in Tuscany and surprisingly is not mentioned in guides. It is run by Antonio de Miccoli, and is full of local goodies. *Prosciutto* from Parma and Siena are hung from the ceiling. There are salamis and cheeses from all over Tuscany, house preserved tomatoes (*pomodori*), artichokes (*carciofi*) and mushrooms (*funghi*). There are also homemade biscuits (*biscotti*), pots of cured meats and wild boar, and the best *panforte* you can buy, made by hand by Signor Miccoli himself. Sandwiches (*panini*) are made to order using very fresh bread. Signor Miccoli gets up every morning at 6am to make it.

Supermarkets *Supermercati*

Consorzio Agrario

Via Pianigian 115

Open Monday to Saturday 08.00 to 19.30

This general food shop (*alimentari*) near Piazza Matteotti sells everything you need to stock your fridge. Its shop window makes it look like a speciality goods shop but behind this is a small supermarket including a deli counter and fresh bread. Prices are not cheap but reasonable for the location and convenience.

Theatres *Teatri*

Information line: (0577) 292225/292141

Teatro dei Rozzi, Piazza Indipendenza. Tel: (0577) 46960

Teatro dei Rinnovati, Piazza del Campo. Tel: (0577) 292265 (closed for restoration until the end of 2004)

Teatro dei Costone, Via del Costone. Tel: (0577) 42073 Monday to Friday 17.30–19.30

Tourist information *Pro Loco*

The tourist information centre in the main Campo has free information in English including an excellent leaflet about the Palio.

Siena Eventi is a free annual publication in Italian and English by the Commune of Siena. It has monthly listings with details of prices including concerts, courses, exhibitions, cinema, markets, guided tours and details about the Palio.

There are two good journals that list all of the local events. They both have a useful telephone number section on their second pages. *Sienadove* is a monthly small magazine costing €1.80 and is in Italian, English and Dutch. *Il Settimanale di Siena* is a free weekly mini newspaper, which is only in Italian.

Writing paper and cards *Cartolerie*

Il Papiro
Via di Citta 37
Tel: (0577) 284241
Open Monday to Friday from 09.00–13.00 and 15.30–19.30
This handmade paper shop sells the typical writing paper, notebooks, photo frames, pens, wrapping paper and cards that Italy is famous for. For the rather high price of €1.75 there are some very nice postcards of the *Palio* (see page 66). *Il Papiro* is part of a chain of shops in the major tourist towns but the paper and cards are still made in the traditional way.

Yoga *Yoga*

La Scuola Italiana di Yoga-Shiatsu at Via Spertini 12. Tel: (0577) 50414. This school runs three-month yoga courses every month except August, costing €45 per month. The school is only open during classes, which are from 18.00 to 20.30 from Monday to Thursday.

Siena City Walk

Finding the best shops, bars, restaurants, amenities and other secrets

This excellent walk has been carefully designed to quickly orientate you to the best amenities, shops, bars, restaurants, sights, viewing points and other secrets. It includes details of the *contrade* (districts), highlighted in the biannual bareback horse race *Il Palio*. If you want to have lunch book a table at **Osteria Castelvecchio** or *pranzo al sacco* (picnic) by the *Duomo* about an hour from the start. The walk is split into sections so it can be made shorter.

We start on the balcony of **Bar La Costarella** Via Di Città 31/33, overlooking the *Piazza del Campo*. From the bar, walk down into the *Campo* to the *Torre del Mangia*.

Piazza del Campo. The *Torre del Mangia* is the bell tower of the *Palazzo Pubblico* Siena's town hall. It was named after the fourteenth Century bell ringer, Mangiaguadagni (spendthrift), who was appointed to climb the 400 steps to ring the bells. It is well worth climbing if you have a head for heights. It is open 10.00–15.15 and they have a maximum of 950 tickets a day. As you walk into the tower the ticket office is straight ahead, the *museo civico* (museum) is to your right and the steps to the tower are on your left. Coming out of the tower, turn right and take the second right off the campo along Via Del Porrione. Walk past the **Osteria Le Logge** at number 33 and take the first left by the *Chiesa di S. Martino*. Walk past the *Logge del Papa* (1462) and turn right into Via di Pantaneto (University Road) which has lots of useful shops. The **Universià per Stranieri** is on the left at number 45 and the 'wash and go' **laundrette** is directly opposite at number 38. Soon after on the left at number 55 is a small mini-market, good for late night or Sunday provisions. There is a **stationer** on the right at number 58, and *Osteria del Coro*, at number 85, which serves good pizza and nightcaps. If you like watching football and rugby, the **Walkabout Pub** at number 90 shows matches from around the world. There is a **cobbler** (*ciabattino*) at number 91 and the Palazzo Bruchi **Bed and Breakfast** at number 105. The excellent **library** (*biblioteca*) is next to the Chiesa di

San Giorgio at number 109. Continue along Via Di Pantaneto past the very simple but fun **Pizzeria Carla e Franca** (number 138) and the **cinema** Flamma (number 143).

Go under the stone arch and take the first right into Via S. Girolamo, heading towards the clock tower at the *Istituto S. Girolamo*. Before you reach it turn right up the hill and follow the signs to Piazza di Mercato and the Campo. Take the first left downhill into Via di Salicotto. There are views of the Tuscan countryside and of *Prato di S. Agostino* across the valley of olive trees. Pass on your left the *Museo Contrada Della Torre* at number 76. The coat of arms for this *Contrada* (district) is an elephant with a tower on its back. Small metal shields of the arms can be seen in numerous places, including outside the museum and outside house numbers 80 and 70. Turn left into Via dei Malcontenti and the **Piazza del Mercato**.

Piazza del Mercato and Old Siena. There is a small antique market at *Piazza del Mercato* on the third Sunday of the month, open from 10.00 to 17.00. Up to the right, there are views of the back of the Palazzo Pubblico and its ancient wooden roof. Walk up Vicolo di San Salvodore which is the road straight ahead of you as you entered the piazza. Take the first left into Via Giovanni Dupre and into the oldest part of Siena. This district is the *Contrada dell'Onda*, symbolised by a dolphin with a blue crown. This can be seen in the bright fresco at the junction with Vicolo della Fontote and at the contada's headquarters at number 66. At the top of the hill walk through the stone arch just past the *Chiesa di S. Giuseppe*. To the left of the arch is a small dolphin fountain. Turn right up Via S. Agata and immediately on the left through the iron gates is one of the **university canteens** (mense). Walk up the hill and take the first right through the arch, Porta All'Arco, into Via S. Pietro. If it is lunch time take the third left which is signed to the **Osteria Castelvecchio** (Via di Castelvecchio number 65). This is a Slow Food *osteria* with a daily changing menu, local specialities and a good wine list. Otherwise take the second left into Via Tommaso Pendola past the small drinking fountain of a baby and a tortoise. The tortoise (*tartuca*) is the district's symbol, and sits in a field of daisies on the coat of arms. The headquarters of the *Contrada della Tartuca* is at number 26, and the museum also at number 26. There are tiny tortoises on the plug covers between the first floor windows. During the Palio these are used for the many painted wooden sconces throughout the city. The large terracotta coloured palazzo at number 37 houses the *Società Dante Alighieri* language school.

At the end of the road there is a tiny church with faded frescoes above the door. Turn right into Via Quirco, entering the snail district (*Contrada della Chiocciola*). Along the road there are small stone plaques with snail illustrations. Walk up past the **cinema** (*Nuova Pendola*) and then bear right along the same road. Turn left at the end and then immediately right into Via Stalloreggi, the panther district (*Contrada della Pantera*) and continue past the fountain to Piazza di Postieria. If you need a *spuntino* (**snack**) or want to *pranzo al sacco* (**picnic**) walk straight down Via di Città rather than deviating left towards the *Duomo*. On your right at number 93 is one of the best delis in Tuscany. Here you can buy *panini* (*sandwiches*) made to order and **fruit** from the *negozio di frutta e verdura* at number 158. The *Accademia Musicale Chigiana* (music academy) at number 89 holds regular concerts. There is a small post office at number 142. Otherwise turn left into Via del Capitano to walk to the Duomo.

Duomo. Turn right as you enter the Piazza del Duomo from Via del Capitano. Walk along the *Duomo's* east side, past the unfinished nave and the *Museo dell'Opera del Duomo*. The nave is accessible from the museum and gives panoramic views of the city. Walk through the tall stone arch to the top of the marble steps that lead down to Piazza Giovani. The building on the right of the steps is the Palazzo del Magnifico, which is where the unmarked *Saena Iulia* **language school** and the **dance school** are based, at number 20. Go down the steep marble steps (no hand rail) at the side of the cathedral. Turn right into Via Pellegrini, in the *Contrada della Selva* and then left onto Via di Città, passing the coffee bar you started in. The small **Caffé Torrefazione Fiorella** is at number 13, although you will probably smell the house roasted coffee before you see it. Try the *caffè shekerato* (shaken with ice) in summer, or splash out on a Blue Mountain coffee (€3).

Continue up Via di Città and when it forks bear left up *Banchi di Sopra* (*sopra* means above and there is also a *Banchi di Sotto* which means below). Walk up Banchi di Sopra towards Piazza Matteotti. You pass an **Odeon cinema** on your left at number 31 (through a stone archway and down the stairs on the left) and the **Moderno cinema** on your right at Piazza Tolomei. On the wall at number 63–65, behind a glass fronted display cabinet, the

CAI (*Club Alpino Italiano*) list the forthcoming walks and excursions. **Fellinelli's bookshop** is opposite at numbers 52 and 64 (number 52 sells language books). The road now splits into three. Take the middle road, Via Pianigiani, and walk up towards Piazza Matteotti past a large **food shop** *Consorzio Agrario Siena* just before the piazza.

Piazza Matteotti. On this piazza, in the district of the dragon (*Contrada del Drago*) there is a **post office**, a **taxi rank** and an UPIM (**department store**). Turn right when you enter the piazza and along the front of the post office. At the right corner of the Piazza turn along Via Malavolti. This takes you to Piazza Antonio Gramsci and the main **bus station**, which has an underground ticket office.

Porta Camollia and the north of Siena. If you want to shorten the walk you can go straight to the *Fortezza* (fortress) from Piazza Gramsci by crossing the park *La Lizza* on the left. Otherwise continue along Piazza Gramsci and take the first right into Vicolo del Sasso di S. Bernardino and then first left onto Via del Montanini. Continue straight ahead, up Via Camolla. You soon pass *Planeta Fitness* **sports shop** at number 19. There is another sports shop at number 201, *Il Maratoneta Sport* which advertises local events. The *Biciclette Bianchi* **bicycle shop** at no 204/6 has information about cycling events. There are superb views of the surrounding countryside from the end of the road at Porta Camollia. Turn right into Via Campansi and take the first right into Via del Pignattello, passing the Siena **motor club** (*Siena Club Auto Moto d'Epoca*) at number 29. After a couple of minutes you emerge in a small square by *Istituto Duca degli Abruzzi* where you turn right into Via Campansi. Walk straight over the crossroads with Via Camollia and walk up Via del Gazzani. The D.F Moto Noleggi at number 16/18 has **bicycles and scooters for rent** (*biciclette a noleggio*). This road leads back to the bus station.

Forte S. Barbara. Cross over the park *La Lizzo* and bear right to the Fort past the statue of Garibaldi on his horse. At the Fort, there is a large enoteca (wine shop) with a separate bar and the headquarters of **Siena Jazz**. From the Fort's walls there are views of the old city and surrounding countryside, which are spectacular at **sunset**. When you leave the Fort turn right into Via XXV Aprile. This runs alongside the right-hand side of the football stadium. At the main road, Viale Vittorio Veneto, turn left into

Viale dei Mille and walk over to the large *Chiesa di San Domenico*. This is opposite a small tourist information centre and the ticket office for **football matches**. Head down Via della Sapenza and past a **walking shop** at number 19 and a **key cutter** next door. Turn right into Via delle Terme which leads back to Il Campo.

Perugia

6

Perugia's internationally renowned University for Foreigners *Università per Stranieri* is the ultimate place to study Italian. It has flexible, good value courses for all levels starting in every month of the year. Perugia is the largest city in Umbria with a population of 158,000. It is a thriving ancient hill town with an altitude of 493m and spectacular views across Umbria. The winding medieval streets, museums, churches, pretty pedestrianised centre and two universities make it a lively place to live. It has a concentrated display of the region's culture within its old city walls and splendid architecture. Perugia has a large number of festivals throughout the year including Umbria Jazz and Eurochocolate. There are good train and bus connections to the rest of Italy making Florence and Rome easily accessible for weekend trips.

Don't Miss *Da Non Perdere*

▶ a *passeggiata* along Corso Vannucci for an early evening *aperitivo*

▶ the floodlights on the *Fontana Maggiore* (1278) fountain

▶ the changing window displays in the Sandri bar and cake shop

▶ sunset over Umbria from Via della Cupa (page 120)

▶ handmade chocolate from Augustina (page 105)

▶ the Medieval Garden (*Orto Medievale*) at the Chiesa di San Pietro (page 104)

▶ the Archaeological Museum in the convent of San Domenico

▶ the Etruscan Well *Pozzo Etrusco*

▶ climbing Monte Subasio from the hermitage of St Francis in nearby Assisi

▶ a weekend trip to Castelluccio and the spring flowers on the plain of Piano Grande

▶ trekking in the spectacular Sibillini Mountains

▶ castelluccio lentils, the best lentils in Italy

▶ fresh black truffles from Norcia and Città di Castello

▶ Perugia's spectacular open air cinema at the *Giardini del Frontone* (page 105)

Perugian festivals

The two most famous festivals in Perugia are Umbria Jazz and Eurochocolate. Half of Europe seems to descend on Perugia for these weeks, when the town goes crazy.

Umbria Jazz

Box office Via Mazzini 9 (off Corso Vannucci)
Tel: 800462311 (from Italy)
Tel: (075) 572 3327 from abroad
Open 10.00–13.00 and 16.00–19.00 and continuously during the festival
Website www.umbriajazz.com (Italian only)
Umbria Jazz was launched in 1973 as a series of small local concerts. Today it is one of the most important jazz events in Europe, hosting top interna-

tional names. The event lasts for ten days in July and has over 200 concerts in historical venues around the town. Since 1993 Orvieto has hosted the winter version, Umbria Jazz Winter, in the last week of December culminating in a New Year's party.

Eurochocolate

Perugia is transformed into a chocolate frenzy during this festival. It is held in October each year. Website www.eurochocolate.perugia.it (Italian only).

University for Foreigners *Università per Stranieri*

Palazzo Gallenga

Piazza Fortebraccio 4
06122 Perugia
Tel: (075) 57461
Website www.unistrapg.it

Student Relations Office (Ufficio Relazioni con lo Studente)

Tel: (075) 5746211 Email relstu@unistrapg.it
Open Monday to Friday 08.15–13.45 and 15.00–17.45
The office is on the left in the main entrance hall as you enter Palazzo Gallenga.

Secreteriat (Segreteria Studenti Stranieri)

Tel: (075) 5746284 Email segrstu@unistrapg.it
Open Monday to Friday 09.00–12.00
The office is on the lower ground floor opposite the police office in Palazzo Gallenga.

Scholarship Office (Ufficio Borse di Studio)

Tel: (075) 574 6285 Email borse@unistrapg.it
Open from Monday to Friday 09.00–13.00
The office is on the right before the stairs leading from the main entrance hall to the lower ground floor in Palazzo Gallenga.

University Bank (*Banca dell'Umbria*)

Open Monday to Friday 08.30–13.20 and 14.45–15.40
On the right as you enter Palazzo Gallenga.

University Library (*Biblioteca***)**
Open Monday to Friday 09.00 to 19.30
On the second floor of Palazzo Gallenga.

University Police (*Polizia***)**
Open Monday to Friday 08.30–13.00
The office is on the lower ground floor past the *segreteria* at the end of the passage.

Atena Service
Via Romeo Gallenga 2
06127 Perugia
Tel: (075) 573 2992 Email info@atenaservice.com
Open Monday to Friday 08.30–12.15 and 14.30–18.15
This university accommodation service is on a small road that leads downhill on the left as you leave Palazzo Gallenga (see accommodation below).

CELI Office
Certificate of Knowledge of the Italian Language (*Certificato di Conoscenza della Lingua Italiana*)
Via Scortili 2
Open from Monday to Friday 09.00 to 17.00
This exam office is on the first floor of a red brick house diagonally left as you leave Pizza Gallenga next to the pharmacy.

About the University *Sull' Università*

The *Università per Stranieri* was established in 1921 by the lawyer Astorre Lupattelli and moved to Palazzo Gallenga in 1927. Palazzo Gallenga is a stunning eighteenth century baroque *palazzo* just outside the famous *Arco Etrusco* (Etruscan Arch) in the old city. It is a large four-storey building with wood panelled frescoed classrooms and is a hub of student activity with its concert hall, library, free Internet access and bar. The university has several smaller buildings including Palazzina Prosciutti, Lupattelli, Orvieto and Valitutti, all about a 15 minute walk from Palazzo Gallenga. These palazzi have spectacular views across the Umbrian hills to Assisi, Monte Subasio and the Vale of Umbria (*Valle Umbra*).

The university's reputation has attracted some of Italy's finest teachers. Furthermore it is open to anyone regardless of educational background. Since the numbers are not closed places on courses are nearly always available. There are two small catches to this excellent University. The enrolment procedure is the most laborious in Italy, made worse by some unhelpful staff in administration and the class sizes can occasionally be as large as 60. For this reason some people combine the University courses with the more personal private language school.

Courses and costs *Corsi e costi*

The courses are the most flexible of any Italian university. It is possible to enrol in any month of the year at any grade. This is achieved by a system of one, two and three-month courses, which are run simultaneously. The courses cost €233 per month.

The **first grade** (*primo grado*) is for complete beginners. The one, two and three month courses have 20 hours of teaching a week, divided into nine hours of Italian language, nine hours of exercises and two hours of *laboratorio linguistico*. The **second grade** (*secondo grado*) courses have 21 hours of teaching a week (three hours in the *laboratorio linguistico*).

The **third grade** (*terzo grado*) courses have a similar content to the first two levels but with the addition of Italian culture lessons. The courses have 22 hours teaching per week divided into nine hours of Italian language, six hours of exercises, six hours of Italian culture and one hour of *laboratorio linguistico*.

The **fourth grade** (*quarto grado*) is termed 'advanced' Italian. The three-month course has 24 hours of teaching a week and students choose between Italian language, culture or technical/business. The intensive one-month course has a mixture of these subject areas and has 30 hours of lessons per week.

The **fifth grade** (*quinto grado*) is considered 'superior' Italian and takes six months to complete. The subjects and number of hours are the same as the fourth grade.

In the **fourth and fifth grades** there is an excellent choice of **subsidiary courses**. These include Dante, economics and geography, medieval and modern history, history of the church, cinema, music and modern art, philosophy, politics, psycholinguistics, sociolinguistics and theatre.

The University also runs **intensive** one-month courses in July, August and September in all five grades. These have 27 hours teaching per week divided into 12 hours of Italian language lessons, six hours of exercise drill lessons, three hours of *laboratorio linguistico* and six hours of conversation lessons per week. These courses cost €310 for the month.

Specialist language courses *Corsi speciali di lingua*

1 **Italian music and opera**. This is a one-month course for singers, conductors and directors. It consists of 25 hours teaching per week and three hours of music practice for reading Italian opera scores. It is run twice a year, in October and February and costs €310.

2 **Professional language courses**. These are one-month courses which focus on the Italian language for biology, chemistry, law, economics, physics or mathematics. They consist of 12 hours teaching per week and can be taken with a basic language course. They are run twice a year, in May and July and cost €208.

3 **Refresher courses for Italian teachers**. These are two-week courses for Italian teachers living abroad. There are two courses each year, in the second week of January and in the middle of July. Each course costs €233.

4 **Advanced courses in humanities**. These two-week courses focus on a variety of fields including contemporary Italian language, Etruscan studies, history of art and Italic studies. They run during the month of July and cost €233 plus an enrolment fee of €18.33.

5 **Supplementary courses for students of European Mobility Programmes**. These one-month courses are aimed at learning Italian for the academic world. They consist of 21 hours of teaching per week and cost €233.

6 **Four degree courses** open to both foreigners and Italians:
   ▶ teaching of the Italian language and culture to foreigners (ILIS)
   ▶ promotion of the Italian language and culture throughout the world (PLIM)

- advertising techniques (TED)

- international communication (COMINT).

7 Two-year Postgraduate Course in Teaching of Italian as a Foreign Language.

Facilities *Attrezzature*

University library *(biblioteca)*
Palazzo Gallenga (second floor)
Open Monday to Friday 09.00–19.30
The university library has over 80,000 books and over 100 magazines specialising in literature, history, history of art, Etruscan studies and linguistics. There are Italian newspapers to read and quiet areas for study. It is a member of the National Library service so data can be gathered from other member libraries.

University computer room *(Aula computer/laboratorio informatico)*
Palazzo Gallenga (fourth floor)
Mondays 09.00–15.00
Tuesdays, Wednesdays and Thursdays 09.00–17.00
Fridays 09.00–13.00
The university's computer room has ten computers and *free* Internet access available for students. This can be booked by the hour using your student card (*tessera*). Printing (*stampare*) is also free but students must bring their own paper.

University sports centre
Via Tuderte 10
Tel: (075) 32120 (rarely answered)
Students at the University for Foreigners can use the University of Perugia's sports centre. You need your student card and a medical certificate confirming your fitness to play your desired sport(s) (see page 24).

The *laboratori linguistici* in Palazzo Gallenga and Prosciutti are used during lessons and are not for independent study.

The University has two friendly **bars** in Palazzo Gallenga and in Palazzina Prosciutti. They serve cheap snacks (*spuntini*), sandwiches (*panini*), cakes (*torte*) and coffee (*caffè*).

Enrolling *Iscrizione*

An application form can be downloaded from the Internet or requested from the student relations office. Postal applications must be made at least one month in advance but it is possible to enrol in person at any stage. The application requires pre-payment of one month of fees, by Western Union Quick Pay System, international postal order or bank transfer (details in the brochure). The University sends a letter of confirmation and a receipt, both of which are needed on the first day. Pay for one month at a time as refunds are difficult to obtain.

Enrolment is completed on arrival at the University. This is a rather laborious process made worse by long queues on the first day and unhelpful administrative staff. Some of the pain can be avoided by arriving a few days early (or late!).

EU citizens require:

▶ passport and photocopy of passport

▶ several passport photos

▶ letter of confirmation of a place on the course

▶ receipt of pre-payment of one month of fees

▶ cash to complete any outstanding payments (the bank does not accept credit cards)

▶ a book to read in the queues.

Non-EU citizens should consult the Italian Embassy in their home country for details of the additional documents required. These may include a study visa, medical certificate, insurance certificate, proof of sufficient funds to finance the stay in Italy and proof of no criminal record. Non-EU citizens also require a revenue stamp (*marca da bollo*) of €18 obtainable from a *tabaccheria/cartoleria*.

Go straight to the student relations office, on your left as you enter Palazzo Gallenga. They will give you an appointment for the police office (in the basement) to arrange your permit of stay (*permesso di soggorno*). There may also be outstanding fees (often unforeseen price increases or tax), which should be paid for in cash at the bank on the other side of the corridor.

Students enrolling for the first grade (beginners) do not need to take an entry test and can now go straight to the *segreteria* (on the lower ground floor) to collect a student card (*tessera*) and timetable (*orario*). All other students first need to take a small entry test to determine their level. The times of these tests are advertised on the notice board outside the office.

The secreteria *Segreteria*

The *segreteria* is on the lower ground floor of Palazzo Gallenga. The entrance for foreign students is through a door on the right at the far end of the corridor, below a small sign *stranieri*. It is open Monday to Friday from 09.00–12.00. They provide a student card (*tessera*) and timetable. It is easy to change levels or classes in the first week.

Where to go for lessons? *Dove andare per le lezioni?*

Most of the lessons for the first grade are held in Palazzina Prosciutti which is a 15-minute walk from Palazzo Gallenga. To get there from Palazzo Gallenga cross over the busy road outside the front entrance and bear right past a basketball pitch (on your left) into Via Pinturicchio. In about five minutes you reach a large stone arch with a laundrette on the left corner. Go through the arch and straight over the round-about, bearing right into Via Settembre XIV. After a few minutes take the second left into a street leading downhill and sign-posted to a car park (*parcheggio*). Palazzina Prosciutti is the second large yellow building on the left about 150 m down this steep narrow road. The building has three name plaques: *Padiglione Adriani, Università per Stranieri* and *Palazzina Prosciutti*. Lessons for the second grade and above are also in other buildings near the Palazzina Prosciutti and Palazzo Gallenga itself.

University organised events *Avvenimenti organizzati dall' Università*

Films

Classic Italian films are shown free of charge every week at Palazzo Gallenga. They are advertised on the University notice boards.

Excursions

The University organises regular, good value weekend excursions. Examples include skiing near Norcia, a long weekend in Sicily, the Carnival in Venice and walking in the Cinque Terre. They are advertised on the notice boards in the University and can be paid for in cash with your *tessera* at the Student Relations Office.

Lectures

There is a series of free Wednesday lectures on Italian culture at Palazzo Gallenga. These are given by academics and public figures and are advertised on the University notice boards. For further information email relstu@unistrapg.it

Exams *Esami*

There is an optional diploma exam at the end of each of the five grades (this is not the CELI exam, see below). To be eligible students must have completed the full three-month course for the first four grades and six-month course for the fifth grade. Only ten days of absence is allowed and teachers keep a register. Your teacher will advise you when to register for the exam. It costs €10 to sit the exam and €18 for the certificate. This is paid for in cash at the University bank. For the shorter courses there is a certificate of attendance, which also allows continuation onto the next level.

The CELI Certificate of Knowledge of the Italian Language (*Certificato di Conoscenza della Lingua Italiana*) is an internationally recognised Italian language qualification (see also page 15 qualifications), organised and run by the University for Foreigners in Perugia. There are 22 exam centres around Italy (including the University at Perugia) and others abroad. The exam has five levels consisting of written and oral tests. It can be taken in June and November each year and costs €78 to sit the exam and €11 for the certificate. Application forms (scheda di iscrizione) are available from the exam office near the University (Via Scortici 2, first floor, next to the pharmacy). The office is open from Monday to Friday from 09.00 to 17.00.

Private Language Schools

ABC Italia Language School

Via Guerriera 13

06121 Perugia

Tel/Fax: (075) 572 3279

Email info@abcitaliapg.com Website www.abcitaliapg.com

This small language school is in a quiet, narrow road a five-minute walk from Piazza Italia. It is on the second floor of a recently renovated old building. The school has wood block floors, white and orange walls and stylish fittings. There is a small seating area by the front desk, with a sofa and a coffee machine. There are three smart classrooms but no other facilities. The school runs a very flexible range of courses and has good value private and one-to-two lessons. These can also be arranged over a weekend. The maximum group size is ten students.

Courses and costs *Corsi e Costi*

The **standard** course of four hours a day (20 hours a week) costs €235 for two weeks and €470 for four. Weekly courses are available as are **weekend courses**. The weekend courses require a minimum of two people and cost just €11 per hour per person. **Individual** lessons cost €20 per hour. The school organises cultural courses and exam preparation for the CELI (see 'qualifications' page 15). There is no enrolment fee.

Accommodation *Alloggio*

The school has a list of local agencies for rooms, flats and bed and breakfast.

Comitato Linguistico Italian Language Courses

Via XIV Settembre 57

06122 Perugia

Tel: (075) 572 1471 Fax: (075) 5734258

Email info@comitatolinguistico.com

Website www.comitatolinguistico.com

Segreteria open Monday to Friday from 09.00–13.00

This small language school is on a busy road not far from the archaeological museum and the ABC school. Once inside, however, one is transported into a quiet school with beautiful views over Umbria. There are five classrooms and a small terrace where classes can be held in the summer. There is also a small seating area in the hall with a coffee machine. There is no *laboratorio linguistico* or library. The group size is a maximum of 12 but there is an average class size of seven.

Courses and costs *Corsi e costi*

The **standard** course of four hours per day (20 hours a week) costs €220 for two weeks or €440 for a month. There is a **conversation** course of two hours per day (ten hours per week) which costs €110 for two weeks or €220 for a month. **Individual** lessons cost €30 per hour. There is a 10% reduction after three months. The **enrolment** fee is €52. **Scholarships** are available by applying directly to the school with a letter of support from an Italian teacher.

Accommodation *Alloggio*

A single room in a shared apartment or bed and breakfast with a family costs €195 for two weeks or €355 for four weeks. A single room half board costs €390 for two weeks or €790 for a month.

Accommodation in Perugia *Alloggio a Perugia*

It is possible to view and book flats and rooms several months in advance. This is ideal if you are planning a longer period of stay. Many people, nonetheless, arrive in Perugia before looking for accommodation and stay at the Youth Hostel. This is fine out of the busy summer period. Try to find a room in the historic centre, as the outside areas are much less pretty.

For longer rents of more than three months a two-person flat in the heart of Perugia costs about €250 per person per month exclusive of gas, telephone and electricity. The main agencies charge one-months rent in commission but it is worth asking for a discount (*sconti*). Many students at the University use Atena Services (the university accommodation service, see below) but there are other options. Rooms and flats are often advertised on the University notice boards and in the weekly newspaper *Cerco e Trovo* ('I look and I find').

Atena Service

Via Romeo Gallenga 2

06127 Perugia

Tel: (075) 573 2992 Fax: (075) 573 0821

Email info@atenaservice.com

This is the University accommodation service. Although it is cheaper than the main agencies it does not take any responsibility for problems or disputes arising over the flats or the landlords. It is vital therefore that you are happy with your accommodation ideally *before* paying. Get written confirmation of the exact type and location of room they have booked, as the standards are variable. Check that the price you have been quoted includes tax (20%) and utilities. The office is extremely busy on the first day of term so it is worth arriving before they open to be first in the queue. Bring all documents, including receipts of any deposit paid. It is best to pay in cash as there is a 5% surcharge for credit cards.

Tecnocasa

Via Baglioni 22

06121 Perugia

Tel: (075) 5733508 Fax: (075) 5720661

Website www.tecnocasa.com

Tecnocasa is a large company with agencies all over Italy. The Perugian office is near Piazza Matteotti.

Real Servizi Immobiliari Perugia

Porta Pesa

Via Pinturicchio

Tel: (075) 572 0666

This small office opposite *Onda blu* laundrette has flats for rent at the lower end of the market (view them before booking).

Immobiliare Biagiotti Bruno

Piazza Italia 4

06121 Perugia

Tel: (075) 572 1244 Fax: (075) 5735150

Email stimimmo@tin.it

Getting to and from Perugia *Andare e tornare da Perugia*

Train

Perugia's main train station, Perugia Centrale, is in Piazza V. Veneto in Fontivegge. This is a 15-minute bus ride from the centre, numbers 6 and 9 from Piazza Italia are the quickest. The information office is open Monday to Saturday 08.10–19.45, website www.trenitalia.com. The ticket office is open daily 06.00–20.40. The station has ticket machines for collecting Internet-booked tickets which also provide information in English about times and costs of trains. The ticket office for buses into the centre (Piazza Italia) is a green building to the left of the main entrance.

Bus

The main bus station is at Piazza Partigiani. This is in the southern end of town just below the old city walls, near the Stadio di Santa Giuliana and athletic track. Escalators (*scale mobili*) lead up to Piazza Italia via ancient covered passageways under the city. These were once the foundations of the sixteenth Century papal fortress Rocca Paolina.

The main bus connections in Perugia are Piazza Italia, Piazza Morlacchi (near the theatre), Piazza Gallenga (by the Università per Stranieri) and the main station at Piazza Partigiani. The word *feriale* on timetables means Monday to Saturday, *festivo* means Sundays and holidays and *sciopero* means strike. If you are unsure of when to get off ask the driver *Può dirmi quando arriviamo a…*

APM (Azienda Perugina della Mobilità)
Tel: (075) 506781
Website www.apmperugia.it (Italian only)
APM is the local bus service. It is cheaper to buy tickets before boarding the bus. They can be purchased from news stands (*edicole*), ticket offices or *tabacchi* (marked with a black T). Singles cost €0.80, ten and 20 ride tickets offer a small discount. Tickets are validated for 75 minutes by inserting them into a machine on the bus.

The **Sulga** Bus Company runs services to Rome's Fiumicino airport (see below), Florence (2 hours), Milan ($6\frac{1}{2}$ hours), Naples ($5\frac{1}{2}$ hours) and Puglia (10 hours to Lecce). Connections include Assisi, Spoleto, Matera, Brindisi and Gallipoli. Most of the services run from the main bus station at Piazza Partigiani. Website www.sulga.it (Italian only) Email info@sulga.it Tel: freephone 800099661 (in Italy only). Tickets can be purchased either on board or from Ag. Viaggi Consul Travel, Perugia. Tel. (075) 5003434 or CTS. per L'Umbria, Perugia. Tel: (075) 5720284.

Plane

The nearest international airports are in Pisa (250km north-west of Perugia), Rome (180km south-west of Perugia) and Ancona (125km north-east of Perugia). Rome's **Fiumicino** airport has the best connections to Perugia. The Sulga bus (above) runs directly to and from the airport. The earliest leaves from Piazza Italia in Perugia at 06.30 and arrives at Fiumicino airport at 10.10 (later buses leave from the main bus station). Buses leave from Fiumicino for Perugia at 14.30, 16.30 and 17.30 on working days (*feriale*). The Leonardo Express train connects Fiumicino to Rome's Termini train station. Rome's smaller **Ciampino** airport is connected to Rome's central Termini station by the airport bus. From Termini station the Eurostar train takes two hours to Perugia and the others with a connection at Foligno take three hours. From **Pisa** there is a train and coach service to Florence (1 hour) and frequent mainline trains to Perugia from there. There is a small airport at **Sant'Egidio** about 15km from Perugia that operates flights from Milan.

Addresses For Easy Living in Perugia

Archaeological Museum and Medieval Garden
Museo Archeologico e Orto Medievale

Museo Archeologico Nazionale dell'Umbria
Piazza G Bruno 10 (next to Basilica di San Domenico)
Tel: (075) 572 7141
Website www.perusia.it (in Italian only but has information about other museums in Umbria)
Open Monday 14.30–19.30 and Tuesday–Sunday 08.30–19.30

Medieval Garden (*Orto Medievale***)**
Chiesa di San Pietro
Monday–Friday 08.00–18.30, Saturday 08.00–13.30

Bakery *Pasticceria*

Pasticceria Lupi Mario e Antonietta
Via della Viola 38 (off Via Alessi, near the Garage internet caffè)
Tel: (075) 572 2409
Open Monday to Saturday 07.30–13.15
This bakery is a local secret. They make delicious fresh bread, cakes and pasta which are snapped up *molto presto* every morning. It is worth the five minute walk from the centre to find it. Walk down Via Alessi away from Piazza Matteotti and turn left into Via della Viola just after the Garage Internet Caffè. You will smell the bread before see the shop.

Basketball *Pallacanestro*

There is a fenced basketball pitch opposite the Università per Stranieri's Palazzo Gallenga where impromptu games are played throughout the day.

Bookshops *Librerie*

La Libreria
Via Oberdan 52
06121 Perugia
Tel: (075) 573 5057
Open Monday to Saturday from 09.00–20.00
From September to June also open Sundays from 10.30–13.30
This is the best bookshop in Perugia. It has a superb selection of books over two floors in a modern building near Piazza Matteotti. They also have English language guide books and an excellent selection of Italian maps.

Libreria Morlacchi
Piazza Morlacchi 7–9
Tel: (075) 5725297
Open Monday to Friday 09.00–19.00 Saturday 09.00–13.00

This bookshop also sells stationery and padded envelopes (*busta imbotitta*) at the back of the shop. There is also a photocopier.

Car parking *Parcheggi*

There are several underground car parks close to the centre. The car park at the main bus terminal, Piazza Partigiani, leads up to Piazza Italia via escalators. The one on Viale P. Pellini connects to Via dei Priori via escalators and the one on Via Tancredi connects to Piazza Matteotti via a lift. They are safe and good value. The tourist ticket (*turistico giornaliero*) costs just €7.50 per 24 hours for the first 48 hours and €5 for every 24 hours thereafter. You should pay for the pass on arrival as this enables you to come and go as you please. If the desk is closed come back the next morning to pay for it. There is free street parking outside the old city walls.

Car rental *Autonoleggio*

Hertz
Tel: (075) 5002439
Website www.hertz.com

Chocolate *Cioccolaterie*

Augustina
Via Pinturicchio 2
Tel: (075) 5734577
Open Monday to Saturday 10.30–22.30 and Sunday 10.30–13.00 and 16.00–20.00. This small family run shop makes some of the best chocolates in Italy. In summer they serve handmade ice creams made with organic milk and have some which are gluten free (see also page 116 'Perugia and chocolate').

Cinemas *Cinema*

Giardini del Frontone
Borgo XX Giugno (next to the Chiesa S. Pietro in the southeast of town)
Tel: (075) 5734794
Email info@microcinema.it Website www.microcinema.it (Italian only)

From June to September, at the end of Borgo XX Giugno, there is a spectacular open air cinema in the public garden (see the Perugia City Walk, page 117). Films start at 21.30 and cost €4.50 for students of the *Università per Stranieri* (bring your *tessera*). There is a small bar, a popcorn seller, and you can even bring a takeaway pizza (*da asporto*) from nearby Pizzeria Pompei.

Teatro del Pavone
Piazza della Republica
Tel: (075) 572 4911
This cinema is in a converted theatre so you can sit in your own box at no extra charge. They show original language films on Monday nights.

Teatro Turreno
Piazza Danti
Tel: (075) 5722110
This mainstream central cinema has discounts for students.

Teatro Zenith
Via Benedetto Bonfigli 11 (just outside Porta S. Pietro)
Tel: (075) 5728588 Closed from June to September
To get to this cinema turn immediately left out of the Porta S. Pietro, 15 minutes from the Archaeological Museum. It has two evening performances and is near the excellent Pizzeria Pompei.

Università per Stranieri
Palazzo Gallenga
The university has weekly showings of classic Italian films *free* of charge. These are advertised on the notice boards in Palazzo Gallenga.

Club Alpino Italia (CAI)

Via Della Gabbia, 9
Tel: (075) 5730334
The Perugian branch of CAI organises weekend trips and walks for all levels of fitness throughout Umbria. The cost of the excursions includes transfer to and from Perugia by minibus or train. The notice board advertising events is on the wall to the left of Sandri's window on Corso Vannucci. A one-year membership of CAI costs €32.

Cobblers *Calzolai*

La Bottega del Cuoio
Via Appia 5 (just before the aqueduct, near Piazza Morlacci)
Tel: (075) 572 4646
Open Monday to Saturday 08.00–13.00 and 15.00–19.30

Delicatessan *Specialità gastronomiche*

Corradi Il Gastronomo (or Casa del Parmigiano)
Via S. Ercolano 36 (opposite the Sant' Ercolano church)
Tel: (075) 572 9935
Website www.ilgastronomocorradi.it (Italian only)
Try this shop's four-year-old Parmesan *parmigiano reggiano* and you will float to heaven. It is so special that it is frequently sold at auction in other parts of the country. Their home-made *pecorino di botte*, a sheep's cheese aged in *barriques*, is equally good. They also have top Umbrian DOP olive oils, Norcian *prosciutto* and salamis, real balsamic vinegar and much more. The owner's son runs the *Univeristà dei Sapori* (University of Tastes).

Università dei Sapori
Clelio Corradi
Via Tornetta 1
06123 Perugia
Website www.universitadeisapori.com (Italian only)

Department store *Grandi magazzini*

Conti
Piazza G. Matteotti 19
Open Monday to Saturday 09.00–12.30 and 16.00–19.00
This small department store sells clothes, bedding, toiletries and a full range of household items at good prices. They have kitchenware and toys upstairs, where an assistant wraps each item in wax paper and accompanies you downstairs to pay.

Electrical shop *Elettrodomestici*

Osram

Via dei Priori 6

Open Tuesday to Saturday 08.30–13.00 and 15.30–20.00

This electrical shop has small items such as plugs, light bulbs and kettles as well as larger items such as fridges, washing machines and ovens. They will deliver and fit items for a reasonable price.

Gyms *Palestre*

Corpus SAS

Via Cortonese 1

Tel: (075) 5056244

This gym is near the main train station.

Olympic Gym

Corso Garibaldi 155

Open Monday to Friday 15.00–20.00 and Saturdays and Sundays 15.00–1900

This tiny gym focuses on weights.

Hotels, hostels and bed and breakfast *Alberghi, ostelli e bed and breakfast*

Hotel Fortuna

Via Bonazzi 19

06123 Perugia

Tel: (075) 5722845 / 46 Fax: (075) 5735040

Email fortuna@umbriahotels.com Website www.umbriahotels.com

This beautiful old hotel has a large roof terrace and an open tea terrace both with views over the valley towards Trasimeno. Some of the rooms have balconies and one has a small private terrace overlooking the valley. There are frescoes on the walls and ceilings. Double rooms start at €120 with breakfast. The nicest rooms are numbers 407 and 309.

Bed and Breakfast di Fabiano Spagnoli

Via Cesare Caporali 17 (just off Via Bonazzi near Piazza Italia)

Tel: (075) 5735127 Mobile: 3405303893 Email fabkation@yahoo.it

This new bed and breakfast is run by a friendly husband and wife team who speak English, French, Spanish and Italian. Their dual level apartment is on the third and fourth floor of a well restored house with wood block flooring in the centre of the old town. The double room has its own fridge and television. There is a panoramic view from the roof terrace and a large airy sitting room where yoga can by practised. Guests have access to a washing machine and the Internet. A single room costs €31, double €48 and a triple €55.

Domus Minervae Bed and Breakfast

Viale Pellini 19
06123 Perugia
Tel/Fax: (075) 5732238
Email info@domusminervae.it Website www.domusminervae.it
This is located at the bottom of the escalators that lead off from the left of Via dei Priori. It is on a busy, noisy road but the rooms are spotlessly clean. Doubles cost €55 and singles cost €35 including breakfast.

Youth Hostel

Centro Accoglienza Ostello Via Bontempi 13
Tel/Fax: (075) 572 2880
Email ostello@ostello.perugia.it Website www.ostello.perugia.it
Open between 16.00 and 23.30
Daytime closure between 09.30 and 16.00
Closed from 15 December to 15 January
This excellent privately owned frescoed youth hostel has 150 beds and is open to everyone. It is in the centre of Perugia and offers cheap, clean, single-sex dormitory accommodation. The smallest rooms sleep four and the largest sleep eight. Beds cost €12 per night plus €1.50 for sheets. It is best to book at least a month in advance for peak periods such as Umbria Jazz, Eurochocolate, Easter and the beginning of the University terms. There are good facilities including a spacious, well-equipped kitchen, sitting room, library, Internet access, outside terrace with wonderful views and shower rooms. Every Wednesday at 21.15 there is a free meeting in the library for Italian conversation practice. During the day it is usually possible to leave luggage. There is a 12pm curfew and a maximum stay of two weeks.

Icecream *Gelaterie*

Gelaterie

Via Bonazzi 3 (the south end of Corso Vannucci)

Open from 11.30 every day until late at night when the ice cream is finished

Closed on random days at the discretion of the owner

This is a very popular central *gelateria*. The owner makes the ice cream in the back of the shop using traditional methods.

Internet Cafés *Internet caffè*

Palazzo Gallenga has *free* Internet access for university students (see above under facilities). Internet cafés in Perugia cost about €1.50 per hour (amongst the cheapest in Italy). Many have phone centres with cheap international calls, fax and Western Union Money Transfer. Some even have a coffee bar attached so you can type away while sipping an espresso.

Garage Internet Caffè

Via Alessi, 80

This small very friendly café next to the church at the bottom of Via Alessi is run by a husband and wife team and their dog Tommy. They treat you with chocolates (*cioccolatini*) and the occasional coffee.

Tempo reale centro sevizi internet and telefonia internazionale

Via del Forno 17

Tel: (075) 5735533

This is just off Corso Vanucci, down a narrow passageway and next to the Merlin pub. It also has a cheap phone centre and printing for only €0.05 per sheet.

Laundrette *Lavanderie*

Onda Blu

Corso Bersaglieri 4 (at the far end of Via Pinturicchio by a large stone arch)

Open every day 08.00–22.30

This is a self-service laundrette where a large wash costs €3.

Libraries *Biblioteche*

Biblioteca Comunale Augusta

Via delle Prome 15

06122 Perugia

Tel: (075) 5772520

Open Monday to Friday 8.30–18.30 and Saturday 8.30–13.30

To register you need a passport and a passport photo.

The library is close to Porta Sole, north of the fountain *Fontana Maggiore*. There is a study room, CD-ROM facilities and photocopying.

Market *Mercato*

Terrazza del Mercato (just off Piazza Matteotti)

Open 08.00 to 13.00 Monday to Saturday

The covered market (*mercato coperto*) is by far the best place for buying food and local specialities. It is on two levels below the terrace viewing point (*luogo panoramico*) off Piazza Matteotti (see page 121). The view across to Assisi, Monte Subasio and the vale of Umbria is spectacular and worth seeing even if you are not shopping.

Musical instruments *Strumenti musicali*

Teresa Papini *Liuteria* classica

Corso Garibaldi 232

Tel: (075) 40054

Website www.papiniteresa.com (Italian only)

Tereas Papini is a classical stringed instrument maker. You can watch her at work in her tiny shop in Corso Garibaldi, not far from the University per Stranieri's Palazzo Gallenga. She also repairs instruments.

Fresh pasta *Pasta fresca*

Bottega Artigiana Pasta Fresca di Paramini Marisa

Via C. Caporali 3 (off Via Bonazzi at the southern end of Corso Vannucci)

Tel: (075) 5727848

Open Tuesdays and Saturdays 08.00–14.00 and 17.00–20.30, Sundays 08.00–13.00.

This tiny pasta shop is next to Café Bonazzi just off Via Bonazzi. It does not have a name over the door. Some of the pastas available are on display on the miniature counter and all are freshly made on the premises. You can often order 'off menu' with only a few hours' notice. Specials include ravioli stuffed with artichoke (*carciofi*), beetroot (*barbabietola*) and truffle (*tartufi*).

Pharmacies *Farmacie*

The Farmacia San Martino
Piazza Giacomo Matteotti (near the central COOP)
Open Monday to Saturday from 08.00–24.00 and Sundays 20.00–24.00 (all year)
There are several pharmacies in Perugia. San Martino has convenient opening hours. There is a rota for Sunday morning opening, the details of which are on a notice board on the right of the entrance. There is a €4 surcharge for medicines purchased after 20.00.

Photographs *Fotografi*

MC Emporio
Ulisse Rocchi (very close to the Etruscan Arch)
Open Monday to Saturday from 09.00–13.00 and 15.30–19.45
This shop takes passport photos and sells small electrical items, mobile telephones and the cheapest hairdryers in Perugia.

Restaurants and bars *Ristoranti e bar*

Alterego
Via Floramonti 2a (leading on from Via Oberdan, five minutes from Piazza Matteotti)
Tel: (075) 5729527
This newly opened restaurant serves local specialities all of which are made on the premises.

Bar Centrale Tea Room
Piazza IV Novembre 35
Open Monday to Saturday 07.00–20.30

This excellent bar has chairs in the Piazza overlooking the *Fontana Maggiore*. They serve a particularly good *latte macchiato*.

Bottega del Vino

Via del Sole 1
06122 Perugia
Tel/Fax: (075) 5716181
Closed on Sundays
This small wine bar overlooks the Piazza Danti from its first floor window. It serves a wide selection of wines and local specialities. Book a table by the window for a view of the Piazza and Cathedral. They often have live music during Umbria Jazz.

Caffè del Gesù

Piazza Matteotti 9
Tel: (075) 5725746
Open Monday to Saturday from 06.00-about 20.00
This cosy café is tucked into a quiet corner of the Piazza Matteotti. It is run by a mother and daughter and is popular with local shopkeepers who pop in for regular fixes. The outside seating lets you sit unnoticed while you watch the comings and goings on the square.

Enoteca Provinciale di Perugia

Via Ulisse Rocchi 18b
Tel: (075) 5724824
This large, friendly off-licence has a large selection of Italian wines. They also have a small wine bar at the back, which serves wine by the glass and platters of cheese and salami.

Pizzeria e Bar Ferrari

Via Scura 1
Tel: (075) 572 2966
Closed on Mondays
Bar open from 08.30–02.00
Restaurant open from 12.00–14.45 and 17.45–02.00
This cosy bar and pizzeria has the longest opening hours in Perugia. The bar (08.30–02.00) serves excellent coffee and the best fresh pastries in

town. They were the first proper pizza restaurant with a wood burning oven (*forno a legna*) to open in Perugia. To find it look for the large sign Hotel Umbria and Pizza Ferrari under an arch on Corso Vannucci.

Pizzeria Pompei

Borgo XX Giugno 14 (just outside the Porta S. Pietro in the southeast end of town)
Tel: (075) 5727931
Closed Monday (*lunedì*)
Open every evening from 19.00 until late
This excellent pizzeria in the southeast of Perugia has outside tables and a wood burning oven. It is midway between the Archaeological Museum and the Medieval Gardens and near the Zenith cinema, so could form part of an afternoon and evening excursion. To avoid queuing arrive before 19.30 or reserve a table (particularly if you want an outside table).

Ristorante da Giancarlo

Via Priori 36
Tel: (075) 572 4314
Open from 12.00–14.30 and 18.30–22.30
Closed on Fridays (*venerdì*)
This restaurant has all the local specialities including white truffles and excellent *antipasti* at good prices.

Sandri

Corso Vannucci 32
Closed on Mondays
This is a Perugian institution. It is on the left as you walk away from the fountain and has its name in green neon above its beautiful window displays. Stand at the bar and ask the lovely Cristina for *una piccola tazza di cioccolato caldo con panna* (a small hot chocolate with cream). If you are an experienced chocolate eater you may be able to manage a standard cup. In the evening try a *prosecco* (sparkling white wine). It will be served in a small glass on a silver coaster accompanied by a selection of nibbles. At the cash desk sipping her own (larger) glass of *prosecco* you may see the owner, who works some of the evening shifts here.

Stationers *Cartolerie*

Magazzine di Egidio Rastelli
Via Baglioni 17 (near Piazza Matteotti)
Open 09.00 to 13.00 and 16.00 to 19.30. Closed Sundays
This large stationer has a photocopier (*fotocopiatrice*) and sells every type of paper, pen and folder.

Supermarket *Supermercato*

COOP supermarket
Open Monday to Saturday 09.00 to 20.00
Piazza Matteotti (near Corso Vanucci in the centre)
The COOP is convenient but pricier than the market. Avoid shopping at lunchtime as the queues are long. Fruit and vegetables must be weighed. Remember to pick up a ticket for the deli counter on the left of the entrance and beware of sweet old ladies queue barging. There is a larger COOP opposite the train station.

Tattoo *Tatuaggi*

Krazy Inc
Via Garibaldi193
Open 14.30–20.00 Monday–Saturday

Theatres *Teatri*

Teatro Morlacchi
Piazza Morlacchi
Tel: (075) 572 2555
Open 4pm–7pm Monday to Friday and one hour before events
This theatre was opened in 1781. There is a regular programme of concerts with international musicians. There are cheap seats available 'in the Gods'.

Tourist information *Pro loco*

Info Umbria
Largo Cacciatori delle Alpi (next to the main bus station)
Tel: (075) 5732933

Open Monday–Friday 09.00–13.30 and 14.30–18.30 Saturdays 09.00–13.00
Email info@guideinumbria.com
Website www.guideinumbria.com (Italian only)
This is the best local source of information about Perugia and Umbria. It
is near the main bus station and provides maps, information about con-
certs and events and can make reservations.

Tourist Office

Piazza IV Novembre 3
Tel: (075) 5736458
Open Monday to Saturday 08.30–13.30 and 15.30–18.30 and Sunday
09.00–13.00
This is the main tourist office and is under the balcony of Palazzo dei Priori.
It is worth walking down to Info Umbria however as they are more help-
ful and will also make reservations.

The monthly Italian magazine *Viva Perugia* has up-to-date telephone numbers for emergencies as well as bus and train timetables. It also has
information about festivals, concerts and other events in and around
Perugia. It costs €0.75 and is available from news stands and *tabacci*.

Enjoying Perugia

Perugia and chocolate *Perugia e il Cioccolato*

Perugia is the birthplace of the famous hazelnut Baci chocolate, made by
the Perugina chocolate factory. The factory was founded in 1907 by
Giovanni Buitoni and Luisa Spagnoli. They developed a fondant recipe,
Luisa, which soon gained local acclaim. They hit the national market with
their cleverly named milk chocolate and hazelnut Baci (kisses). These are
individually wrapped in blue and silver starred foil containing a message.
In the early advertising campaign the 'Baci' was seen as a punch rather
than an affectionate kiss. The factory was bought by Nestlè in 1988 and
moved to modern premises in Via Pievaiola, on the outskirts of Perugia.
Free guided tours of the factory and museum can be arranged by telephoning (075) 527 6796. The best times are Monday to Thursday
mornings. To get to the factory take bus number 7 from Piazza Italia. With

discretion the chocolate can be purchased at a big discount from the staff shop. This is in an unmarked squat concrete building on the opposite side of the car park from the main public entrance to the factory and museum. Alternatively chocolates can be purchased at less of a discount from the museum shop.

Two ex-long-term employees of Perugina have opened a small chocolate shop near the university, called Augustina (page 105). They produce delicious handmade chocolates and organic ice creams using traditional methods. Their own version of the Baci, made with plain chocolate, is even better than the original and their chocolate covered chestnuts are superb.

Four places to sit and enjoy the sun *Quattro posti per prendere il sole*

▶ *Le scale* (the steps) in front of the cathedral. The stones heat up during the day and stay warm after sunset.

▶ Piazza San Francesco. This is a tiny meadow in front of a pink and white Franciscan church and a small Renaissance masterpiece, Oratorio di San Bernardino. The piazza is at the bottom of Via dei Priori, on the right after passing through the Porta Trasimeno city gate.

▶ The Medieval Garden at the Church of S. Pietro. This cosy garden has spectacular views, a fountain and secluded courtyards.

▶ The grass in front of the beautiful Tempio St. Angelo church, at the top of Corso Garibaldi.

Perugia City Walk *La Passeggiata*

Finding the best shops, bars, restaurants, amenities and other secrets

Perugia has a twisting medieval street plan that makes it easy to become disorientated. This excellent walk has been carefully designed to quickly acquaint you with the best restaurants, shops, amenities and sights. It takes about two and a half hours with stops for drinks and a quick look at the monuments.

The walk starts in Piazza IV Novembre, the social and historical heart of Perugia. Bar Centrale is a good place to sit with a latte machiatto and look at the square. In the centre of the sloping piazza is *Fontana Maggiore*, one of Italy's most important thirteenth century sculptures and fountains. The inner basin rests on 36 carved columns, which can be seen from the top of the cathedral steps. To the left is the gently curved façade of Palazzo dei Priori, which holds the National Gallery of Umbria. Halfway up the wall above the Palazzo's door are two thirteenth century bronze statues. One statue is of a lion and the other of a griffin, which is also the symbol of Perugia. The **tourist information** office is under the balcony of the Palazzo. The wide pedestrianised Corso Vannucci runs south to Piazza Italia like a giant out-door corridor.

Turn right out of Bar Centrale, walk into Piazza Danti and then up Via del Sole on the right-hand side of the cinema. You pass the Bottega del Vino wine bar on your right (number 1), which has a window seat on the first floor overlooking the Piazza. The street soon divides. The road uphill to the right leads up to Piazza Michelotti, the highest part of Perugia. The area around this Piazza is worth exploring for its tiny medieval streets and piazzas. For now, however, bear left and continue to the end of Via del Sole where there is an excellent **viewing point**. The public **library** *Biblioteca Augusta* is on the right just before the end of the road. The terrace looks north along the Trevi valley towards Città di Castello, Gubbio and the Apennine mountains. Below to your left you can see the large University building Palazzo Gallenga with its central white columns. The street below running from left to right is Via Pinturicchio.

Turn left down the wide, bowed steps that zigzag down to Piazza Fortebraccio and the **Università per Stranieri.** On the way down there are views of Assisi and Monte Subasio to the east. The steps lead out onto Piazza Fortebraccio. On the left is the massive *Arco Etrusco* (Etruscan Arch), built in the third Century BC as the main city gate. Straight ahead is the *Università per Stranieri* in the eighteenth Century baroque Palazzo Gallenga, which has a good view from the top floor terrace. The first road on your right from the bottom of the steps is Via Pinturricchio, which has Internet cafés, international phone centres and book shops. At number 1 there is a fabulous **chocolate** and ice cream shop Augustina (see page 116 'Perugia and Chocolate'). There is a fenced **basketball** pitch next to the shop where informal games are played. The MC Emporio shop just through the Etruscan Arch takes **passport photos** and sells the cheapest hairdryers in Perugia.

Turn left out of Palazzo Gallenga and walk up Corso Garibaldi. This narrow street leads to the northern-most reaches of medieval Perugia. You pass a small Conad supermarket at number 8, a **laundrette** at number 43 and several bars and Internet cafés. The classical stringed instrument maker at number 232, *Liuteria Classica*, also repairs and restores instruments. You pass several convents, including on your left the convent of Sant'Agnese, which has a fresco by **Perugino** of the Madonna and Saints. Near the end of the road turn right into Via del Tempio to visit the secluded Tempio di Sant'Angelo. This beautiful fifth Century church has a circular interior with a ring of Roman columns and faded frescoes. As you come out of the church cut down the small street on your right which leads back onto Corso Garibaldi. At the end of the road is the Porta San'Angelo city gate through which you can see the Monte Ripido convent at the end of the road. Retrace your steps for a few minutes down Corso Garibaldi. Turn right into Via Benedetta and at the San Benedetto Monastery walk down the stone steps on your right (Via del Fagiano). Follow this small road until the crossroads with Via Ariodante.

To visit the main **University buildings** (not the University for Foreigners) turn right and follow the road to Piazza di Università (a two minute walk). Otherwise, cross over the road and bear right down Via dell' Acquedotto. This aqueduct used to carry water from Monte Pacciano to the fountain at Piazza IV Novembre. There are pretty gardens down on your right and Palazzo Gallenga soon comes into view on your left. Continue up the stone steps at the end of the aqueduct. There is a **cobbler** on the left immediately under the bridge (La Bottega del Cuoio, Via Appia 5). At the T-junction turn right and walk into Piazza Cavallotti. Piazza Morlacchi is the adjacent piazza on the right with a superb **theatre** (*Teatro Morlacchi*), a **book and stationery shop** (Libreria Morlacchi) and Caffé Morlacchi which has **live music** (08.00–01.00). From Piazza Cavallotti bear left up Via Maestà delle Volte to Piazza IV Novembre.

From Piazza IV Novembre walk down Corso Vannucci and turn right though the large arch into Via dei Priori. On your right is a **photo developing** shop and on your left at number 6 is the Osram **electrical appliance** shop which also sells batteries, screwdrivers and so on. You pass the tiny church of Sant'Agata (1290–1314) on your left which has pretty **frescoes**. Turn left into Via della Cupa, opposite the Baroque church of San Filippo Neri. This road overlooks the Campaccio Gardens and there are views west towards the Lago di Trasimeno (particularly nice at sunset). Continue alongside the gardens until Piazza Mariotti, home of the Music Conservatory and then through Porta Eburnea, also called Porta della Mandorla. Follow Via S. Giacomo into Via del Parione. This passes the church of S. Spirito and eventually leads out onto the busy Via Luigi Masi. There are views to the right of the athletic track near the main **bus station**. Turn left and enter the tunnel leading to the escalators (*scale mobili*) that lead into Piazza Italia. The escalators pass through a maze of ancient streets and passages that were covered over in the sixteenth Century as part of the foundations of the **papal fortress**, *Rocca Paolina*. There is a bookshop among the passageways which has English guidebooks. The escalators emerge in Piazza Italia.

Turn left at the top of the escalators and walk to the balustrade of the **Carducci Gardens** near the Hotel Brufani. From here there are **views** south along the Tiber valley, east towards the Vale of Umbria and Assisi and west towards Tuscany and Largo Trasimeno. There is an outdoor **bar** on the old city wall on your left. It is expensive but has fabulous views of Assisi. Walk back past the escalator and after the Banca d'Italia turn left down a flight of stone steps to Via Bonazzi. Turning left and then imme- diately right takes you to a tiny unmarked **fresh pasta** (*pasta fresca*) shop at number 3 Via Caporali. Otherwise turn right into Via Bonazzi from the bottom of the steps, passing an excellent ice cream shop just before reach- ing Piazza della Repubblica. On the left is the Teatro del Pavone **cinema**, which is a converted theatre and shows original language films on Monday nights.

Cross over Corso Vannucci and turn right into the narrow Via Danzetta, passing an **optician** at number 13. The street comes out into Piazza G. Matteotti and Via Baglioni. There is a **stationers** Magazzini di Egidio Rastelli at Via Baglioni 17 just beyond the Banco di Napoli. In the far-right hand corner of Piazza Matteotti there is a small road Via G. Oberdan. This leads towards the excellent **archaeological museum** *Museo Archeologico Nazionale dell'Umbria*, the Basilica di S. Domenico, and the **medieval gar-**

dens of S. Pietro (see below). It also leads to Perugia's best bookshop (La Libreria, number 52) and deli (Casa del Parmigiano, page 107).

In the Piazza itself the Antica Spezieria Bavicchi at number 32 sells every type of rare ingredient and spice for keen cooks. Should you be getting withdrawal symptoms it also stocks Marmite, Lyons golden syrup, and Fortnum and Mason's marmalade. The **pharmacy** at number 26 is open from 8am until midnight. Next to it is Café Oscar where your cappuccino will have a heart-shaped swirl of coffee on it. Conti at number 19 sells household and kitchen items on the second floor, the baker at number 16 is good for lunchtime sandwiches and the butcher next door sells exceptionally good Umbrian sausages and hand-sliced prosciutto. There is also the ever-popular COOP supermarket. Opposite these shops is the main **post office**, which also sells boxes to send larger items.

Turn right through the large archway next to the *Palazzo del Capitano del Popolo* signed to the *Terrazza del Mercato* from Piazza G. Matteotti. The terrace has magnificent views over Umbria, including the distant Monte Vettore, the Sibillini's highest peak (2478m). To the right is the large flood-lit bell tower (*il campanile*) of San Domenico and the Archaeological Museum. Palazzina Prosciutti (part of the Univeristy for Foreigners) is straight ahead on the other side of the main road, hidden behind a clump of trees. The busy road ahead is Via XIV Settembre, which sweeps up to the left to join Via Pinturicchio leading to Palazzo Gallenga.

There is a superb daily **food market** on two floors below the terrace. The upper level has butchers, a baker, a cheese seller from Campagna and a fishmonger. The lower level has fruit and vegetable sellers. Signora Antonietta Penchini runs a small stall at the southern end selling delicious home grown vegetables and salads (*produzione propria*), including fresh garlic (*aglio fresco*), spinach (*spinaci*), artichokes (*carciofi*), wild asparagus (*asparagi di bosco*), mushrooms (*funghi porcini*), and huge bunches of herbs (*erbe aromatiche*). She also gives cooking advice in Italian.

After visiting the market retrace your steps to Piazza Matteotti. Before going back to Piazza IV Novembre you could walk up the narrow Via delle Volte which leads uphill to the right and which has interesting medieval vaulting.

Archaeological Museum and Medieval Garden afternoon

For another half-day stroll you shouldn't miss is walking to the National Archaeological Museum (*Museo Archeologico*) by the Basilica di San Domenico and to the excellent nearby Medieval Garden (*Orto Medievale*) at the Chiesa di San Pietro. The walk from Piazza Matteotti takes about 30 minutes and passes through a *bellissimo* part of Perugia. From Piazza Matteotti walk down Via G. Oberdan. Go straight down the stone steps of Via S. Ercolano (passing the famous Casa del Parmigiano deli at number 36) and at the large church of S. Ercolano turn left onto Corso Cavour. In a few minutes you reach the Piazza G. Bruno and the huge Basilica di S. Domenico, Umbria's largest church. The Archaeological Museum is in the next-door cloisters. It has an extensive display of Etruscan and Roman artefacts including the famous *Cippo Perugino*, a stone with one of the longest inscriptions in the Etruscan language. It is open on Monday from 14.30–19.30 and Tuesday to Sunday from 08.30–19.30. Entrance is €2. To get to the Medieval Gardens, continue to the end of Corso Cavour. Walk through the stone Porta S. Pietro and straight ahead along Borgo XX Giugno to the beautiful bell tower and church of San Pietro. The gardens are free and have spectacular views east over Umbria. There is a free English guide available on request. The adjacent Church of San Pietro has concerts throughout the year. In summer the adjacent public gardens, Giardini del Frontone, are used as an open air cinema. There is also excellent pizzeria (Pizzeria Pompei) at number 14, near the Zenith cinema.

ROME

ROMA

7

Rome is a city of contrasts. When you first arrive it is easy to see only traffic and hear only the hooters of vespers and cars. Over ten million tourists visit per year so you frequently hear English voices and see people clutching their maps. Prices are higher than in other parts of Italy and it can be difficult to see past this big loud first impression. There are, however, many areas where you can see another side of Rome. There are quiet shady parks, hidden piazzas and spring water fountains among the world famous monuments and museums. We have devised a walk through the Trastevere region and up to a viewpoint over Rome where you can see this side of the city. There are five universities in Rome but none of them have language courses for students outside their own programmes. We have included a Rome chapter because of its importance as the capital of Italy.

Don't Miss *Da Non Perdere*

▶ the view across Rome from Piazzale Garibaldi (see our walk on page 149)

▶ Bernini's floodlit fountains

▶ drinking from water fountains on street corners

▶ the perfect circle of light that comes through the roof of the Pantheon

▶ the frescoed ceilings of Sant' Ignazio di Loyola and Gesù (illusions of perspective)

▶ a Sunday walk on Via Appia, Rome's oldest road, lined with cypress and catacombs

▶ a day trip excursion to the Tivoli gardens and waterfall

Drinking fountains *Fontane di acqua potabile*

On most streets in Rome you can hear the calming noise of spring water splashing onto the pavement from one of the many waist-high water fountains. Many locals use these fountains not only for drinking but also for washing fruit from the market, sprucing up in the heat of the day and washing their cars. In the summer heat it is one of the real pleasures of walking around the city. Put your mouth by the small hole above the end of the pipe and block the water's exit so it shoots up out of the small hole into your mouth. You will be mistaken for a real Italian.

Table comparing Rome's Language Schools
Le Scuole di Lingua

School	Arco di Druso	Centro Prolingua	Ciao Italia	Dilit International House	ItaliaIde	Società Dante Alighieri	Torre di Babele
Two-week Course	€186#	€420	€300	€330	€256#	–	€325
Four-week Course	€270#	€650	€525	€597	€465#	€245#	€588
Individual lesson	€25	€36	€32	€35	€44	–	€36
Single room two weeks	–	€240	€230	€235	€250	–	€225
Single room four weeks	€350	€440	€420	€400	€400	€320	€390
Enrolment fee	€30	€50	€30	€40	€35	€36	€40
Maximum group size	10	8	12	15	10	No maximum	12
Air conditioning	One room	Yes	Yes	Some rooms	Yes	No	Yes
Laboratory	Yes	Yes	No	Yes	No	No	No
Discounts	No	Some special packages	After one month €130/week	5% after four months paid in advance	10% after three months paid in advance	No	No
Scholarships	Yes	Yes	Yes	No	No	Yes	Yes

Three hours per day, Monday to Friday

Accommodation prices are approximate

Private Language Schools *Le Scuole di Lingua*

Arco di Druso

Via Tunisi 4

00192 Roma

Tel: (06) 39750984 Fax: (06) 39761819

Email info@arcodidruso.com Website: www.arcodidruso.com

This is one of Rome's budget options. It is a tiny school on the second floor of a modern block a few meters from the entrance to the Vatican Museums. The entrance is on your right as you go down the wide stone steps leading to Via Tunisi opposite the entrance to the Vatican Museum. The area is full of tourists and souvenir sellers and is loud, busy and chaotic. The school, in contrast, is quiet. It consists of three small classrooms coming off a narrow corridor and some computers with Internet access and Italian CD-ROMs. The classes are limited to a maximum of ten students. The friendly director does not speak much English.

Courses and costs *Corsi e costi*

The **standard** courses are three hours teaching a day (15 hours a week) and cost €186 for two weeks and €270 for four weeks. The school also runs **evening** courses of two hours teaching three times a week, from 19.00–21.00, costing €276 per month. The **individual** lessons are possibly the cheapest in Rome. They are €25 an hour but a three week 'lunch time' course of two hours twice a week costs €216 (€18 an hour). This can be taken in addition to group course. The enrolment fee is €30. **Scholarships** are available via the Italian Cultural Institutes (see page 13).

Accommodation *Alloggio*

A single room in a shared apartment costs €300 per month.

Centro Prolingua

Via Angelo Ranucci 5 and 9

00165 Roma

Tel: (06) 39367722 Fax: (06) 39367723

Email info@prolingua.it Website www.prolingua.it

Open Monday to Friday 09.00–19.30

This small school has been running since 1992. It is located a few hundred metres southwest of the Vatican, on the corner of Via Angelo Ranucci where it meets the large, busy main road Via Gregorio. It is not our favourite area of Rome and highlights the contrasts of the city. Although it is close to the centre of the Catholic Church and one of Rome's biggest tourist attractions it is an ugly traffic-filled area of residential apartment blocks and shops. The school, however, has three advantages over its competitors: it has a good *laboratorio linguistico* (multimedia classroom), a maximum group size of eight and wheelchair access.

The offices and a couple of classrooms are located at number 5, on the first floor above some shops. The newer, nicer, half of the school is in the basement of number 9. This is a modern air-conditioned building with an excellent multimedia classroom and two further classrooms overlooking the back of the building. The multimedia classroom has several computers with CD-ROM Italian exercises for recording answers and playing them back to improve pronunciation (see page 7 *laboratorio linguistico*). The steps down to the basement have a stair lift for wheelchair users.

Courses and costs *Corsi e costi*
The **standard** course of four hours a day (20 hours a week) costs €420 for two weeks and €650 for four weeks. There are **non-intensive** courses of between six to 20 hours a week, priced according to the number of hours. There is a free test on their website if you are interested in getting an idea of your level before you arrive. There are courses for CILS and IT exam preparation and **specialised** courses in business, legal and medical Italian. A free guided visit each month is included in the price of an intensive course. There is a €50 enrolment fee. The school is unusual in offering refunds for lessons cancelled due to bank holidays (see page 17). **Scholarships** are available by applying directly to the school.

Accommodation *Alloggio*
The school owns an apartment with five bedrooms, some of which have a balcony (*un balcone*). A single room costs €450 per person per month.

Ciao Italia

Via delle Frasche 5 (off Via dei Serpenti)

00184 Roma

Tel/Fax: (06) 481 4084

Email info@ciao-italia.it Website www.ciao-italia.it

Open Monday to Friday from 09.15 to 18.30

This small school is in the centre of Rome within walking distance of the train station and Colosseum. It has been running for more than ten years and currently has about 300 students per year. The school is on the second floor of a cosy building in a quiet cobbled street near the busy main road of Via Nazionale. The school is light and airy. There are four classrooms which are painted cream and grey and which are hung with black and white photos of *Roma*. There is a notice board with student information and a small seating area. Monica, the course organiser, speaks excellent English and will tailor courses to individual needs. The school is particularly good for those who are employed as well as studying Italian as there is a range of evening classes. There is no *laboratorio linguistico* or library but there are televisions and videos.

Courses and costs *Corsi e costi*

The **standard** language course of four hours teaching per day (20 hours a week) costs €300 and for two weeks or €525 for four weeks (minimum of two weeks). The **intensive** courses have four hours of group teaching and two hours of individual lessons per day. These cost €715 for two weeks or €1,320 for four weeks. There is a **non-intensive** course of two hours a day two or three times per week for a minimum of eight weeks which costs €242 for two months. This course is ideal for au pairs or people working as the classes can be in the mornings or evenings. **Individual** lessons cost €32 per hour and there is an enrolment fee of €30.

The school also runs **holiday courses** in the small medieval village of Cetona in Tuscany. These include accommodation in small apartments, three hours of teaching per day, half-board and extracurricular activities. They cost €740 per week but can be taken for a long weekend.

There are **specialised** courses in Italian for opera singers, history of art and business; these last 16 hours over one month but only run with four or more students.

The school organises a programme of cultural activities including films, lectures, parties, wine tastings and guided tours. There are also outings to theatres, opera, concerts, restaurants and sports clubs.

Qualifications *Titoli*

Students receive a certificate of attendance at the end of the course. The school is a training centre for the CILS and IT exams (see page 15 'exams').

Scholarships *Borsi di Studio*

The school offers scholarships of 50% of the course fees for a one-month course. Applications require a letter of support from a language school/teacher/university or Italian Cultural Institute.

Accommodation *Alloggio*

The school can help you find accommodation either with an Italian family, in a shared apartment or in a hotel. All rooms include the use of a kitchen. Prices start at €420 for a month in a single room or €335 per person in a double room. A €80 deposit is required.

DILIT International House

Via Marghera 22

00185 Roma

Tel: (06) 4462592 Fax: (06) 4440888

Email info@dilit.it Website www.dilit.it

This large school has been open since 1974. It is part of International House, a worldwide organisation of 120 schools. It occupies a pretty palazzo on a quiet road close to the Termini railway station. Coming from the station the school is on the left, tucked back from the pavement behind a small front terrace. There are four bright spacious floors, two terraces and a cosy bar serving drinks and food. There is also a wide screen television for Italian films. All of the classrooms have large windows. There is a tiny *laboratorio linguistico*, which has several very small TVs for watching Italian videos and tape recorders for interactive Italian exercises (see page 7 *laboratorio linguistico*). A computer room is being built next to the *laboratorio*, which will have Internet access. There are English, French and German classes for Italian students so it is easy to meet other language students for conversation practice.

Courses and costs *Corsi e costi*

The group courses are 15, 20 or 30 hours a week for a minimum of two weeks. Each group has a maximum of 15 students. The **standard** course of four hours teaching a day (20 hours a week) costs €330 for two weeks or €597 for four.

The **afternoon** course of three hours a day (15 hours a week) costs €254 for two weeks and €455 for four weeks. There is an enrolment fee of €40.

The school also runs courses for CILS exam preparation and specialised courses on business Italian, art, culture, cooking, cinema and opera.

There are free weekly seminars on literature, art, cooking, wine and regions of Italy, which are open to all. They also organise a full programme of social activities including films, excursions, concerts and operas.

Accommodation *Alloggio*

There is a free accommodation service. A single room with an Italian family (with use of the kitchen) or in a shared apartment is €235 for two weeks or €400 for four weeks. A double room costs €178 per person for two weeks or €380 for four.

Italialdea

Via dei Due Macelli 47 (near the junction with Via Capo le Case)
Roma 00187
Tel: (06) 69941314 Fax: (06) 69202174
Email info@italiaidea.com Website www.italiaidea.com
This modern school is a stone's throw from the Spanish Steps on the first floor of newly refurbished premises. It could win a design award with its high quality furnishings and bathroom fittings. The school has been open since 1984 and attracts about 800 students per year. The age group is slightly older but there are a range of courses to suit anyone from holidaymakers, students, business people and those immigrating to Italy. On the first day of your course there is a *giro sotto casa*, a tour of the neighbourhood to orientate you to the sites and useful amenities. There is a library with a range of videos and books for loan.

Courses and costs *Corsi e costi*

The school runs an extensive range of courses.

The **group courses** have a maximum of ten students and include 'intensive', 'full immersion' and 'extensive' courses. The 'intensive' group course is three hours per day (15 hours a week). The full course lasts a month and costs €465 but you can attend for two or three weeks only. The two-week 'full immersion' course is the same group course as the intensive course but with the addition of two hours a day of individual lessons and costs €970. The 'extensive' group course is a ten-week course of three hours twice a week in the morning or afternoon and costs €465.

There are small group **evening** classes that consist of two hours twice a week from 18.30–20.30. This course runs for eight weeks starting in any month between October and June. The maximum group size is four people and the cost is €582.

There are **specialised** one-month courses in business Italian, Italian cinema and history of art. Each has 24 hours of lessons divided into two-hour sessions three times per week and cost €310. The business Italian course focuses on understanding professional relationships, job hunting and the business environment of Italy. The Italian cinema course explores the last 100 years of Italian cinema including Neorealism, comedy, Fellini, Benigni, silent films and the New Italian Cinema Movement. The history of art course covers art from 1700 to the present day and includes visits to churches and museums.

The **individual** lessons cost €44 per hour or €925 for 25 hours (€37 per hour). They can be scheduled for evenings or weekends and can take place in your office or hotel.

There is an unusual **'walking Italian'** course of 15 hours of individual lessons that are held while walking around the sites of Rome. This allows you to see the sites with a teacher of history of art and learn Italian at the same time. The course costs €824.

Qualifications *Titoli*

An attendance certificate is given to everyone who finishes a course. Individual courses can be arranged to prepare for the CILS exams.

Accommodation *Alloggio*

The school can organise accommodation either in a shared or private apartment or with an Italian family. The school regularly checks all accommodation. A single room in a shared apartment costs €400–€500 per person per month or €250–350 for two weeks. To stay with an Italian family costs €720–840 per month. Apartments start at €800 per month per person.

Società Dante Aligheri (Rome branch)

Piazza Firenze 27
Roma 00186
Tel: (06) 6873722 Fax: (06) 6873691
Email dantealighieri.roma@libero.it Website www.dantealighieri-roma.it
Secretariat: Monday to Friday 09.30–12.00 and 17.30–19.00
Library: Tuesdays, Wednesdays, Thursday 09.30–12.30 and
Tuesdays and Wednesdays 15.30–18.30
This school is one of Rome's bargains (see page 126 *Arco di Drusco*). It is in the centre of ancient Rome within easy walking distance of the main sites. The school occupies the second floor of a grand palazzo surrounded by a maze of quiet cobbled streets. As you enter the courtyard, turn right up a large flight of stone steps. On the second floor, as you enter the school there is a pretty windowed hall with four large carved wooden tables and views down into the courtyard. This would be a good place to do homework (*compiti*) or play their grand piano. Up to the right is a small library with a frescoed ceiling and a small collection of books for loan. The view from the library's balcony onto the garden is worth seeing even if you are not studying here. The classrooms have large whitewashed walls and high ceilings. The main disadvantage of the school is that there are no limits to the number of students in the class (unlike *Arco di Druso*).

Courses and *costs Corsi e costi*

The school runs Italian language courses and Italian culture courses that can be taken together or separately. The shortest language course is one month and they are only run with a minimum of ten students. There is a €36 **enrolment** fee. **Scholarships** are available by applying directly to the school. There are no courses in August or September.

Language courses

There are three types of **one-month** language course in all levels.

1 **Intensive** one-month courses of three hours per day (15 hours a week) from 11.00 to 14.00 Monday to Friday. These courses run in October, November, January, February, March, April, May and June and cost €245.

2 **Conversation classes** of 20 hours a month divided into two-and-a-half hours twice a week. These courses are based around discussion of topics about life in Italy and cost €100.

3 **Post-advanced courses** for people with almost perfect grasp of Italian. This course is 16 hours divided into two hours twice a week and costs €88.

There are two types of **two-month** language courses in all levels.

1 **Ordinary courses** of 32 hours over two months. Lessons are divided into two-hour sessions twice a week from 09.00 to 11.00 and 18.00 to 20.00 and cost €135.

2 **Semi-intensive courses** of 48 hours over two months. Lessons are divided into three-hour sessions twice a week from 15.00 to 18.00 and cost €200.

These courses start in October, December, February, April and June.

Italian culture courses in Italian literature, art and history

1 **Italian literature**. This course is 20 hours over one month (two-and-a-half hours twice a week) and costs €100. Literature from the thirteenth to the twentieth century is studied as well as Lectura Dantis (*Hell*, *Purgatory* and *Paradise*).

2 **History of art**. There is both a one-month and a two-month course. The one-month course is 20 hours (two-and-a-half hours twice a week) and covers the seventeenth century from Caravaggio to Bernini. The two-month course is 32 hours (two hours twice a week) and covers Raffaello, Michelangelo, Caravaggio, Bernini, Borromini and the origins of Rome.

3 **History of Italy**. There is both a one-month and a two-month course. The one-month course lasts 20 hours (two-and-a-half hours twice a

week) and looks at Italian political parties and the first Republic. This costs €100. The two-month course lasts 32 hours (two hours twice a week) and looks at medieval history from the end of the Roman Empire to the beginning of the second millennium. The courses include the use of old films and documentaries and costs €88.

Qualifications *Titoli*

A certificate of attendance is given to all students. The school is also a centre for the *Progetto Lingua Italiana Dante Alighieri* (PLIDA) exams (see page 16). This exam can be taken in May and November and the closing date for registration is 10 April and 10 October respectively. It is also possible to take a diploma exam at the end of all intensive and semi-intensive courses.

Accommodation *Alloggio*

The school does not offer an accommodation service but can give advice.

Torre di Babele

Via Bixio 74

00185 Roma
Tel: (06) 7008434 Fax: (06) 70497150
Email info@torredibabele.com Website www.torredibabele.com
This small school is located in the Esquilino district, in a quiet road near the Termini train station. It was founded in 1984 and occupies a pretty city house over four narrow floors with a small third floor terrace and a shady ground floor garden. The classrooms are modern and bright and have good quality tape recorders and CD players and/or televisions with videos. There is one computer available for students in the main office but this is limited to only ten minutes use at any one time. There is no library or *laboratorio linguistico*.

Courses and costs *Corsi e costi*

Groups are a maximum of 12 students. The **standard** course of four hours teaching a day (20 hours a week) costs €325 for two weeks or €588 for four. There is a 'mini-group' course which has a maximum of three students and a two-week **senior class** for the over 50s. The school can also arrange a CILS exam preparatory course. **Scholarships** are available by applying through the Italian Cultural Institutes.

The school organises regular extracurricular activities and weekend excursions that are paid for separately. Cultural seminar programmes only take place with a minimum of five students.

Accommodation *Alloggio*

A single room in a shared apartment costs €225 for two weeks or €390 for four weeks. A double room in a shared apartment costs €160 for two weeks or €306 for four weeks. The prices quoted for finding a private apartment were very expensive.

Getting to and from Rome *Andare e tornare da Roma*

Trains *Treni*

Rome is the centre of an excellent train network with express trains for destinations all over Italy. The main Termini train station is in the city centre on Piazza D. Cinquecentro. The ticket office is open from 07.00–21.45 seven days a week. Information about train times and costs can also be had from the automated ticket machines in the station. The website has timetable information in English www.trenitalia.com Tickets for Eurostar trains (Italy's fastest trains) must be booked in advance of travelling.

Bus *Pullman*

Local buses leave from behind the train station. Buy your ticket from a news stand (*edicole*) or *tabacchi* and validate it by using the machines on the buses. There is an information office for buses in the square behind the station or ask the bus drivers.

Air *Aerei*

Rome has two airports, Fiumicino and Ciampino. Fiumicino (Tel: (06) 65954455) is the larger of the two and has regular trains straight to Rome's main Termini station (30 minutes). Ciampino (Tel: (06) 794941) is about one-and-a-half hours from Rome by bus or by bus then train.

Addresses For Easy Living in Rome

Au pair work *Lavoro alla pari*

This is a good way of learning Italian if you enjoy looking after children. The European Au Pair Programme is a cultural exchange that enables EU members to live and work in Italy for a year or more. Non-EU members can work as an au pair for a maximum of three months using a study visa. As an au pair you receive board and lodging and pocket money of between €55 to €80 a week in return for light housework and looking after the children. You should expect to be working between six and eight hours per day for six days a week including some evening baby-sitting. This is not a job for the faint-hearted. During school holidays the au pair is expected to work longer hours and will be paid extra, in the region of €90–110 per week.

Roma Au Pair

Via V. Bellini 10
Rome 00198
Tel: (06) 85354549 Mobile: (339) 7794126 Fax: (02) 95441254
Website www.romaaupair.it
This agency places au pairs with families in Rome, Bologna, Milan and Florence. You will need a lot of *documenti* including two references, a medical certificate, passports photos and a handwritten letter to the host family about yourself. There is no agency fee. The application form is detailed and even includes questions about your parents' occupations. Most families want an au pair for a year at least although there are shorter contracts.

Bakeries *Panetterie*

Il Fornaio

Via Natale del Grande 4
00153 Roma
Tel: (06) 5806408
Open Monday to Saturday 08.00–20.00 Sundays 08.00–13.00
This tiny bakery in the Trastevere district will entice you with the smell of freshly baked bread.

Il Pane di Trastevere

Piazza di San Cosimato 53

Roma

Open 07.30–14.00 and 17.00–20.00. Closed on Sundays and Thursday afternoons

This bakery on the pretty Piazza San Cosimato (Trastevere district) is where many Italians come to buy a fresh slice of *pizza bianca* (white pizza) and biscotti for lunch. There is a small mini market at the back selling fresh milk (*latte fresco*), groceries (*provviste*) and soft drinks (*bibite*).

Bike rental *Biciclette a noleggio*

Eco Move Rent

Via Marghera 47D (100metres from the Termini station)

Tel: (06) 44704518

Email info@ecomoverent.com Website www.ecomoverent.com

Open every day 08.30–19.30

This shop rents bicycles, scooters, cars and even helicopter rides. Bicycle hire is from €11 a day.

Romarent

Vicolo dei Bovari 7/a (30m from Campo di Fiori)

Tel/Fax: (06) 68 96 555

Website www.romarent.net

Open every day 08.30 to 19.00

This company rents scooters, bikes, cars, sailing boats and video cameras. Bicycle hire is from €9 a day.

Bookshops *Librerie*

The Almost Corner Bookshop

Via del Moro 45 (Trastevere district)

Tel: (06) 5836942

Open Monday–Saturday 10.00–13.30 and 15.30–20.00

Sundays 11.00–13.30 and 15.30–20.00

This shop sells English language books.

Liberia 4 Fontane

Via delle Quattro Fontane 20/a

Tel: (06) 4814484 (next to the British Council Library)

Open Monday to Friday 09.00–13.00 and 15.30–19.30 Saturdays 09.00–13.00

This shop sells English and international books.

Mondadori Trevi (near the Trevi fountain)

Via San Vincenzo 10

Roma

Tel: (06) 6976501

Open every day from 10.00 to 22.00

This three-storey air-conditioned bookshop stocks English art books and international titles. On the top floor there is computer software and a bar on the ground floor.

Childcare *Babysitting*

Baby Park/ Verba espressioni digitali

Via Merry del Val Cardinale 20

Roma

Tel: (06) 581 3208

Open every day 09.00–23.00

This child-minding facility is newly opened, spotlessly clean and air-conditioned. Children from 3 to 10 years of age can play and learn about computers. There is Internet access on state of the art computers and DVD rental. There is a maximum of 15 children per day. The prices range from €30 for three hours, €90 for ten hours, €160 for 20 hours to €280 for 40 hours. There are discounts if more than one child attends from the same family, 20% for one extra child, 30% for three children and 50% for four children.

Cinemas *Cinema*

Pasquino

Piazza S. Egidio 10

Tel: (06) 581 5208

This cinema looks like a green garage door when it is closed and has no sign outside. It is opposite the Museo di Roma in Trastevere and shows daily English films.

Alcazar

Via Merry dal Val 14 (Trastevere district)

Tel: (06) 5880099

This cinema shows Italian films daily and original language films on Mondays.

Dance schools *Scuole di danza*

La Piroetta

Viale Leonardo da Vinci 307

Tel/Fax: (06) 5404663

The *segreteria* is open every day from 16.00–21.00

There are classes in flamenco, jazz and even baby jazz for 8–10 year olds.

Delicatessans *Nogozi di specialità gastronomiche*

Antica Caciara Trasteverina di Roberto Polica

Via San Francesco a Ripa 140 a/b (Trastevere district)

Tel: (06) 5812815

Open Monday to Saturdays 07.30–14.00 and 16.00–20.00

This speciality food shop has been run by the same family since 1900. The friendly Roberto Polica whose grandparents started the shop will tell you about his specialities and point out his many awards. He sells a wide selection of cheese, including *castelmagno* (matured on cave floors in Piedmont), *pecorino di fossa* (a strong sheep's cheese matured underground), and the infamous *pecorino Romano* (*del Lazio*) and *ricotta di Pecora* (made from the same milk as the pecorino Romano). They even sell *burrate Pugliesi* (a type of Puglian mozzarella stuffed with butter). They stock pre-soaked salt cod (*baccalà*) and chick peas (*ceci*) and over 100 wines.

Fishmonger *Pescivendolo*

Pescheria da Danilo

Via Natale del Grande 34

This tiny shop sells fresh fish from 08.00–13.00 daily. Closed on Sundays.

Galleries *Gallerie*

Galleria Spada

Piazza Capo di Ferro 13

Tel: (06) 686 1158

Open Tuesday to Sunday 08.30 to 19.30

This gallery has works collected by Cardinal Bernardino, his great nephew Cardinal Fabrizio Spada and his other nephew's wife Maria Veralli. There are paintings by Reni, Titian, Baciccia and Rubens and others. Entrance costs €5.20 and guided tours in English or Italian are available by appointment only (Tel: (06) 8555952).

Gyms and sports centres *Palestre e centri sportivi*

Farnese Fitness

Vicolo Grotte 34

Tel: (06) 6876931

This newly renovated gym just south of Campo di Fiori has the latest fitness machines.

Roman Sport Center

Via del Galoppatoio 33

Tel: (06) 3201667/3218096

This huge sports centre (70,000 square feet) is located under the Villa Borghese park, next to a large underground car park. They have aerobic rooms, gyms, squash courts, swimming pools (including a 25m pool), saunas, steam rooms and a beauty centre. There is a bar and restaurant at the centre. A day pass costs €26 and a monthly pass costs €200.

Hotels and *hostels Alberghi*

Family House Bed and Breakfast

Via Bixio 72

00185 Roma

Tel: (06) 7000770 Fax (06) 70497996

Website www.family-house.it

Email info@family-house.it

Rooms cost €62 a night with a shared bath, €72 with private bath. They also offer apartments at about €400 a week for two people.

Hotel Pensione Cortorillo

Via Principe Amedeo 79a

Tel: (06) 4466934 Fax: (06) 4454769

This family run hotel near the Termini train station is one of Rome's bargains. A double room with a bathroom within the main hotel costs €70 a night including breakfast. There are cheaper double rooms with a communal bathroom from €50 including breakfast. These rooms are located in separate buildings near the main hotel. Bring earplugs as some of the cheaper rooms are on busy roads.

Hotel Trastevere

Via Luciano Manara 24a/25

00135 Roma

Tel: (06) 5814713 Fax: (06) 5881016

Email hoteltrastevere@tiscalinet.it

This hotel is in the heart of the Trastevere district. It was completely renovated in 1998. Most of the rooms face out onto Piazza San Cosimato and the bustling daily food market. There are also some rooms a few minutes walk from the hotel on the ground floor. Double rooms start at €103 including television, private bathroom and breakfast.

Other accommodation options

The English magazine 'Wanted in Rome' (see below).

www.bedroma.com is a site for Rome bed and breakfasts.

www.hotelreservation.it is a site for hotels in Rome, Venice, Florence, Naples, Milan, Viterbo, Siena, Tivoli, Sorrento and Capri. This service is free and run from a small office in Termini train station. The office and call centre is open from 07.00 to 22.00 seven days a week. Tel: (06) 6991000. Email hr@hotelreservation.it

Ice cream *Gelateria*

San Crispino

Via Della Panetteria 42
Tel: (06) 6793924
Open 12.00–24.30, closed on Tuesdays
This is the ultimate ice cream in flavours including hazelnut, Chilean grape, pear and pink grapefruit. The cost of €1.70 for a tiny cup is worth it. The taste is different from the usual ice cream and surprisingly a small cup is enough (*basta*).

Grattachecca is an icy drink which takes its name from *gratta* from *grattugiare* (to grate) and *Checca* short for Francesca, the name of the woman who invented it. A good place to try it is from the green kiosk next to the Ponte Cestio (see our walk on page 150).

Kitchen shops *Negozi di casalinghi*

Ditta Peroni Vittorio

Piazza dell'Unita 29
00192 Roma
Tel: (06) 3211662
Open 09.00–13.00 and 16.00–19.00 Closed on Sunday
This good little kitchen shop is near to the Piazza dell'Unità market.

Rosati

Via A. Depretis 71/74 (near Basilica di Santa Maria Maggiore)
Tel/Fax: (06) 4880819
Open Monday–Thursday 09.00–19.30, Fridays 09.00–14.00 and Saturdays 09.00–17.00
This shop sells all of the best known Italian makes.

Laundrettes *Lavanderie*

There is no shortage of laundrettes in Rome. Many of them have Internet access as well, so you can surf while your washing is being done.

www.Holidayinrome.it (website under construction), Via Varese 33, just behind the Termini station have Internet access at €1.50 an hour (or €1 an hour if you are a language student at DITILS).

Library *Biblioteche*

The British Council Library
Via delle Quattro Fontane 20
Tel: (06) 478141
Open Monday, Tuesday, Thursday and Friday from 10.00–17.00, Wednesdays from 12.00–17.00 and Saturdays from 10.30–12.30.

Markets *Mercati a Roma*

Every zone in Rome has its own market, so you are never far away from a regular supply of delicious, good value food. We have listed some of the best.

▶ *Campo di Fiori*: the daily market in Campo di Fiori is one of the most picturesque in Rome. It has a reputation with the locals as being a market for the tourists (*i turisti*) but it is still one of Rome's best.

▶ *Vecchia Porta Portese market zona Trastevere*: this huge Sunday market is a Roman institution among locals and tourists alike. Take the number 170 bus from Termini, hop off at Ponte Sublicio and walk along to Via Luciano Manara. It is called *vecchio* (old) because it outgrew its location, so some of the traders were relocated to new premises at Via Palmiro Togliatti. If you would like to go to this *nuovo* (new) Porta Portese market, take tram number 14 in the direction of Via Farini.

▶ *Piazza di San Cosimato*: there is a small daily food market on this pretty piazza in the Trastevere district. It is open from about 07.00–14.00 every day except Sundays.

▶ *Ex-Piazza Vittorio Emanuele market*: there is a large daily food market on Via Principe Amedeo near the Termini train station by the junction with Via Lamarmora. This is known by some as the 'ex-Piazza Vittorio Emanuele market' because it used to be held in the nearby Piazza Vittorio Emanuele. The new market is covered and good value.

▶ *Mercato di Via Sannio*: this popular clothes market is open every day except Sundays from about 06.00–13.00.

▶ *Piazza dell'Unità*: there is a daily food market in the large white building on Piazza dell'Unità, just off Via Cola di Rienzo, a 15-minute walk from the Vatican.

Opera *Opera Lirica*

Teatro dell'Opera di Roma
Biglietteria (ticket office), Piazza Beniamino Gigli 1 (close to Piazza della Repubblica)
Tel: (06) 48160255/06 4817003 Fax: (06) 4881755
Open Tuesday–Saturday 09.00–17.00 and Sunday 09.00–13.00
The opera house is in Via del Viminale.
Website www.amitonline.it (in English with ticket information) or www.opera.roma.it (in Italian only)
The Teatro dell'Opera was opened in 1880 and has 1,600 seats. Tickets are also for sale from the opera house on the day of the performance one hour before the start of the performance. Students and people under 25 or over 65 are entitled to a 50% discount on tickets.

Pet shop *Negozi di animali*

La Boutique del Cane Chic
Vicole Grotte 16
Open Monday to Saturday from 09.30–13.30 and from 16.00–20.00. Closed Sundays.
This shop sells everything you could need for your pet including the pet itself. There are rabbits in the window (*vetrina*) waiting for a home.

Post offices *Poste*

Via di Monte del Gallo
(next to the Roma S. Pietro train stop exit)
Open Monday–Friday from 08.30–14.00 and Saturdays from 08.30–13.00

Via Della Scrofa 61
Open Monday to Friday from 08.30–18.30 and on Saturdays from 08.30–13.00

Via di Porta Angelica 26/27

(just off St Peter's Square)

Open Monday–Friday from 08.30–14.00

Piazza di San Cosimato

(on the corner with Via Luciano Manara and Via Giacomo Venezian)

Open Monday to Friday from 08.30–14.00 and Saturday from 08.30–13.00

Piazza di Sidney Sonnino

Open Monday to Friday from 08.30 to 14.00 and Saturday from 08.30 to 13.00

Restaurants and bars *Ristorante e bar*

Sacchetti

Piazza di San Cosimato 61, Roma

Tel: (06) 5815374

Open from about 06.00–22.00

Closed on Mondays

This bar is a couple of doors down from the Il Pane di Trastevere bakery (above) and has outdoor seating. They make particularly good fresh cream cakes. Try their *caffè con panna* (espresso with fresh whipped cream) for a mid-morning perk up.

Piccolo Bar di Zhor Guoying

Via di San Vito 13

This Chinese run bar, ten minutes from the Termini train station, serves one of the cheapest cappuccinos in Rome: €0.75.

Cul de Sac Enoteca

Piazza Pasquino 73

00186 Roma

Tel: (06) 68801094

Open 12.00–16.00 and 18.00–24.30 seven days a week

This is one of our favourite wine bar/eateries. It has a vast range of wines that line the walls above the small tables with bench seating. The wines are pulled down from the high shelves with an extendable 'grabber' by the helpful and knowledgeable staff. They serve speciality cheeses (*formaggio*) and salamis (*salame*), as well as simple plates of pastas, seasonal vegetables and other tasty morsels. They have seating outside and run a ticket system for the inevitable queue. If you book a table they may give you a number so you can breeze in like a film star.

Ristorante Cinese Lago Azzurro
Via di San Vito 15–16
If you feel the need for noodles Chinese style this place may hit the spot. It is usually packed with Chinese people and serves good value, tasty food.

Stationer *Cartoleria*

Risparmio, Cartoleria, Libreria di Veroli
Piazza Vittorio Emanuele II 141
Tel: (06) 4469693
Open 09.00–13.00 and 16.00–20.00. Closed Saturday afternoon and Sunday
This is a good general stationer in the Esquilino district.

Supermarkets *Supermercati*

Supermercato Rocca
Piazza Santa Maria Maggiore 1–5 (next to the UPIM department store)
Tel: (06) 44360225. Open every day from 08.30 to 20.00
This is a good quality, cheap supermarket that sells fruit, vegetables, groceries, wines, bread, meat, fish, cleaning products, toiletries, house goods and has a large deli counter.

'Dì per Dì' (Day After Day)
Via di Monte del Gallo 15
Open Monday–Saturday from 08.00–20.00
This small supermarket is southwest of the Vatican, near the Centro Prolingua language school.

GS Supermarket
Under Villa Borghese
Open 09.00–21.00 including Sundays
This supermarket is 300m from the Spanish Steps under Villa Borghese.

Tourist information for living in Rome *Informazioni per vivere a Roma*

Wanted in Rome

Via dei Delfini 17

00186 Roma

Tel: (06) 6790190 Fax (06) 6783798

Email info@wantedinrome.com

Website www.wantedinrome.com (a very good website also listing accommodation).

This English magazine has a large classified section and interesting articles about living in Rome. There is an up-to-date list of telephone numbers for all the museums, cinemas, information lines and theatres. It has a 'what's on and where to go section' listing events including exhibitions, music, festivals, dance, opera, theatre and cinema and lectures. There are several pages of advertisements for all types of accommodation at much better prices than the language schools offer. The magazine only costs €0.75 and is widely available from news stands and the bookshops listed. You can also subscribe to it from abroad.

Pagine Utili

Website www.pagineutili.it (in Italian only)

These are the Italian equivalent of *Yellow Pages*. They are published in Italian for every region of Italy.

Rome City Walk

Finding the best shops, bars, restaurants, amenities and other secrets

This walk has been carefully designed to quickly orientate you to Rome's most interesting areas and useful amenities. It includes a viewing point, shops, markets, churches, cafés, restaurants and monuments. There is a roundabout for children, an ancient fountain used as a car wash and even a Virgin Mary in blue neon. We have used the street names from the road signs, which are sometimes different from those on the street maps. It may be worth checking the opening times of shops and churches before setting off (see below). The walk can be divided into two sections. The first part starts at Piazza Bocca della Verità (near Ponte Palatino) and finishes at the Isola Tiberina (Ponte Fabricio). The second part continues through the heart of the Jewish quarter to Campo di Fiori and ends at Piazza Navona. The walk takes about three hours allowing for coffees and short visits into the churches.

The walk begins at Piazza Bocca della Verità (bus number 170 from the Termini train station) near the Ponte Palatino Bridge. The Piazza is best known for the medieval drain cover that is supposed to snap shut on the hands of liars. This is set into the portico of Santa Maria in Cosmedin on the Piazza. Unless you want to visit the church, climb the steps passing between two small temples, with the circular second century BC *Tempio Rotondo* on your left. These are two of the best-preserved Republican temples in Rome. Cross over the main road and turn right to walk along the edge of the River Tiber. There is a view of Isola Tiberina from this shady beech-lined road. Cross over the pedestrainised Ponte Fabricio (Rome's oldest bridge) on to the Isola Tiberina passing a **pharmacy** (*farmacia*) and a sign to the **Accident and Emergency** (*pronto soccorso*) on your right. The island has been a place of healing since Roman times. Leave the island by the Ponte Palatino, cross over the busy Lungoteverre degli Anguillara and go down a flight of steps into Piazza Piscinula. From here turn right into Via Lungaretta and continue straight until you come out at the busy Viale di Trastevere in Piazza Sidney Sonnino. There is a **cinema** here on your left. Cross over Viale di Trastevere, passing a **tourist information centre** and a **post office** on your left. Continue walking straight ahead to the Piazza S. Maria in Trastevere. If you need an **English bookshop** (*libreria inglese*) the Almost Corner bookshop is at number 45 Via Moro. This road comes off the very small Piazza on your right just before Piazza S. Maria in Trastevere.

In Piazza S. Maria in Trastevere there is the thirteenth century **Basilica of Santa Maria**, which has a mosaic facade and distinctive bell tower. The polygonal pond and fountain date back to the Jubilee Year of 1450. Turn left out of the church into Via Della Paglia, which is a quiet residential street. Take the first left into Via Giacomo Venezian and then the second right, at the **post office**, into Via Luciano Manara. At the end of this street you can see a large carved arch over a lion's head that was once used as a fountain. Turn left when you reach the arch and after 20m turn right up a flight of steps leading to views of Rome. After a couple of minutes climbing you come out to a road. Cross over to the flight of steps opposite and continue up until you reach Via Garibaldi. Turn right at the top and walk up to the **Church of San Pietro Montoria**. From the steps of this church you can begin to see some views of the city about 40 minutes from the start of the walk.

Continue uphill on Via Garibaldi passing the Memorial (1849–1870) on your right. Soon there is another **viewing spot** from a balustrade with stone balls on top. Take the next right turning through a large iron gate onto a cobbled road. This is called *Passeggiata del Gianicolo* and is a shady walk with views over Rome through the beech trees. Just before reaching Piazzale Garibaldi there is a **merry-go-round** and **bouncy castle** for children (*bambini*). There is also a series of busts, some wearing ornate hats, leading to the Piazzale G. Garibaldi with a statue of the proud man on his horse. From here there is almost a 360° view of Rome. There is a small café selling the usual over-priced drinks and snacks, and public toilets. It is worth the climb to see this view. Bus number 270 comes up to this Piazzale if you are not a walker.

Retrace your steps along the cobbled road back through the large iron-gate at the T-junction with Via Garibaldi. From here you can either continue retracing your steps back to Via Luciano Manara and then right into Piazza S. Cosimato or take a slightly less pretty short cut. For the short cut take the flight of steps immediately down to your left leading into Via di Porta S. Pancrazio. At the bottom, on the right, is an ancient Roman fountain that is used as an informal car wash. Turn right on to Via Garibaldi and take the steps leading down immediately on your left. At the bottom of these go down the rather dank Vicolo della Frusta leading to the right. At the T-junction at the end of this road turn right and follow the road round into Via Luigi Masi. This is a wide road that is used as a resident's car park. At the T-junction with Via G. Venezian (water fountain on your right) turn right towards the post office and into Piazza S. Cosimato. This will have taken about an hour from the start of the walk. There is a delightful **market** selling fruit, vegetables, meat, fish and local specialities. If you are in need of **lunch** you could buy a picnic or a slice of *pizza bianca* from Il Pane bakers. Next door is the **Sanchetti Bar**, which sells good fresh cream cakes and a delicious *caffé con panna* (espresso with cream). These are ahead and to the left as you enter the Piazza. The Hotel Trastevere is directly to your left overlooking the Piazza.

Having refuelled, cross the Piazza into Via Natale del Grande. On the corner there is an *Ave Maria* in blue neon. Via Natale has every type of shop. The Todis **supermarket** is on the right, a **fishmonger** is on your left and a there is a **fresh pasta** shop at number 140A. If you need some speciality **cheese** turn right at the bottom of this street to visit Antica Caciara Trasteverina. Otherwise, cross straight over Via S. Francesco into Cardinale Merry del Val. At number 15, on your right, there is the Alcazar **cinema** and on your left, at number 20, the 'baby park' **childcare facilities** which have a smart (and expensive) Internet point and 24-hour DVD rental machine.

Keep going straight and cross over Viale Trastevere into Piazza Mastai with its pond and fountain. At the far end turn right into Via della Luce and continue along until you reach Piazza S. Francesco D'Assisi. In front of you is the **Chiesa di S.Francesco a Ripa** that has Bernini's rarely visited *Beata Lodovica* in the last chapel on the left. After visiting the church turn right out of door, along the less pretty Via Anicia and take the first right into Via della Madonna dell'Orto. The large white *Scuola Elementare Maschile* runs along the whole length of this road. At the T-junction turn left along Via S. Michele until you reach **Piazza S. Cecilia**. Santa Cecilia is the patron saint of music. The Basilica has mosaics, frescoes and a pretty courtyard (see below for the opening times). On your right is the pretty Piazza de Mercanti. Continue straight ahead along Via S. Cecilia. Continue on to Piazza Ponziani and bear left across into Via della Botticella, which leads to the river. Bear left at the river and walk along to the Ponte Cestio. On the left of the bridge is a kiosk which sells a Roman speciality the **Grattachecca** (see page 142) costing €1.60. It is a type of Roman slush puppy but less sickly. To arrive here should take about two-and-a-half hours from the start of the walk.

Continue crossing back over both bridges and over the busy main road into Piazza di Monte Savello on the left of the **Teatro di Marcello**. After a look around this ancient Roman theatre continue left along Via Del Portico d'Ottavia into the heart of the **Jewish quarter**. You pass *La Dolceroma* **chocolate shop** at number 20 and the Kosher Taverna del Ghetto **restau-**

rant at number 8, where you can try Jewish artichokes and other specialities. Between numbers 2 to 4 there is the Casalinghi **multi-purpose shop**
where you could stock your entire house. At the end of this road turn right
if you need another post office, a bookshop or the theatre. Otherwise leave
the Jewish quarter by crossing over Via Arenula into Piazza Cairoli and
along into Via Giabbonari.

There is a multitude of small boutique shops selling **trendy designer
clothes**. Continue going straight until you come to Campo di Fiori. If you
are in the mood for going to the **Palazzo Spada Gallery** take the small
Vicolo Grotte to the left before the Campo. This road like its name is a bit
grotty, but leads past a pet shop at number 16 and gym opposite at
number 34. At the end of this street turn right into the Piazza Capo di
Ferro. The entrance to the Spada Gallery is on your left opposite a fountain. It is worth looking into the courtyard even if you are not an art-lover.
When you come out of the Gallery turn left and then immediately right
into Via dei Balestrari and onto **Campo di Fiori**. Useful amenities here
include the Farnese **cinema** and the **wine bar** La Vineria at number 15. At
the back of this bar is a TV for football lovers. Campo di Fiori is where the
philosopher Giordano Bruno was burned at the stake for suggesting that
the earth revolved around the sun. His statue here serves as a reminder.

From Campo di Fiori take the middle right turning into Via dei Baullari
and follow it straight ahead. If you need **car** or **bike hire** turn right into
Vicolo dei Bovari just before you get to Corso V. Emanuele. At number 7A
is a rental shop for bicycles, motorbikes, sailing boats, video camera and
cars. Otherwise cross over Corso V. Emanuele and go straight into Via
della Cuccagna. The end of this road leads out into **Piazza Navona** and
Bernini's Fountain of the Four Rivers (1651).

The churches *Chiese*

Basilica of Santa Maria
Piazza S. Maria (Trastevere district)
This thirteenth century church is open from Monday to Friday 09.00 to
17.30, Saturdays from 17.30 to 20.00 and Sundays 08.30 to 10.30 and 12.00
to 17.30.

Chiesa S. Francesco in Ripa

Piazza di S. Francesco (Trastevere district)

Open 07.00–12.00 16.00–19.30.

This church contains Bernini's *Beata Lodovica*.

Basilica di Santa Cecilia in Trastevere

Piazza di Santa Cecilia (Trastevere district)

Open for visits 09.30–12.30 and 16.00–19.00

This is a pretty church near the quiet and picturesque Piazza di Mercanti. The church has an attractive courtyard (*antico cortile*). The frescoes (*affreschi del Cavallini*) can be seen on Tuesdays and Thursdays between 10.00–12.00 and on Sundays between 11.15–12.00. So don't be late!

Santa Maria in Cosmedin

Piazza Bocca della Verità (Trastevere district)

09.00–12.00 and 15.00–17.00 (*bocca della verita* open 09.00–17.00)

Just across the river from the Trastevere district, near Ponte Palatino. This pretty church is best known for the medieval sewer cover *bocca della verità* which is supposed to bite off the hand of liars.

Reggio di Calabria, the Land of the Bergamot

8

Il Paese dei Bergamotti

This seaside town is almost at the bottom of the 'toe' of Italy, on the Straits of Messina and next to the wild mountainous National Park of the Aspromonte. It is a cheap town in which to live, study and explore Calabria and Sicily. Reggio is often underrated but has much to offer. It has the cheapest University for Foreigners in Italy, excellent trekking opportunities and easy access to some of Italy's finest beaches. There are many unusual buildings that were rebuilt after a devastating earthquake in 1908. The beautiful Duomo had to be built completely afresh on the same site as its Norman predecessor. There is a stunning seaside promenade to stroll along from which the smoking peak of Mount Etna in Sicily can be seen. There are frequent ferries running to Messina in Sicily (*Sicilia*) for day trips or longer holidays. There are also excellent transport links with the rest of Italy including an overnight train to Milan.

Reggio is famous for its museum (Museo Nazionale), which has relics from the region including the two magnificent fifth century BC bronze warriors *Bronzi di Riace*. They were only discovered in 1972 in the town of Riace. Reggio's main street, the pedestrianised Corso Garibaldi, is 3km long and runs parallel with the sea. Here is where the people stroll and have their ice creams while enjoying the views of the mountains and the sea. There are a host of designer shops as well as cheaper fashion stores in between the older buildings with their ornate iron balconies and carved stone cornicing. Reggio's population is 189,000 and growing to match the investment in the area. The bergamot's bittersweet fruit has become the symbol of the town and is used for perfumes, alternative medicine, ice cream and confectionery. It was known as 'green gold' and was once used in smelling salts. Calabria is also known for its honey, almonds, dried figs and other citrus fruits. For highlights and further details about the region of **Calabria** see page 254.

Don't Miss *Da Non Perdere*

▶ Reggio's Duomo (1908) in the evening light or floodlit

▶ the Museo Nazionale and the *Bronzi di Riace*

▶ the sea front *passeggiata* on Lungomare Giacomo Matteotti

▶ the Aspromonte National Park

▶ cross-country skiing along the Tosso Ski Trail on Monte Curcio

▶ the September fireworks ending the Festival of the Madonna della Consolazione

▶ nights at the opera in Cosenza and Messina

▶ the beautiful beach town of Scilla

▶ sailing among the Aeolian Islands.

University for Foreigners
Università per Stranieri Dante Alighieri

Via del Torrione 95
Reggio di Calabria 89125
Tel: (0965) 312593 Fax: (0965) 323637

Email priolo.tutor@unistrada.it Website www.unistrada.it (Italian only)
Open Monday to Friday 09.00–13.30

University Sports Centre (CUS)
Via Baracca Trav. De Salvo 8
Tel/Fax: (0965) 891162
Email info@cusreggiocalabria.it

The University for Foreigners in Reggio was founded in 1984. It is one of
the smallest and most personal universities in Italy and is also the cheapest. The university palazzo is two minutes from the sea in the centre of the
old town. It has a small library, a computer room, a pretty inner courtyard
and airy classrooms. The groups tend to be small (less than 15) and anyone
over the age of 16 can enrol.

Courses and costs *Corsi e costi*

1 The standard **three-month** language courses consist of four hours of teaching per day (20 hours a week) and cost €103 per month plus a €52
enrolment fee. Courses start at the beginning of January, April and October.

2 The standard **one-month** course runs every month throughout the year as
long as there are ten students enrolled. There are four hours of teaching per
day (20 hours a week) and it costs €103 for the month plus a €52 enrolment
fee. It is possible to attend for two or three weeks but there is no discount.

3 **Intensive** summer courses lasting one month start at the beginning of
July, August and September. The course has 20 hours per week but the
teaching moves at a quicker pace than the standard courses.

4 Courses for **teachers of Italian** last six months and start at the beginning of
January and the end of June. There are also one-month refresher courses.

5 **Specialised** courses are run when more than ten students are enrolled
and include archaeology, history of Italian art, cinema and music,
singing, translating, and Calabrian politics and linguistics.

Extra-curricular activities *Attività extra*

There is a full programme of outings to local sites as well as one and two-day
coach trips. Outings are organised by teachers with specialised interest in the

different areas. At the end of each course there is a party (*festa*) or concert (*concerto*). At Easter and Christmas there is a special *festa* where students make a speciality dish from their home country to share with their group.

Qualifications *Titoli*

The University is a registered centre for the Progetto Lingua Italiana Dante Alighieri (PLIDA) examinations held in May and November (see page 15 'qualifications'). An end of course certificate is given to all students at a cost of €5.

Scholarships *Borse di Studio*

Scholarships are available from October to June and cover the cost of tuition. The application should be addressed to the dean (*preside*) of the university and should include a curriculum vita in Italian, a letter of support from an Italian language teacher, school or cultural institute and a letter explaining your reasons for learning Italian.

Study vouchers

A study voucher is given to the student who gets the best end of term exam result. This voucher entitles the winner to attend a free course of the same length as the one attended within one year of winning.

Accommodation *Alloggio*

Mr Nino Loitta
CTS Mediterraneo
Via Demetrio Tripepi 7/e
89125 Reggio Calabria
Tel: (0965) 897969
Email reggio@cts.it Website www.ctsmediterraneo.it (under construction)
The University accommodation consists of shared apartments with two or three bedrooms. A single room costs €195 per month and a double €135 per person per month, not including electricity and gas. It is difficult to find an Italian family to live with in Calabria. Requests for accommodation must be received at least two weeks before arrival.

Getting to and from Reggio di Calabria

Arrivare e Partire da Reggio di Calabria

Buses *Pulman*

Buses leave from Piazza Garibaldi opposite the train station next to the Dì per Dì (Day after Day) supermarket. Information is available on (0966) 57552 from Monday to Saturday between 08.45–12.30 and 14.45–19.30 and on Sunday mornings from 08.45–12.30. The night bus for **Perugia**, **Siena** and **Florence** leaves at 21.00 and arrives in Siena at 08.30 and in Florence at 09.30. The **Rome** bus leaves at 07.00 and arrives at 15.00. There is also a night bus to Bologna, Milan and Lake Como leaving at 18.45 and arriving at 06.55, 10.00 and 11.15 respectively.

Vacovatour
Via Aspromonte 10 (opposite the train station)
Open Monday to Friday 09.00–13.00 and 16.00–20.00 and Saturdays 09.00–13.00
This travel agent sells commission-free long distance bus and train tickets.

Trains *Treni*

The main station (*stazione centrale*) is in Piazza Garibaldi. The ticket office (*biglietteria*) is open every day from 05.35–20.30 (see also the general website www.trenitalia.com). Within the station there is a bar, cash point, Internet access, newsagent, passport photo machine, *tabacchi*, telephones, ticket information, toilets, tourist information and self-service ticket machines.

Avoid the queues by using the **self-service** machines to pick up pre-booked tickets and for information on timetables and costs. The **toilets** are hidden at the very end of platform one (*binario uno*) in area E. The **cash point** is just before the toilets on platform one between areas D and E. **Left luggage** is on platform one area D and costs €3.87 per piece of luggage for 24 hours. It has strange opening times even by Italian standards: Mondays 08.00–12.00 and 15.00–18.12 and Tuesday to Saturday from 06.18–20.42. They are closed on Sundays. The opening times are not a misprint!

There are excellent **connections** across Italy. The overnight train to **Milan** leaves at 19.30 and arrives at 10.15. A one-way ticket costs €70.39 for a bed in a sleeper carriage or €52 for a seat. There are five express trains to **Rome** (six hours, €41) and **Naples** (four hours, €31) a day and an overnight service. Trains leave at 06.05, 07.55, 09.57, 13.57 and 16.42. The overnight train leaves at 22.30 and arrives in Rome at 06.00.

Ferries *Traghetti*

Reggio's port is run down, with potholed roads and few signposts, but it is well served with ferries to Sicily and the Aeolian islands. It is a short walk from the Lido Comunale and the Lungomare/Corso Vittorio Emanuele. On foot it is best approached from Viale G. Zerbi and then Viale Florio. From here there is a short-cut past the Hotel Continental through large iron gates (closed to cars) into the port.

Hydrofoil foot passenger service to Messina *Servizio aliscafi per Messina*

The ticket office is poorly marked. Entering the port through the iron gates off Viale Florio (and Viale Zerbi) you pass a small bar/*tabacchi* on the left. Turn left just beyond the bar and the ticket office is on the right in a one-storey concrete building. Ferries leave from the mooring next to it regularly from 06.40 until 20.40 (06.40, 07.30, 08.00, 08.50, 09.15, 10.15, 1140, 12.45, 13.10, 14.25, 15.40, 17.00, 18.45, 19.45, 20.40). The crossing takes 25 minutes and costs €2.60 single, €4.30 return or €38 for a monthly pass.

Car ferry service to Messina *Servizio traghetti per Messina*

Meridiano Lines
Via dei Pritanei 12
Tel: (0965) 810414
This is a cheap car ferry and foot passenger service, located about 100m away from the hydrofoil service. It is opposite the pizza restaurant and bar on the left hand-side of the port when entering by car or the right-hand side of the port when entering by foot from Via Zerbi and is sign posted *Autotraghetti per Messina*. It costs €8 per car and takes 45-minutes. The

ferries leave every two hours from 06.00 throughout the day and night. It is possible to arrive 15 minutes before the ferry departs without booking. This ferry is much cheaper than the car ferry running from San Giovanni up the coast (which is better signposted and advertised). The Meridiano dock in Messina is difficult to find for the return trip but is worth the effort as the ferry to San Giovanni costs €16 for a one-way ticket. Make a note of where it is when you arrive at Messina (it is under a large Campari sign).

Day trips to the Aeolian Islands *Gite di un giorno alle Isole Eolie*

Eurolines
Tel: (0965) 810724
Website www.sneuroline.com (Italian only)
This company runs boats trips to the Aeolian Islands (Lipari, Salina and Vulcano), Taormina, Catania and Taoromina throughout the year but more regularly in the summer. Tickets cost from €23.

Addresses for easy living in Reggio di Calabria

Bakeries *Panetterie*

Panificio Fazia
Via Tommasini 26
Tel: (0965) 23823
Open Monday to Saturday 07.00 to 13.30
Fresh breads and hot pizza are made in the back of the shop. There is a fruit and vegetable shop next door (open Monday to Saturday from 07.00–13.00 and 16.00–20.00).

Pane e Delizie
Via de Nave 124
Tel: (0965) 812731
Bread, biscotti, cakes, fresh cheese and fresh pasta are available to order.

Bookshops *Librerie*

Libreria Nuova AVE snc
Corso Garibaldi 206

89125 Reggio di Calabria

Tel: (0965) 23533

Email nuovave@yahoo.it

Open Monday to Saturday 09.00–12.45 and 16.00–20.30

This is an excellent central bookshop. It has a wide range of books including language textbooks and a large range of maps and books on the Aspromonte National Park. The owners offer lots of local advice (in Italian).

Butchers *Macellerie*

Rosse e Bianche

Via de Nave 116 A/B

Fresh *panini* are made to order from a range of tasty specialities.

Cheese shop *Negozi, di Formaggi*

Fiore di Calabria

Via De Nave 95

Open Monday to Saturday from 08.30–13.00 and 17.00–20.00

The owners of this shop make their own mozzarella and caciocavallo. It also stocks a selection of local olive oils, potted tomatoes and peppers, pastas and other goodies.

Cinema *Cinema*

Odeon Cinema

Via Settembre 3 (close to the museum)

Hairdresser and beautician *Parrucchiera e istituti di bellezza*

Figara di Paris 26

Via Cattolica dei Greci 24

Tel: (0965) 813220

This hairdresser and beauticians has two shops next door to each other, one for men and the other for women.

Hotels *Alberghi*

Hotel Noel

Via Genovese Zerbi 13

Tel: (0965) 890965

This basic budget hotel is near the port on a busy road but has sea views. A double room costs €37 with private bathroom. Rooms on the first floor have balconies and televisions.

Hotel Lungomare

Viale Zerbil 13/b

Tel: (0965) 20486

This modern three star hotel, near Hotel Noel, is good value and has a roof terrace with sea views. A double room costs €80 including breakfast.

Internet *Internet*

Sweet@web

Via Giudecca (open 24 hours but sometimes closed!)

Via de Nave 142

Tel: (0965) 21134

The nicer of the two branches is Via de Nave, which is open from 09.00 to 21.00.

System House Internet Access

Stazione Centrale, Piazza Garibaldi (main train station)

Tel: (0965) 324 744

Open Monday to Friday 09.00–13.00 and 14.00–20.30 and Saturdays 09.00 to 13.00

This Internet café is in the main train station.

Key cutting and photocopying *Duplicati chiavi e fotocopie*

CLIK

Via de Nave 126

The shop has a fax, photocopying and key cutting service.

Markets *Mercati*

Palazzo del Popolo

Open every morning

This excellent daily food market sells fruit, vegetable, cheeses and salamis.

Museum *Museo*

Museo Nazionale della Magna Grecia Park
Piazza de Nava 26
Tel: (0965) 81 22 55
Open every day (except the first and third Mondays of each month) 09.00 to 19.00.
Tickets cost €4 or €2 for 18–25s. Free for under-18s and over-65s (bring passport).
This museum holds the famous bronze statues of two Greek warriors *Bronzi di Riace*. These larger than life figures have been superbly restored and stand in a room with the Greek *Head of the Philosopher*. The museum also has a number of artefacts from *Magna Grecia* (Greater Greece) and a *sezione subacquea* recovered from the Ionian Sea. Visit the museum late in the afternoon to have the museum to yourself.

Off licence *Enoteca*

Enoteca Tripodi di Tripodi Giovanni
Via Veneto 46
Tel: (0965) 895009
Open Monday to Saturday 09.00–13.00 and Tuesday to Friday 17.00–20.15
The owner of this wine shop (*enoteca*) will arrange wine tasting for groups on request.

Opera houses in Messina and Cosenza *Opera lirica a Messina e Cosenza*

Teatro Virrorio Emanule di Messina
Via Pozzoleone 5
98122 Messina
Tel: (090) 5722111
Open Monday to Friday 09.00–13.00 and 16.00–18.40
Website www.teatrodimessina.it (Italian only)
Messina is an easy day trip from Reggio (25 minutes on the hydrofoil). The opera season runs from November to June and tickets cost from €6.

Teatro Rendano

Piazzo XV Margo

87100 Cosenza

Tel: (0984) 813229/813220/813331

Open Monday to Friday 10.00–13.00 and 17.00–20.00

Website www.comune.cosenza.it/rendano (Italian only)

Cosenza is a three-hour train journey from Reggio. The glamorous Rendano theatre (1895) was completely rebuilt after WWII. Its opera season runs from October to December and has hosted the likes of José Carreras. The theatre season runs from January to May.

Post offices *Poste*

Main office

Via Miraglia 14 (near Piazza Italia)

Open Monday to Friday 08.00–18.30 and Saturday 08.00–12.30

There is a smaller branch post office at Via V. Vento 54 (near the museum).

Restaurants and bars *Ristoranti e bar*

Agorà

Via Cattolica dei Greci 24 (near the University)

Tel: (0965) 331700

This excellent pizzeria, with a *forno a legna* (wood burning oven), is open for lunch and supper.

Baylik

Vico Leone 1,3 and 5

Tel: (0965) 48624

Email info@baylik.it Website www.baylik.it (Italian only)

Closed on Thursdays

This award-winning restaurant serves fresh fish and other local specialities.

Caffetteria Antica Reggio

Via Torrione 93

This café near the University has black and white photos of old Calabria, and serves a cappuccino in thick cream coloured 'moca' cups.

Da Giovanni

Via Torrione 77

Tel: (0965) 814900 Closed in August and on Sundays

This delightful fish restaurant is near the University.

Napoli and Napoli

Via S. Caterina 90

Tel: (0965) 45324

Closed on Wednesdays and Sundays

This simple pizzeria with a wood-burning oven is in the scruffy western reaches of town.

Stationers *Cartolerie*

Buffetti Business

Via Missori 7

Tel: (0965) 331961

Website www.buffetti.it (Italian only, possible to buy online)

Open Monday to Saturday from 08.30–13.00 and 16.00–19.30

Stationary, computer softwear and Internet access.

Supermarkets *Supermercati*

Dì per Dì supermarket

Piazza Garibaldi 58

Via De Nave

Tel: (0965) 330259

Open Monday to Saturday 08.00–13.00 and 17.00–20.30

This supermarket is opposite the station and stocks groceries, toiletries, nappies, fruit and vegetables and lots of special offers.

Gigad

Via Osanna (near the University for Foreigners)

Open Monday to Saturday from 09.00–13.00 and 16.00–20.00

This small supermarket does not sell fruit and vegetables.

Tourist information *Pro loco*

Via Roma 3
Tel: (0965) 892512

Corso Garibaldi 329
Tel: (0965) 21171
Website www.comune.reggio-calabria.it (Italian only)

These offices give out a useful free local guidebook (*Guida alla Città di Reggio Calabria*) with a map in the back. This is written in Italian and English. Both offices are open Monday to Friday 09.00–13.00.

Walking in the Aspromonte *Andare a piedi in Aspromonte*

Carte Escursionistiche della Calabria: Associazione Loisir
Piazza S. Nicola 1
88100 Catanzaro
Tel/Fax: (0961) 480616
Email loisir@abramo.it
Website www.loisir.it
This is one of the most detailed maps and costs €9.30.

Club Alpino Italia (CAI) sezione Aspromonte Reggio Calabria
Via S. Francesco da Paola 106
89100 Reggio Calabria
Casella postale 60
Tel: (0965) 898295
Email info@caireggio.it
Website www.caireggio.it (in Italian only)
The office is near the train station (one block further inland). It is only open on Thursdays from 20.30. The club has a range of books and organised trips. The books include the excellent *Il Parco Nazionale d'Aspromonte* by Francesco Bevilacqua, edited by Alfonso Picone Chiodo (Italian only).

Reggio City Walk *La Passeggiata*

Finding the best shops, bars, restaurants, amenities and other secrets

This walk has been carefully designed to quickly orientate you. It takes about two hours with stops for coffee and a quick look at the monuments.

The walk starts at the **University for Foreigners** (*Università per Stranieri*), Via Torrione 93. The *Caffetteria Antica Reggio* bar next door serves good coffee and fresh pastries if you are in need of a primer. Across the road from the University is the back of the Teatro Comunale. This recently restored **theatre** was built in the 1920s by Francesco Cilea and once hosted Maria Callas. Along Via Torrione to the right is Da Giovanni's smart fish restaurant (at number 77). Just beyond the restaurant on the right there is a 24-hour Internet café Sweet@web (at 35 Via Giudecca).

Start the walk by turning left out of the University along Via Torrione. Take the first right into Via Cattolica dei Greci passing the excellent Agora **pizzeria** (named after the ancient Greek and Roman city) and the unisex hairdressers and women's **beauticians** *Figara de Paris* next door. Continue down this road crossing Corso Garibaldi, the main **shopping** street of Reggio. This 3km promenade runs parallel to the sea and curves gently uphill at its northern end to views of the surrounding hills (*colline*).

Cross straight over Corso Garibaldi into Piazza Italia and walk over to the central white marble *Monumento all'Italia* (*Monument of Italy* 1968), where Italy is represented as a woman. The square's ornate 1920's palazzi have recently been superbly restored. If you face the same way as Italy (the statue), on your left is the Palazzo San Giorgio (1921) with a clock tower on top. It is the seat of the Mayor and the Town Council and it is worth asking at the front desk to see the beautiful inner chambers. Behind you is the Palazzo della Prefettura (Palazzo del Governo) with frilly iron doorways, and on your right is the Palazzo della Provincia.

Cross over the piazza and turn left into Via Miraglia (in the far left-hand corner of the piazza if facing the sea). This road is crossed by Via S. Sales, which gives views down to the sea and the WWI memorial, *Monumento ai Caduti*. Continue along Via Miraglia, passing the main **post office** on your right and coming to the small Piazza Genoese with a monument to Federico Genoese in a small, grassed area surrounded by palm trees.

There is a small **bookshop** on your right. At the far end of the square turn left up Via Cavour into Piazza Duomo. The **Duomo** was built in 1908 after an earthquake destroyed its Norman predecessor and is floodlit at night. Turn left out of the cathedral along Corso Garibabdi. There is a good **ice cream** shop (*Gelateria di Stefano*) on the corner with Via Tommasini. In Via Tommasini itself is the award winning **bakery** *Panificio Fazia* (number 26) which sells tasty slices of pizza to take away (*da portare via or da asporto*). There is a fruit shop next door.

Continue along Corso Garibaldi (east, away from the centre) to the **city park**, Villa Comunale, which is surrounded by iron railings. It was built in 1896 and is full of tropical plants and trees. If you want to see where the **train** and **bus station** is, walk through the park to the southern end, and exit onto the busy Corso Vittorio Emanuele. Turn left and continue for 50 metres or so to the station where there is a **supermarket** (Dì per Dì) and an Internet café. The CAI (**Club Alpino Italiano**) office is also near by. If you do not want to go to the station, retrace your steps along Corso Garibaldi and turn left into Via Foti, heading towards the sea. This comes out onto the busy and often traffic jammed Corso Vittorio. To the left is the **Roman Terme**, floodlit at night, just beyond a huge ancient *quercus ilex* (leccio) tree. To the right is the WWI *Monumento ai Caduti* (*Monument to the Fallen*).

Cross over to the **sea** and turn right to walk along the recently restored **promenade** Lungomare. This is a wide stone promenade above the beach with views to Sicily and the smoking **Mount Etna**. Across the road from the **Monumento ad Atena** are the Gothic arches of **Villa Zerbi**. Walk up the stone steps on the right between the pizza restaurant and the public toilets (*gabinetti da toletta*). Cross over Corso Vittorio Emanuele and walk straight up into Via D'Annuzio.

When Via D'Annuzio meets Corso Garibaldi turn left and walk the short distance into Piazza De Nava and the **Archaeological Museum**. The museum is one of the best in Italy. Its famous bronze statues *Bronzi di Riace* have been superbly restored and stand in a room with the Greek **Head of the Philosopher**. The museum also houses numerous artefacts from *Magna Grecia* and there is an interesting *sezione subacquea* recovered from the Ionian Sea. If you visit late in the afternoon you can often have the museum to yourself.

Turn left out of the museum and walk down Via De Nave. This is the **foodies** road with many cafés and interesting food shops. There is an excellent

gelateria on the corner, a new **Internet café** at number 142, a **key cut-ters**/fax/photocopy shop, a **bakery** (*Pane e Delizie*), a **butcher** (Rosse and Bianche) who sells Calabrian meats, salamis, cheeses, *panini* and pizza slices, a **stationers** (number 114), a **fishmonger** (number 109) and further down the **supermarket** *Dì per Dì* (day after day). At number 95 is an *ottimo* (ultimate) cheese shop (*caseificio*) called Fiore di Calabria which sells home produced caciocavallo and mozzarella.

Continue along Via De Nave, past Via 3 Settembre, where there is an **Odeon Cinema**, and turn right into Via XXV Luglio. This ends at Palazzo del Popolo where there is a superb daily **food market** selling fruit, veg-etable, cheeses and salamis (mornings except Sunday). From here you can head back to the University area, by walking along Via Lorenzo as far as Piazza de Nava and Via Torrione.

Lecce (Puglia)

9

L ecce is rightly described as the most pure Baroque (*Barocco Leccese*) walled town in the whole of Italy, a small Florence without the tourists. It is a lively university town with a population of 97,000 and is the power base of the Salento peninsula in Puglia. The buildings in the pedestranised walled centre are made from a special type of soft carved stone called *tufigna*, which is stunningly floodlit. There are two theatres, an opera season with top international names, fantastic restaurants and bars. It is an excellent place from which to explore the rest of Puglia. See also page 249 for a description of Puglia and the region's highlights.

Don't Miss *Da Non Perdere*

- the flood-lit stone of Lecce's architecture (*tufigna di Lecce*)

- the Roman amphitheatre discovered and excavated in 1938

- an evening *aperitivo* of *latte di mandorle*

- the rose window of the Santa Croce church

- a day trip to Gallipoli for some of the best seafood in Italy

- the perfection of *pasticciotto* custard tarts, Lecce's answer to the Portuguese *natas*

- a drive down the olive oil road (S611) between the sea and ancient olive groves

- the opera season (February to May) which attracts top names.

University for Foreigners

Università degli studi di Lecce, Scuola di Italiano per Stranieri

Centro Linguistico d'Ateneo
Via Vito Cartuccio 2 (five minutes from Porta Napoli on the western city wall)
Tel: (0832) 300841 Fax: (0832) 247531 Mobile: 3393003767
Email patguida@italianoperstranieri.lecce.it
Website www.italianoperstranieri.lecce.it/corsi.shtml (the site is in Italian but the descriptions of the courses are in English).
The small language school at the University of Lecce is our top choice for those who have a month or more in Puglia. It is the most expensive of the Universities for Foreigners but this is offset by cheap accommodation in the halls of residence and a lower cost of living. The school has modern facilities and an extensive summer programme of extracurricular activities.

There are 20,000 students at the University scattered in various buildings around the town. The language school for foreigners has just 150–200 students a year, less than many private language schools. It is housed in the CLA (*Centro Linguistico d'Ateneo*) building just outside the western city walls near a busy main road ten minutes walk from the historic centre. The school is on the fourth floor (via a lift) with the secretariat, facilities and classrooms together in one place. It is air conditioned, modern and has the atmosphere of a private language school. There are two *laboratorio linguisticos*, a small classroom, a computer room and a small library. There are no vending machines or coffee facilities, however, so breaks are often taken at a nearby café.

Students on the language course can use the University's facilities including the sports centres (closed in summer), halls of residence and canteens (*mense*). The groups have a maximum of 12 students.

Wheelchair access *Accesso ai disabili*

Although there is no wheelchair access in the CLA building, classes can be held in the brand new university campus just outside Lecce, which has good facilities. Lecce is one of the easiest towns for wheelchair users. It is flat, the centre is pedestrianised and the stone roads are wide with ramped pavements.

Courses and costs *Corsi e costi*

There are four levels of courses from beginners to advanced. A test on the first day establishes the student's level.

The school has four **intensive** one-month courses each year in February, June, July and August. These consist of four hours teaching a day (20 hours a week) and cost €400. It is also possible to attend for only one, two or three weeks at a cost of €100 per week. In June, July and August there is an optional **extracurricular** programme which costs an extra €250 (see below).

There are two **ordinary** courses starting in January and October each year. These consist of three hours teaching per day (15 hours a week) for ten weeks and cost €990. Extracurricular activities are organised depending on demand and are priced individually.

In July there is a two-week **history of art** course. Students have guided visits to the local monuments, buildings and galleries that have been discussed in class. Each weekday consists of a two-hour class and a two-hour guided visit. The course runs from the second week in July and costs €250.

When more than five students enrol there is a special course on Italian for **business** and throughout the year language courses can be tailor-made.

Individual lessons cost €21 per hour. There is no **enrolment** fee.

Extracurricular cultural programme *Le attività culturali*

In summer (June, July and August) there is an optional extracurricular programme that provides an excellent introduction to the region. Activities are organised every afternoon (except Friday) and at the weekends. These include guided visits to nearby towns, days at the beach, lectures, a weekly film and one afternoon a week of cooking, painting, stone carving or papier-mâché (*cartapesta*). The towns visited may include Otranto, Gallipoli, Matera and Alberobello (with the *trulli*). There are also parties and theatre performances (*spettacoli*). The extracurricular pro-gramme costs €250 per month (not including meals). The full timetable of activities changes each month and can be obtained by email from the course director Patricia Guida: patguida@italianoperstranieri.lecce.it

Facilities

The school has two language laboratories, a computer room with free Internet access and a small library. In theory they are available for inde-pendent study when the school is open (Monday to Friday from 09.00–13.00 and afternoons depending on demand). In practice this means finding a time when the rooms are free as they are also used by Italian stu-dents for their English lessons.

There are two University canteens (*mense*) which serve lunch and dinner from Monday to Friday for €2.50 per meal. They are both closed in August. The *mense* are at the *Maria Corti Residenza*, Via Lombardia 11 (near the train station) and EDISU Residenza, Via Adriatica 6 (just off the roundabout leading to the Brindisi superstrada opposite the University Sports Centre).

University sports centre *Palazzetto dello sport Universitario*

Palazzetto dello Sport Universitario 'Mario Stasi'
Superstrada to Brindisi (next to Hotel Tiziano on the Piazza del Bastione roundabout)
Open Monday to Friday 09.30–11.30 and 16.30–19.30 from November–end May
Closed from June–October
Tel/Fax: (0832) 309115
Email cusle@mail.clio.it
Website www.unile.it/cusl (in Italian, lists course times)
Students from the University language course are entitled to use the University sports centre (open from November until the end of May) at minimal cost. This is more like a school sports hall than a sports centre but

it is extremely cheap and there are weekly sessions of cardiovascular circuits, gymnastics, dance, free weights, tennis and swimming. The centre is housed in a square, windowless concrete building with bright blue doors and drainpipes a 15-minute walk from the centre. There is an indoor pitch for basketball and gymnastics and two floodlit outdoor tennis courts. Students can also use a local five-lane swimming pool at the ICOS sports centre (see below). The notice board in the centre and the above website advertise activities and courses such as trekking, diving, skiing, climbing and fencing. The centre does not have a bar.

Students wishing to use the facilities should arrive at the sports centre with a recent medical *and* dermatological certificate (see also page 24 'what to do before arriving'), proof of enrolment on the language course, two passport photos and a revenue stamp (*marche da bollo*). The medical certificate should state that the person is medically fit to play their chosen sport. The dermatological certificate is required for swimming and gymnastics and should state that the person has no contagious skin conditions. Both of these can be obtained from your GP before you leave and should ideally be written in Italian. The revenue stamp can be bought from a *tabaccheria* or post office. The cost changes but in 2003 it was just €24 for the whole season (November–end of May). The university tennis courts may soon be available out of season (June to October). There are plenty of other options in Lecce for sports including a private tennis club, swimming pool, sports centre and gym.

Scholarships *Borse di studio*

Various scholarships are available to people who can demonstrate financial or physical hardship or merit in Italian. Preference is given to developing countries. Applications should be made to the Italian Cultural Institute in the student's home country (see page 13 'scholarships').

Accommodation *Alloggio*

A single room in a shared apartment costs €140–170 per month per person. Independent apartments cost a similar amount to shared apartments depending on the location and season. There are also places available in the University **halls of residence** (see below) that cost just €90 per month for a single room. There are no cooking facilities but the two University canteens (closed in August) serve lunch (*pranzo*) and dinner (*cena*) for €2.5 from Monday–Friday.

University halls of residence *Residenza Universitaria*

There are three halls of residence for the University of Lecce. Italian students have priority over foreigners (*stranieri*) for the rooms but there are usually some places available. By far the nicest of the three is 'Maria Corti' (see below) so specify when booking. To check availability, the central number for the University halls of residence is (0832) 387311, open Monday to Friday from 09.00–12.00.

Residenza Universitaria 'Maria Corti'
Via Lombardia 11 (southern end of town near the train station)
This is by far the nicest of Lecce's University halls of residence. It is also the only one to remain open in August. It is housed in an attractive stone palazzo close to the train station a ten-minute walk from the old centre. The palazzo was completely renovated two years ago with modern fittings. There are about 70 rooms over three floors, a small canteen and some vending machines. The canteen (closed in August) serves cheap, tasty meals from Monday to Friday.

EDISU
Via Adriatica 6 (just off the roundabout leading to the Brindisi superstrada)
This hall of residence is housed in an ugly concrete building with dark orange window frames next to one of the main roundabouts into town. The building is rundown and except at sunset the surroundings are rather bleak. It is however only 200m from the old city wall and a 15-minute walk from the centre. There is also one of Lecce's best cafés opposite (*caffetteria Santa Posa*, page 184).

Residenza Universitaria 'Ennio De Giorgi'
Via del Salesiani, no number (adjacent to the modern Basilica S. Domenico Savio)
This is an ugly building in a grim part of town, half-an-hour's walk from the centre. It is not suitable for a holiday.

Enrolment *Iscrizione*

It is possible to enrol online on the University website.
The secretariat's office is open Monday to Friday from 09.00 to 13.00.

Exams *Esami*

The University is currently developing an exam. A certificate of attendance can be obtained at the end of the course.

Private Language Schools

Scuola D'Italiano Per Stranieri: Maria D'Enghien Lecce

Viale Lo Re 59
73100 Lecce
Tel/Fax: (0832) 306253
Email info@mdelecce.it
Website www.mdelecce.it
This small school has an excellent central location and a wide range of courses. When we visited they were just transferring from their old premises. There are spacious classrooms and a small library which also has a selection of Italian audio cassettes and CDs. There is a computer with free Internet access and a small kitchen with a coffee machine. One coffee per day is free of charge (*gratis*). Groups have a maximum of ten students.

Courses and costs *Corsi e costi*
The school has a 'high season' from June to August when prices increase. A **standard** course of four hours per day (20 hours per week) costs €300 for two weeks (€450 from June–August) or €600 for four weeks (€700 from June to August). **Individual** lessons cost €25 per hour. The **weekend courses** have four hours of lessons a day from Friday to Sunday, a guided tour of Lecce and an afternoon excursion to a nearby town. This costs €350 (€450 from June to August). There are also courses for **children** (with a supplement of €50) and **childcare** facilities. Discounts are available for group bookings. There is no enrolment fee.

Accommodation *Alloggio*

A single room in a shared apartment costs €100–120 for two weeks and €200–220 for four weeks.

Centro Caritas, S. Luigi Gonzaga

Scuola per Stranieri

Via G. Palmieri 78 (near Porta Napoli)

Lecce

Tel: (0832) 240439

This church-run school gives **free language lessons** every Monday, Wednesday and Friday from 17.30–20.00. The building has a dark, dusty, church-like atmosphere but the groups are small. There is no formal enrolment procedure, just check when the next course is starting.

Getting to and from Lecce *Andare e tornare da Lecce*

Train *Treno*

The train station is at Piazzale Oronzo Massari. The ticket office (*biglietteria*) is open every day from 07.35–14.15 and 14.50–21.25. Tel: (0832) 301016. The automated ticket machines also provide information in English. Outside the station there is a bar, newsagent and a small post office with wheelchair access. There are no left luggage facilities. The general Italian train website: www.trenitalia.com has timetable information in English.

There are good services to Bari, Brindisi, Gallipoli, Otranto, Reggio di Calabria and the rest of Italy. **Bologna** is seven-and-a-half hours away (€52.99), **Milan** ten hours (€65.13), **Naples** five-and-a-half with one change (€35.32), **Rimini** six-and-a-half (€47.88) and Rome six hours (€44.16). These prices are for a single journey on a Eurostar train. There is an overnight service to Bologna, Milan and Rome with cabins (*cuccetta*). The bus service for Naples is cheaper than the train and avoids a connection.

Bus *Pulman*

Iurlano Tourist Agency

Viale Ugo Fascolo 41 (between the roads Via Gaetano Argento and Via Giammatteo)

Reservations Tel: (0832) 303016 Fax: (0832) 245055

Open Monday to Saturday 09.00–13.00 and 16.30–20.00

This company sells tickets for buses to Bologna, Milan, Naples, Rimini, Rome and connecting towns. It is next to Caffè Foscolo, which is open Monday to Saturday from 07.00–21.00. Most of the buses leave from outside the front door. There are three buses a day to **Naples** via **Potenza** and **Salerno** which takes five-and-a-half hours and costs €23 (single). There are four buses a day to **Rome** (€35, seven hours) and others to **Bologna** (€48), **Milan** (€48) and **Rimini** (€38).

Local buses: there is an information booth (Tel: (0832) 340898) in front of the train station in the pedestrianised centre of Viale Oronzo Quarta, the main road leading from the station to the city wall. This is open every day from 07.00–20.30. Timetables are displayed on the front and side windows. Single tickets cost €0.52 and books of six cost €2.58. From Monday to Saturday there are four buses a day to the beach (*spiaggia bella*) from Porta Napoli.

Salento in Bus (www.salentoinbus.it) runs from 21 June to 14 September to all of the main tourist towns on the Salento peninsula. The website is only in Italian but has a timetable of all of their services. The bus stop is outside the closed Grand Hotel on Viale Oronzo Quarta, near the train station and the bus information booth.

Addresses for Easy Living in Lecce

Art courses *Corsi di Arte*

Marini Centro D'Arte
Palazzo Marini
Piazzetta S. Giovanni dei Fiorentini 9
Tel/Fax: (0832) 307841
Email info@palazzomarini.it Website www.palazzomarini.it (in Italian)
This private art school is housed on the second floor of a prettily restored palazzo in the centre of Lecce. They organise a wide range of art courses.

Bakeries *Panetterie*

Il Fornaio
Piazza Oronzo 23 (oppostite the Roman Ampitheatre)
Tel: (0832) 300 064

Open Monday to Saturday 05.00–14.00 and 17.00–20.30

This bakery sells bread that has been cooked in a stone oven (*pane cotto al forno di pietra*). The local speciality *pizzo*, made with olives (*olive*), tomatos (*pomodori*), onions (*cipolle*) and chilli (*peperoncino*) is delicious.

Bicycles for hire *Biciclette a noleggio*

Piazza S. Oronzo and Porta Napoli
Mobile: (347) 871 0717
Open every day 09.15–13.15 and 17.00–21.30
Closed Saturday and Sunday mornings
Prices start at €1.5 per hour, €8 per day or €30 for six days.

Bookshops *Librerie*

Liberrima
Via Corte dei Cicata 1 (next to the Chiesa di Sant'Irene)
Tel: (0832) 24 26 26
Email liberrima@mail.clio.it
Open Monday to Friday 09.15–13.00 and 16.30–20.30
Saturdays 09.15–13.00 and 16.30–24.00
This shop has an excellent range of books and cards. It also stocks a range of guidebooks and novels in English.

Butchers *Macellerie*

Macelleria
Via Fazzi, 6
Open Monday to Saturday 07.00–14.00 and 17.00–20.30
Closed on Monday and Thursday afternoons.

Cinema *Cinema*

Cinematografo Odeon
Via Lebertini, 4 (near Porta Rudiae in the east of town)
Tel: (0832) 302068
This cinema is located in the Spedale dello Spirito Santo, which dates back

to 1392. The building was once used by Dominican friars to nurse sick pilgrims. There are student reductions from Monday to Thursday.

Multisala Massimo
Viale Lo Re 3 (off Viale Marconi, near the castle)
Tel: (0832) 307433
This multi-screen cinema is near the excellent Cotognata Leccese *pasticceria* (see under 'restaurants and bars').

Car parking *Parcheggi*

There is free parking around Via Montegrappa. Other street car parks are marked with blue boxes and cost €0.5 per hour.

Cobblers *Calzolai*

Calzoleria
Via G. Libertini 9 (near Porta Rudiae)
Open Monday to Saturday from 08.30–13.30 and 16.30–20.00

Dance schools *Scuole di danza*

Tropicalia
Via Ribezzo 8
Tel: (0832) 277700 Closed from June to September
Website www.tropicalianet.it (In italian only)
This small dance studio runs courses in Latin American dance, as well as the local traditional *pizzica*. There are also courses for children (*bambini*).

Laboratorio di Danza
Palazzo d'Amore
Via A. Galateo 61
Tel: (0832) 246292
Website www.elektranet.it/elektraballet.asp (in Italian, click on 'laboratorio di Danza').
This is a small central school that runs courses in traditional and modern dance.

Discount clothes shops *Negozi con sconti*

Aspen Stock House

Via 95° Reg. Fanteria on the corner with Via Michelangelo Schipa

Tel: (0832) 340 843

Open Monday to Saturday 09.00–13.00 and 17.00–20.30

This shop has designer jeans such as Voyage and Diesel for as little as €15. There is also a good range of shoes particularly in sizes 36 and 37.

The Blue Family Benetton shop

Next to Chiesa Irene on Via Vittorio Emanuele

Open Monday to Saturday 09.00–13.00 and 17.00–21.00

This shop sells discount Benetton and Sisley clothes at bargain prices.

Diving, snorkelling and fishing *Sport subacquei e pesca*

Mazzotta Mare Pesca Subacquea Nautica

Via di Pettorano 32

Tel: (0832) 398501

Open Monday to Saturday 08.30–13.00 and 16.30–20.30

This shop sells everything you need for diving, snorkelling or fishing. They also advertise local diving courses.

Padi Courses

Corall Center Diving Sub Salento

Via Valzanni 23, 73010 Surbo (north of Lecce)

Mobile: 3495824940

Email corallcenterdiving@libero.it

This centre organises Padi diving courses (in Italian).

Fishmongers *Pescherie*

Fish in Puglia *Pesci in Puglia*. The sea around Otranto is clean and full of delicious fish. The best fish restaurants are in and around Gallipoli and one of the best fish markets is in Trani. Some of the local specialities include: *il sarago* (white bream), *la cernia* (grouper), *il dentice* (dentex), *lo sgombro* (mackerel), *l'orata* (gilthread), *il cefalo* (grey mullet), *l'occhiata* (saddled bream), *la spigola* (bass), *lo scorfano* (scorpion) *la triglia di scoglio* (surmullet), *il pesce S Pietro* (dory), also *i ricci di mare* (sea urchins), and *molluschi*: *calamari* (squid), *seppie* (cuttlefish), *polpi* (octopus) and *pesce azzurro* (*sarde e alici*) (blue fish: sardines and anchovies), *pesce spada* (swordfish), *cozze* (mussles), *crostacei* (shellfish).

Pescheria

Via Non Bosco (on the corner with Via Montegrappa near the train station)
Tel: (0832) 300 751
Open Monday to Saturday mornings only.
This fishmonger has a brilliant photograph of a puff fish at close range.

Pescheria

Piazza Porta Rudiae (on the western city wall)
Open mornings from Monday to Saturday.
This small fishmonger is on the outside of the covered market at Porta Rudiae.

Hotels *Alberghi*

Hotel Cappello

V. Montegrappa 4
73100 Lecce
Tel: (0832) 308881 Fax: (0832) 301535
Website www.hotelcappello.it
This hotel is next to the railway line about five minutes walk from the station. The rooms that face the street are much quieter and numbers 25 and 31 have their own balconies. All rooms have a private bathroom, a fridge and a television. There is centrally timed air-conditioning which is switched off at midnight, a bar and free street parking. Singles €28, doubles €45 and triples €58 and breakfast €3. Pizzeria Regina di Cuori (via Alfieri 21, Tel: (0832) 231810) will deliver Lecce's cheapest pizza to your room (or ask the night porter).

La Suite Bed and Breakfast

Via Acaya 14
Mobile: 328 0973058
Email lasuite@clio.it Website www.lasuitebeb.it (with online booking)
This bed and breakfast has an excellent central location, just off the main Piazza dell'Oronzo and the Roman Amphitheatre. Double rooms with balconies, televisions and kitchenettes cost €80 per night including breakfast or €50 for a single room.

Information on living in Salento *Informazioni per vivere in Salento*

The Best of Salento Lifestyle

This book is published several times a year and lists local events, concerts, festivals and includes articles of local interest. It costs €6.50 and is available from local *tabacci*. Website is being constructed www.thebestofsalento.com

Internet *Internet*

Associazione Multimediale Chatwin

Via Isabella Castriota 8

Tel: (0832) 277 859

Website www.chatwin-netcafe.it

Open Monday to Friday from 10.00–13.30 and 17.00–22.00

This Internet café and bar also has newspapers and guidebooks. Internet access costs €3 per hour.

A new Internet café is due to open in late 2003 in Via Vito Fassi, 15 to 19 (near the Roman amphitheatre).

Laundrette *Lavanderia*

Via dell'Università 49

Open Monday to Friday 08.30–20.30 and Saturdays 09.00–13.00 and 15.00–19.00.

The laundrette is self-service but there is someone to help, so you can sit in the next door bar (*Bar Antica Lupiae*). The cost of a large load is €4.

Library *Biblioteca*

Via Adriatica 6a (under the EDISU University halls of residence)

Open Monday to Friday from 09.00–12.00

Tuesday and Thursday afternoons 15.00–17.00

Markets *Mercati*

Piazza Libertini Market

There is a clothes market every morning from 07.30 around the walls of the castle and in Piazza Libertini by the central post office. There are also one or two fruit and vegetable sellers.

Porta Rudiae Market

Open Monday to Saturday 06.30–13.00 and 16.30–20.30. Closed Sunday afternoons.

There is a small covered food market just outside the pretty Porta Rudiae on the east side of the town. Inside the squat stone building there are stalls of fruit, vegetables, meats, plants and flowers, and house cleaning items. There is a fishmonger on the outside wall and a café.

Opera season *Stagione di Opera Lirica*

Teatro Politeama Greco

Viale XXV Luglio opposite the Banca di Napoli near the junction with Via S. Trinchese

Teatro Paisiello

Via G. Palmieri (near Porta Napoli)

The annual opera season runs from the beginning of February to the beginning of May. Information and booking is available from the *Ufficio Relazioni col Pubblico della Provincia di Lecce*, Via Umberto I°, 13a. Tel: (0832) 683 398 or free phone 800242815 (in Italy). Returns can be bought on the day of performances from the box office. Many of the 'standing' tickets have bench seating and are a bargain at €15.

Pharmacy *Farmacie*

Farmacia

Piazza S. Oronzo 18
Tel: (0832) 307 469
Open 08.30–13.00 and 17.00 to 20.30
This pharmacy is in the main central square, next to the Roman amphitheatre.

Post office *Poste*

Via dei Fedele at the corner with Piazza S. Oronzo (main square)

Open Monday to Saturday 09.00–13.00 and 17.00–21.00
This post office has the longest opening hours and wheelchair access.

Via Piazza Libertini

Open Monday to Friday 08.00–18.30 and Saturdays 08.00 to 12.30
This is the central post office. It is a large square building with iron dragons holding lanterns in their mouths, a symbol of the old fascist regime.

Train station

There is a small post office next to the train station. Open Monday to Friday 08.00–13.30 and Saturdays and the last day of each month from 08.30–12.30.

Restaurants and bars *Ristorante e bar*

Alle due Corti

Corte dei Giugni, 2
Tel: (0832) 242223 Closed on Sundays
This family-run restaurant is five minutes walk from Porta Napoli and owned by Rosalba de Carlo. She closed her leather goods shop (*pelletteria*) as she had always dreamt of running a restaurant. Her husband takes care of the administration and her son is one of the waiters. They have a daily changing menu of the season's tastiest morsels. There is a toilet for wheelchair users.

Bar Costa Rica di Sabato Armando

Viale d. Studenti 1 (outside the city wall near Porta Napoli)
Open Monday to Sunday from 06.00–20.30 (closed Sunday afternoons)
This corner bar serves delicious warm home made 'Chelsea' buns and one of the cheapest *cappuccini* in Lecce (€0.70). It is on the corner of Viale d. Studenti and Viale S. Nicola, near the University language course.

Caffetteria Santa Posa

Via Brenta 10–12 (just off Via Adriatia opposite the University hall of residence).
Open Monday to Saturdays from 07.00–22.00

This small bar is a good place for a morning coffee and fresh pastry. In the evening it is transformed into a mini trattoria/pizzeria and serves economical *aperitivi* as the sun sets. Pizza is also served for lunch on Wednesdays and Thursdays.

Cotognata Leccese de Matteise Oronzo

Viale Marconi 51 (near the castle)

Tel: (0832) 302800

Open Monday to Saturday from 07.00–21.00

This family run bar and *pasticceria* near the castle sells the ultimate coffee and sweetmeats. The food is handmade on the premises and their specialities include *Confettoni*, *Torta Maria* and *Cotognata Leccese*. The *Confettoni* are individually cellophane wrapped delicacies of chocolate mixed with almond and cinnamon, coated with tiny white sugar balls. The *Torta Maria* is a sponge cake layered with strawberry, pistachio, sour cherry, pine nuts, pineapple and glazed chestnut. Try a slice (*fetta*) with a cappuccino. The cleverly packaged *Cotognata Leccese* is a very sweet jam made from slow cooked local quince (*mela cotogna*) and sold by the block in wicker boxes. There is outside seating in the shady street opposite the castle and daily market and no table charge.

La Cicala di Perulli Luigi

Corte dei Cicala (at the side of Chiesa di Sant' Irene on Via Vittorio Emanuele II)

Open from about 10.00 until late seven days a week

This small central bar has seating outside. In summer glasses are chilled for an ultra refreshing *aperitivo*. Inside there are old black and white photos of local characters, including one of the grinning owner himself. There is no table charge.

Pasticceria Alvino

Piazza S. Oronzo 30 (opposite the Roman Ampetheatre)

Tel: (0832) 247436

Open from 06.30–22.00. Closed on Tuesday and Sunday

This bar and *pasticceria* has been in the square by the Roman Ampetheatre since 1908. It is *the* place for a mini cappuccino (*espressino*) and a *pasticciotto,* a boat-shaped custard tart that is Lecce's answer to the Portuguese *natas*. Their daily changing window display tempts in passing business while the *baristi* nonchalantly knock out one of the widest range of speciality drinks in Italy. In summer try the *caffè con ghiaccio e latte di mandorle*, a sweet espresso mixed with almond syrup poured over ice. The iced tea with a scoop of sorbet made from locally grown lemons is equally addictive.

Speciality food shop *Negozi di specialità gastronomiche*

Antica Panetteria
Via Vito Fassi 4 (just off Piazza S. Oronze)
Tel: (0832) 309981
Open Monday to Saturday from 06.30–14.00 and 17.00–21.00
This delicatessen sells local cheeses, cured meats, pasta, bread and milk.

Sports centres and swimming pools *Centri sportivi e piscine*

ICOS
Via Luigi Einaudi 12 (off Via Taranto which is west of Porta Napoli)
Tel: (0832) 240084 Fax: (0832) 307055
Email segricos@tiscalinet.it Website www.icosport.it (in Italian)
Open Monday to Friday from 09.00–22.30
Closed from mid-July to mid-September
This small, modern sports centre is a 20-minute walk from Porta Napoli. It has a five-lane swimming pool, a modern gym with step and aerobic classes, a beauticians and a small bar. Enrolment costs €30, the gym €42 per month and the pool €50 per month. Bring a passport photo and a recent medical and dermatological certificate confirming fitness for sport and the absence of contagious skin conditions (see page 24 'sports'). The University sports centre (page 172) has regular sessions here for students enrolled with them (see above).

Palestra Eraklion
Via Montegrappa 2
Tel: (0832) 244448
Open from Monday to Saturday, hours variable according to season
This gym is near the train station, next to Hotel Cappello. There is a hall for

gymnastics, step, power strike, spinning and aerobics, and a good range of exercise machines and free weights. Membership costs €33 per month. Bring a passport photo and a recent medical and dermatological certificate.

Stationers *Cartoleria*

Cartomax
Via B. Cairoli 1
Tel: (0832) 308 411
Open Monday to Friday 08.00 to 13.00 and 16.30 to 20.00.
Saturdays 08.00–13.00 only

Supermarkets *Supermercati*

Minimarket Bergamo 'Tutto Igiene'
Via Don Bosco 26
Tel: (0832) 245 408
Open Monday to Saturday 07.00–14.00 and 17.00–21.00
This small supermarket has fruit, vegetables, fresh bread and pasta, meats, cheeses and a small variety of groceries.

Conad
Via A. Galateo (near Porta Rudiae)
Open Monday to Saturday 07.00–14.00 and 17.00–20.30

There are a number of discount supermarkets on Via Taranto (leading away from Porta Napoli).

Tennis *Tennis*

Circolo Tennis Mario Stasi Lecce
Porta Napoli (with the obelisk outside)
Secreteria is open Monday to Friday from 10.00–13.00 and 15.00–18.00
This club has eight clay courts and a smart clubhouse and bar. Tennis coaching is from €15/hour and there are summer courses available for children (*bambini*).

Tourist information *Pro loco*

Via Umbero I° no. 13
Tel: (0832) 683 398 or free phone 800 242 815
Open Monday to Saturday 09.00 to 13.30 and 16.00 to 19.30.
Sundays 10.00 to 13.30 and 17.00 to 19.30
There are other TICs around the town but this office has the longest opening hours and the most helpful service.

Yoga *Yoga*

Anna Purna Yoga Centre
Via A. Galateo 19–21 (near Porta Rudiae)
This centre has yoga classes and also runs massage courses. The opening hours are erratic.

Leece City Walk

Finding the best shops, bars, restaurants, amenities and other secrets

This walk has been carefully designed to quickly orientate you to the most important parts of Lecce. It includes all of the best amenities, sights, parks, cafés and even a school offering free language lessons. It takes about two hours with short visits to the churches and coffee stops.

The walk starts from the Alvino **Pasticceria** (number 30) in Piazza Sant' Oronzo. Straight ahead is the Column of St Oronzo (*Colonna di Sant'Oronzo*) and the second century Roman amphitheatre (*anfiteatro Romano*). The amphitheatre, which would have held around 20,000 people, was discovered in 1901 when the Banca d'Italia was being built. Half of the amphitheatre is covered by the Church of Santa Maria delle Grazie. Turn left out of the café and left again at the corner of the square after the Church of Santa Maria delle Grazie into the unmarked Via Fazzi. There is a **speciality delicatessen** on your left at number 4 and a **butcher** (*macelleria*) at number 10.

At the end of the road cross over the busy Via XXV Luglio. With the Castello Carlo V (the castle) on your left, walk straight ahead towards the *Fontana dell'Armonia* (Fountain of Harmony) in Largo dell'Aeronautica. The trapeze-shaped castle in its present form was built between 1539 and 1549 from two medieval towers. Since this time it has been used as prison, a court, a military headquarters and is now used for exhibitions. Inside there is a shady central courtyard and a **TIC** centre. Continue along the palm-lined pedestrian area that runs parallel with Via Marconi. There is a multi-screen **cinema** on the right as you approach the fountain. At the far corner of the castle on the other side of Via Marconi is the superb **pasticceria** Cotognata Leccese. After trying one of their speciality *confettoni* chocolates, cross the road into Piazza Libertini with the statue of Guiseppe Libertini facing you. During the mornings and some afternoons there is a busy **clothes market** here. Continue straight ahead, passing a large four-storey building on your right which is the **post office**. The iron dragons on either side of the doors are old symbols of Mussolini's fascist regime. Continue past the castle until a T-junction with Via Salvatore Trinchese and the Oviesse clothes shop on the right.

Turn right and then immediately left into a shady pedestrianised area parallel with Viale F. Cavallotti and continue straight ahead. At the traffic lights (*semaforo*) turn left and immediately right into **the park** (*Giardino Pubblico*) opposite the school *Scuole Elementari Cesare*. Continue along an avenue of lime trees. Turn left, past a playground, a bandstand with a green-tiled roof and the café *Caffé del Parco*. Walk between the busts of C. Libertini and A. Panzera (at 90° to the path you came into the park on) and stroll down to the gates to leave the park.

Cross over Via XXV Luglio and into the Palazzo dei Celestini, which is marked '*La Resistenza*' on a stone plaque on the left of the entrance. Cross the courtyard where there are often **concerts** and walk out on to Via Umberto I°. Turn left to visit the **Basilica di Santa Croce**. This was commissioned between 1548 and 1695 and is famous for its rose window above the entrance.

Turn right out of the basilica, soon passing the excellent Centro Turismo Culturale **tourist information centre** on the right at number 13a. Take the first left into Via Idomeneo which forks after about 30m at number 75.

Bear left and continue straight through a small piazza. After a couple of minutes there is another fork with Via C. Gaufrido. Bear left, continuing along Via Idomeneo until a T-junction with Via Guiseppe Palmieri. Turn right at this T-junction, passing the parish church (*parrocchia*) of Santa Maria della Parta before reaching Porta Napoli.

Porta Napoli is over 20m high and was built in 1548 in honour of Charles V. Passing through Porta Napoli there is a **tennis club** on the right and an interesting central stone obelisk with fish carvings. This was erected in 1822 in honour of Ferdinand I of Boubon. Retrace your steps back through Porta Napoli and turn right, back into Via G. Palmieri. On your right at number 78 is the church-run Centro Caritas, which organises **free languages lessons** (see page 176). The **Teatro** Paisiello is almost opposite and was inaugurated with the Masked Ball Opera (*Il Ballo in Maschera*) in 1870. It is a small theatre with just 320 seats, decorated in mint green, restored and reopened in 1993. It is also the oldest theatre in the town and has regular concerts and plays, some of which are free.

Take the third right into Piazzetta Ignazio Falconieri. Straight ahead is the Palazzo Marrese with its striking eighteenth century façade and long balcony with supporting consoles. On either side of the main door are two pairs of caryatids. Acanthus leaves decorate the lower windows and shells the upper windows. Turn left around the Palazzo into Vico Della Cavallerizza. At the T-junction with Via Malennio turn left. At the next T-junction with Via Sumno, turn right, but before doing so look left to see the top of the bell tower (*campanile*) near the Duomo. At the next T-junction with Luigi Scarambone turn left. Continue straight ahead, passing a **dance centre** on the left at number 61 and a Conad **minimarket** opposite. Continue going straight passing a drinking fountain on the right and a **yoga** centre on the left between numbers 19–21.

At the crossroads with Via G. Libertini turn right past a **cobbler** at number 9 (on the left). Also on the left is the Chiesa di San Giovanni Battista/ Rosario d'Ajmo. This was built between 1691 and 1728 and has winged horses on its façade. The pulpit is the only church in Lecce to use local stone. Next to the church is the eighteenth century Accademio delle Belle Arti, which was once a monastery. Opposite is the Spedale dello Spirito

Santo, which dates back to 1392. It was previously used by Dominican friars to nurse sick pilgrims and is now a **cinema**. Continue straight ahead through Porta Rudiae which is the most western point of the town walls. The gate once led to the now destroyed Messapian town of Rudiae where the Latin poet Quinto Ennio was born. It was rebuilt in 1703 and has the Saints of Oronzo, Irene (see below) and Domenico on the arch of the gate. Through the arch on the left is the Caffè Rudiae Gelateria and Pasticceria. Behind this lies the **covered food market**. If you need a **laundrette** turn right along Viale dell'Università: it is a five-minute walk away on the left-hand side of the road.

To continue the walk, return through the Porta Rudiae and along Via Giuseppe Libertini back past the Chiesa di San Giovanni Battista/ Rosario d'Ajmo. The next church on the right is the Chiesa di Sant'Anna built in 1680. The statues of St Peter and St Paul are on each side of the door but have been badly eroded. The Conservatorio di Sant'Anna next to the church was for 'virgins, widows and ill-married woman' to find shelter and live a life of prayer and good works. Continue straight ahead, along the main **shopping street** with cafés and cheap pizzerias, until you reach the Piazza del **Duomo** on the right. The double façaded Duomo is in front of you as you enter the Piazza and the seventeenth century bell tower (*campanile*) is on the left. The Duomo was rebuilt between 1549 and 1695 replacing an earlier Norman church dating from the twelfth century. The Bishop's Palace *Palazzo Vescovile* and *Episcopio* on the right of the Duomo were homes to eunuchs that were sent to the Vatican for their highly prized singing voices. Above the door of the Bishop's Palace is a clock by Domenico Panico. On the right of the Piazza is the *Seminario*, which houses the Innocentian Library which has over 10,000 books.

Leaving the Piazza del Duomo, turn right into Via Vittorio Emanuele II. The church of Sant' Irene is on the left opposite an excellent **bookshop** and the cafe *La Cicala di Perulli Luigi* where the owner chills the glasses in summer. Opposite the church is the Blue Family discount Benetton shop. Continue along Via Vittorio Emanuele which leads back to Piazza Sant'Oronzo and the start of the walk.

Monuments in the walk *Monumenti lungo la passeggiata*

Basilica di Santa Croce
Open every day 08.00–13.00 and 16.00–19.30

Duomo dell'Assunta
Open 06.30–12.00 and 17.00–19.30

Basilica S. Rosario
Mass 08.00 weekdays, 19.00 Saturdays and 09.30 Sundays
The Basilica is open for visits before and after the services.

Public gardens Giardini pubblici
Open 1 October to 31 March every day 09.00–18.00
Open 1 April to 30 September every day 09.00–21.00

The Patron saint of Lecce *(Il Santo Patrono di Lecce)*

Sant' Irene was the Patron saint of Lecce until she was usurped by Sant'Oronzo in 1656. During the time of the plague a visionary Calabrian mystic, sent to Lecce from the Holy Office in Rome, reported that Sant'Oronzo's miracles had spared the city. As a result of this publicity, Sant'Oronzo was promoted. Drums of stone were taken from the Sant'Oronzo column in Brindisi (which marks the end of the Appian Way) and brought to Lecce. The statue of wood and copper that was placed on top is seen at the start and end of this walk. The Saint's day is celebrated on 26 August with fireworks and live music.

Language Schools by Area

Piedmont *(Piemonte)*

Landlocked Piedmont is home to white truffles, Barolo wine, beautiful mountains and the stunning baroque town of Turin (*Torino*). The magnificent Western Alps stretch from the border with France to Largo Maggiore and include Italy's oldest national park, the *Parco Nazionale del Gran Paradiso*. The region's cultural capital, Turin, is nestled in the shadows of the Alps. It forms the beginning of the Po Valley and the paddy fields that supply nearly two-thirds of Italy's rice. In the south there are the vine-covered hills (*colline*) of Barolo and the white truffle valleys around Alba. We have listed language schools in Turin, including the University, which also offers a skiing and language course in the Winter Olympic resort of Bardonecchia.

Highlights of Piedmont *Da non perdere del Piemonte*

▶ the ultimate hot chocolate can be sipped in Turin, the birthplace of modern chocolate

▶ Turin's magnificent Baroque architecture

▶ truffle-hunting and the white truffle markets in Alba

▶ Barolo, Asti and Barbaresco wines

▶ the shimmering rice fields of Vercelli

▶ the cheese fair in Cuneo every November

▶ *castalmango*, the cheese matured on swept cave floors in Piedmont's Alps.

Turin *Torino*

Turin is a magnificent Baroque city that sits at the start of the Po Valley, under the Western Alps. It is Italy's fourth largest city with a population of just under 1,000,000. It was the birthplace of modern chocolate and is one of Italy's coffee capitals with Lavazza roasting like there is no tomorrow. More recently it was the centre of the Risorgimento, the movement that united Italy under the King from Piedmont, Emanuele II. It was even the early capital of this newly united Italy. Turin is still a bustling hive of economic, political, academic and gastronomic activity. It is home to the Fiat car company, the Juventus football team and one of Italy's best glass elevator rides in the National Cinema Museum. In 2006 it will host the Winter Olympic games, the first Winter Olympics in Italy since the 1956 games in Cortina d'Ampezzo.

University of Turin

Information about the course:
Segreteria Relazioni Internazionali
Sezione Relazioni Internazionali
Via Bogino 9
10123 Torino
Tel: (011) 6702955 or (011) 6702457 or (011) 6702486 Fax: (011) 6702453

Email summerschool@rettorato.unito.it
Website www.summerschool.unito.it

University Hall of Residence

Residenza Cavour
Via Cavour 32
Torino
Tel: (011) 6531800

Location of the lessons (subject to change)

Palazzo Gorresio
Via Giulia di Barolo, 3/A,
Torino

The University of Turin runs an excellent 18-day **summer course** in Italian language and culture in July and a nine-day **skiing and Italian language** course in Bardonecchia in February/March.

Summer course and costs *Corsi estivi e costi*

The 18-day **summer course** in July consists of 50 hours of teaching (four hours a day from Monday to Friday and three hours on Saturday morning) and an extensive extracurricular programme for the afternoons and weekends. A typical week might include a guided tour of the town, visits to local sights and museums, a weekend outing to the Valle D'Aosta's mountains and seminars on Italian culture. The course is well organised and includes a welcome party and celebratory dinner on the first day. Students have free access to a **swimming pool** and **tennis courts** and can study in the large University **library**. There are normally about 40 students of all ages with a maximum of 15 per class. Lessons take place in Palazzo Gorresio, a beautiful white palazzo with taupe shutters near the River Po. The classrooms have high frescoed ceilings and modern fittings. The course, including extracurricular activities, costs €400. The full package of the course, extracurricular activities, a single room in the halls of residence, breakfast and lunch in the canteen costs €940.

Accommodation *Alloggio*

The University halls of residence, *residenza Universitaria cavour*, is in the centre of Turin. It is housed in a restored palazzo on a quiet road a ten-minute walk from the lessons. The rooms are modern and basic. A **single room** costs €400 and a double €225 per month. The cost of breakfast and lunch is €140 per month. The University has arrangements with a number of local cafés and restaurants for these meals.

Skiing and Italian language course *Corso di lingua di Italiana e di sci*

The nine-day **skiing and Italian language** course is held in Bardonecchia in early March. Bardonecchia is one of the venues of the Winter Olympics 2006. The course consists of 30 hours of language lessons, which are held in the late afternoon after skiing. It costs €420 including half-board in an apartment. Extra costs include €70 for a six-day ski pass, €45 for ski and boot hire and €60 for skiing lessons.

Enrolment for summer and winter courses *Iscrizione*

An application form can be downloaded from the Internet or requested from the *Segreteria Relazioni Internazionali*. Postal applications must be made at least two weeks in advance of the course and places are limited.

Dialogo +

Via Santa Teresa 10

(near Piazza San Carlo)
Torino
Tel: (011) 561 3695 Fax: (011) 563 7114
Email info@dialogoplus.com Website www.dialogoplus.com
This tiny language school is on the second floor of an attractive eighteenth century palazzo in the centre of Turin. It is on a busy main road but the school is quiet. The entrance is almost opposite the Church of Santa Teresa, near the junction with Via XX Settembre. There is an inner courtyard with curly iron gates and large marble stairs flanked with carved columns and colourful coats of arms. The school consists of just two small modern classrooms, newly painted with white walls and blue doorframes. There are videos and a small selection of Italian books for studying after lessons. The school is very expensive for its facilities but the group size is a maximum of six.

Courses and costs *Corsi e costi*

A **standard** course of four hours teaching a day (20 hours a week) costs €430 for two weeks and €860 for four weeks. A **'two-to-one'** course (one teacher to two students) of four hours teaching a day costs €650 for two weeks. **Individual** lessons cost €31 an hour. There is an **enrolment** fee of €52 which includes one guided visit.

Accommodation *Alloggio*

The school can arrange accommodation with an Italian family or in bed and breakfast. A **single** room with an Italian family costs from €170 a week and includes the use of the kitchen.

Instituto Linguistico Europeo

Via Assarotti 4

10122 Torino

Tel/Fax: (011) 548 951

Email istitutoile@libero.it

This is the cheaper option in Turin. The school is on a busy main road a 15-minute walk from Piazza Castello (the hub of the city). It is on the second floor of an unattractive building. The school has three small classrooms with old carpeting and a rather gloomy atmosphere. There are no intensive courses in July or August.

Courses and costs *Corsi e costi*

The '**intensive**' course of four hours teaching a day (20 hours a week) costs €420 for four weeks. Lessons take place either in the morning or in the afternoon. The **non-intensive** three-month courses consist of three hours teaching a week (two 90-minute classes) either in the morning or early evening and costs €180. **Individual** lessons cost €20.66 per hour and two-to-one lessons €22.72 per hour. There is an **enrolment** fee of €35.

Accommodation *Alloggio*

There is no accommodation service.

Liguria

Liguria has one of Italy's most spectacular coastlines. It stretches for 350km along the Mediterranean between France and Tuscany and includes the famous *Cinque Terre* and *Riviera di Levante*. Tiny villages rise from seemingly impossible spaces, steep slopes and mountains are cultivated with vines and olive trees and well-marked paths run through isolated country-side with views of the sea. Genoa, the region's capital, blends this history, sea and vertical drama into an intoxicating mix. The region is renowned for its basil (*basilico*), table olives and the world's best pesto.

We have chosen the University of Genoa's excellent summer course in Santa Margherita Ligure (page 199) and a private language school in Genoa (page 199).

Highlights of Liguria *Da non perdere della Liguria*

▶ Genoa's spectacular fountain in the Piazza dei Ferrari

▶ the oriental market in Genoa, with a fine selection of fresh herbs

▶ the bright green Ligurian pesto

▶ the tiny black Ligurian olives

▶ James Bond-style driving along the coast

▶ a weekend in San Fruttuoso, which is only accessible by boat from Portofino

▶ walking along the marked trails on the Riviera Levante

▶ the University summer language course at Santa Margherita

▶ the Cinque Terre, the coast is so dramatic that not even the tourists can spoil it.

Genoa *Genova*

Genoa is one of Italy's most important commercial ports. The town is nes-tled in the middle of the Italian Riviera. Its port has been a source of wealth since the eleventh century and provides lavish palaces, churches, parties and museums as well as a fascinating medieval quarter. The city was refurbished prior to the G8 summit in 2001 and is an excellent base from which to explore Liguria.

A Door to Italy

Via P.E. Bensa 2/4°
16124 Genova
Tel: (010) 246 5870 Fax: (010) 254 2240
Email info@adoortoitaly.com Website www.adoortoitaly.com
This small private language school has an excellent central location close
to the main sights. The school is at the top of the medieval quarter near the
university and above the old city port (*porto vecchio*). It is on the fourth
floor of a restored seventeenth century palazzo complete with a beautiful
spiral staircase. It is a small L-shaped school with three plain classrooms,
facing a small inner courtyard. There is a coffee machine and a small selection of Italian books for loan but no other facilities.

Courses and costs *Corsi e costi*
The **standard** course of four hours teaching a day (20 hours per week)
costs €290 for two weeks and €570 for four weeks. The school runs an
intensive course of six hours of teaching a day (30 hours a week) which
costs €370 for two weeks and €730 for four. There are **evening** courses
which consist of two hours teaching twice a week in small groups which
cost €15 per lesson. There are a number of **specialised** courses in business,
opera, theatre and cinema as well as a practical cooking course.

Accommodation *Alloggio*
The school can organise a wide variety of accommodation. A single room
with an Italian family with breakfast costs from €260 for two weeks or
€416 for a month. In some cases this also includes use of the kitchen. The
cheaper family stay option costs €265 for a single room with use of the
kitchen or €455 for half-board per month. Apartments cost from €160 per
week per person.

University of Genoa (Università degli Studi di Genova)

Centro Internazionale di Studi Italiani
Palazzo dell'Università
Via Balbi 5
16126 Genova

Tel: (010) 2099868 Fax: (010) 2099869

Email centrint@unige.it Website www.unige.it/centrint/

Location of the course (only open during the course):

Villa Durazzo

Piazzale S. Giacomo di Corte 3

16038 Santa Margherita Ligure (Genova)

Tel: (0185) 288128

The University of Genoa organises a superb five-week Italian language course in August and September. It is held in Santa Margherita Ligure, a small twelfth century seaside town four kilometres from Portofino on the famous Riviera di Levante. There are extensive opportunities for walking, trekking, swimming, boating and designer shopping. The language course is held in the stunning seventeenth century hilltop Villa San Giacomo (next to Villa Durazzo). This has frescoed ceilings, sea view balconies and shady outside seating. It is surrounded by landscaped parkland with exotic trees, flowers, marble statues, monuments, tree lined avenues and views down to the town and the coast. It is one of the most spectacular locations of any language school in Italy.

Courses and costs *Corsi e costi*

The University suggests that students have at least an elementary knowledge of Italian. The course consists of 25–30 hours of teaching a week. The time is divided into grammar and conversation classes in the morning and a choice of afternoon subjects. These include history of art, cinema and theatre, contemporary Italian political history, law in contemporary Italy, Dante and Middle Age civilisation, and Italian literature and music.

Enrolment *Iscrizione*

Application forms can be downloaded from the website or requested by email. The application requires prepayment of €200 via bank order and two passport photos.

Scholarships *Borse di studio*

The University offers a limited number of scholarships from €400–€517. Applications should be sent to the Director of Centro Internazionale di

Chapter Ten – Language Schools by Area **201**

Studi Italiani, Via Balbi 5, 16126 Genova (Italy) by the end of June. The application should be accompanied by a short curriculum vita in Italian and a letter of support from either a university language teacher, a director of an Italian Cultural Institute or by a director of a Dante Alighieri Society (see page 2).

Accommodation *Alloggio*

Information regarding accommodation can be obtained from local tourist services:

Ms Morena Lelli
Bureau of Tourism
Santa Margherita's Town Administration
Piazza Mazzini 46
16038 Santa Margherita Ligure
Tel/Fax: (0185) 205423

Tourist Office
Via XXC Aprile 2B
16038 Santa Margherita Ligure
Tel: (0185) 287485

Agenzia Cairoli
Piazza Cavour 12, 16035
Tel: (0185) 50129
This is only for accommodation in Rapallo, near Santa Margherita.

Lombardy *Lombardia*

Lombardy falls from the Alps bordering Switzerland into the vast flat plain of the Po Valley and the industries around Milan. It includes the magnificent Lake Districts of Como, Garda and Maggiore. The region is one of Italy's economic powers, leading the way in fashion, design, business and large-scale agriculture. We have chosen the excellent University of Milan Summer Course on Lake Garda (page 207), the University of Bergamo (page 205) and private language schools in Milan (page 202).

Highlights of Lombardy *Da non perdere della Lombardia*

▶ opera in Milan, at the *Teatro degli Arcimboldi*, while La Scala is renovated

▶ shopping in Milan, one of the fashion capitals of the world

▶ the Lake Districts of Lakes Como, Garda and Maggiore

▶ the pretty towns of Bergamo and Mantova

▶ Cremona, where the violin was first developed and Stradivarius had his workshop.

Milan *Milano*

Milan is the undisputed capital of Lombardy and one of the fashion and design centres of Italy. Its Duomo is one of the largest Gothic churches in the world and sets the tone of the city: everything is BIG. Streets are double width and have treble the traffic, buildings are domineering and distances large. No photograph can do justice to the scale and beauty of the Duomo with its 3,400 statues, 135 spires and grimacing gargoyles. The city is also home to the *Teatro alla Scala*, Italy's most prestigious opera house and the AC and Inter football teams. If you like it large, Milan is the place.

Società Dante Alighieri

Via Napo Torriani 10
Milano 20124
Tel: (02) 6692816 Fax: (02) 6693098
Email info.mi@societadantealighieri.org
Website www.societadantealighieri.org
Open Monday to Friday 09.00–12.00 and 14.30–17.30
This small school is the bargain option in Milan. It is located on the third floor of a shared office block a five-minute walk from the central train station and a short bus ride from the centre. There are four plain classrooms with modern fittings, televisions and air conditioning. Groups have a maximum of 12 students.

Courses and costs *Corsi e costi*

The school runs both language and cultural courses. The language courses have varying levels of intensity from two to 15 hours per week. The **hyper-intensive course** has 15 hours per week, divided into three hours of lessons from Monday to Friday. The course costs €180 for two weeks, €365 for four weeks and each extra week costs €100. There are two **intensive courses** that run from October to January and from January to May. They have three hours of lessons three times a week and cost €630. The **annual course** runs from October to May and has two hours of lessons per week and costs €630. There is a placement test for this course at the end of September. **Individual lessons** cost €33 per hour.

There are **cultural courses** that run from October to May. Each course meets once a week for two hours and can be combined with a language course. The overview of Italian literature covers the history of Italian literature from its origins to the present day. The course costs €365. The overview of Italian history of art course looks at art from the Middle Ages to the present day with particular focus on the Lombardy regions. Slides are used in the classes and on request visits can be organised to local galleries. The course costs €415.

Accommodation *Alloggio*

There is no accommodation service but the school recommends two agencies.

El Flaco, Via Ampere 11. Tel: (02) 236 0144 www.elflaco.com. This website has information on the latest apartments and rooms to let all over Milan. A single room for a month costs from €350.

Euro Home S.R.L. Via Camperio 14. Tel: (02) 8029 9182 Fax: (02) 8698 4556

International House

Piazza Erculea 9
(just off Corso di Porta Romana)
Milano
Tel: (02) 805 7825 Fax: (02) 869 11097
Email infomilano@ihmilano.it Website www.ihmilano.it
Open Monday–Friday from 09.00–19.30

This excellent school is a ten-minute walk from the Duomo. It is on the third floor of a smart office block with good facilities. There are ten modern air-conditioned classrooms and computers with free Internet access. The student common room has a sofa, wide screen television, free video library, magazines, newspapers and a coffee machine. The school runs English lessons and a joint programme of social activities making it easy to meet other Italians. Every Tuesday there is an international evening for conversation practice in a local café. The free movie club shows an Italian film every Wednesday afternoon and every Friday there is a free guided visit to somewhere of interest in Milan. The school also organises day trips to local sites such as Lake Como, the beach at Varazze and pizza evenings. These trips are charged for separately. The group size is limited to eight people.

Courses and costs *Corsi e costi*

The **intensive course** has either three of four hours of lessons from Monday to Friday. The three hours a day course (15 hours per week) costs €362 for two weeks and €692 for four weeks. The four hour a day course (20 hours per week) costs €480 for two weeks and €920 for four weeks. Each additional week costs €173 or €230 respectively. **Evening classes** have 40 hours of teaching over ten weeks. The sessions are on Mondays and Wednesdays from 18.45–21.00 and cost €465. **Individual lessons** cost €44 per hour. The **CELI exam** course consists of two evenings per week for six weeks and costs €350. The mock exam costs €40 for International House students or €60 for external students. The enrolment fee of €52 includes a course book, a discount card for use in local shops and restaurants and an end of course certificate. There is a discount of approximately 20% after six months at the school. No scholarships are available.

Accommodation *Alloggio*

A single room in a shared apartment costs €140 per week. Half-board with an Italian family costs €205 per week.

Bergamo

Bergamo is a pretty medieval hill town near the foot of the Orbic Alps. It is 35 kilometres northeast of Milan and is within striking distance of Lakes

Como and Iseo. The old town, *Città Alta* (high), crowns the top of the hill and has some of the finest medieval buildings and churches in the region. From here there are views to the modern and spacious *Città Bassa* (low) lying on the vast plain below and to the Alps in the north. The *Galleria dell'Accademia Carrara* in *Città Bassa* houses important works of art. The University has an excellent location in the old part of town.

University of Bergamo

Information and location of the course:
Centro di Formazione Permanente
Università degli Studi di Bergamo
Via Salvecchio 19
24129 Bergamo
Tel: (035) 205 2232 Fax: (035) 205 2238
Email alliub@unibg.it Website www.unibg.it/cis

Segretaria (lower ground floor, *scale* 'C') open Monday, Wednesday and Friday 15.00–18.00, Tuesdays and Thursdays 09.00–12.00

Linguistic Centre (fourth floor, *scale* 'B') open Tuesday, Wednesday and Friday 09.00–18.00 and Mondays and Thursdays 09.00–14.00

The University of Bergamo has been organising Italian language courses throughout the year since 1978. All the courses include self-access to the language laboratory, library and use of the University canteen. The University is in a restored palazzo in the centre of the Città Alta, the high ancient part of Bergamo. There is an internal cobbled courtyard overlooked by balconies. There are views from some of the air-conditioned rooms of the nearby Orbic Alps.

Courses and costs *Corsi e costi*
In July there are **intensive summer courses** of two, three and four weeks. These consist of five hours teaching a day (25 hours a week), three in the morning and two in the afternoon. There are a wide choice of afternoon classes to choose from including films, conversation, grammar, writing, Italian Internet and business Italian. For more advanced students, there are afternoon lectures on contemporary Italian culture. There are a maxi-

206 Learning Italian in Italy

mum of 75 participants and 15 per group. The courses cost €300 for two weeks, €430 for three weeks and €500 for four. This includes access to the linguistic centre, a guided tour of the town, a day trip to a local city and dinner on the last night.

There are two **non-intensive** 15-week courses starting in October and March. These have four hours of teaching a week (two afternoons) and cost €370. They can be taken for shorter periods at a reduced cost.

Business Italian courses run if there are more than ten people interested. These can be combined with the three-week intensive summer course (see above) where afternoon lessons focus on business Italian. This option costs €470 for three weeks. Alternatively the afternoon lessons can be taken on their own (two hours a day) and cost €160 for three weeks. The university can organise courses for private companies and groups on request. **Individual** lessons cost €24 per hour. Special courses in writing and in teaching Italian as a foreign language are organised on request.

Facilities

Students have free access to the University's excellent **linguistic centre** with the *laboratorio linguistico*, computers, Italian videos and cassettes. There is an extensive range of material available for independent study. There is a teacher available to help on Wednesdays from 15.00–18.00. There is a **library** with a wide selection of Italian language books and a University canteen (*mensa*) providing lunches costing €3.

Accommodation *Alloggio*

The coordinator of the course at the above address books accommodation for students with Italian families and in the halls of residence. There is a booking fee of €27 and at least one month's notice is required. A **single room** with an Italian family with breakfast costs €155 per week. A single room with half-board in the **halls of residence** costs €26 per day. A single room with breakfast in the **youth hostel** costs €19 per night and should be booked by the student by telephoning 035 361724 or emailing hostelbg@spm.it. Shared **mini apartments** for two to three people cost from €300 per person per month and should be booked through the *Segreteria Alliub* (Via Salvecchio 19, 24129 Bergamo. Tel: (035) 2052232) who allocate on a first come first served basis.

Enrolment *Iscrizione*

An application form can be downloaded from the Internet or requested from the *segretariat*. Postal applications must be made at least one month in advance but it is possible to enrol in person at any stage. The application requires pre-payment of one month of fees, by Western Union Quick Pay System, international postal order or bank transfer. The University sends a letter of confirmation with a receipt, which is needed on the first day.

Lake Garda *Lago di Garda*

Lake Garda is the largest of the Italian Lakes with 370 square kilometres extending through the regions of Veneto, Lombardy and Trentino. It is bordered by snow-capped peaks in the north and unspoilt dense green hills in the centre. This is where the superb University of Milan Summer Course is based. In the south the lake has been ruined by theme parks and camping sites. There are numerous opportunities for water sports and trekking in all areas.

University of Milan's Summer Course at Lake Garda

Information about the course:

Segreteria dei Corsi Internazionali di Lingua e Cultura Italiana
Università degli Studi di Milano
Dipartimento di Filologia Moderna
Via Festa del Perdono 7,
20122 Milano
Tel: (0250) 312812 Fax: (0250) 312656
Email gargano@unimi.it Website http://studenti.unimi.it/
Address of the course (only open during the course):

Palazzo Feltrinelli
Via Castello 3
25084 Gargnano del Garda (Brescia)
Tel: 036571101 Fax: 036572832

The University of Milan runs two summer courses in Italian language and culture. These are held in a beautiful palazzo overlooking the lake in the tiny village of Gargnano del Garda. The courses are open to all foreigners over 21 who already have at least an intermediate level of Italian. There are no courses for beginners.

Palazzo *Feltrinelli*

Palazzo Feltrinelli is the University's summer seat. It is a stunning nineteenth century palazzo on the west banks of Lake Garda. The grounds extend to the waterfront where meals are served. There are frescoed ceilings and walls, ornate iron fittings, marble stairs and large windows overlooking the lake. It is one of the most spectacular locations of any language school in Italy.

Courses and costs *Corsi e costi*

There are two month-long courses in July and August. They consist of three hours of language lessons each morning (15 hours a week) and two hours of seminars on Italian culture and society each evening from 17.30–19.30 (ten hours a week). The course costs €827 which includes full board from Monday to Friday and accommodation. There are a maximum of 60 students with approximately ten to 15 per class.

Exams *Esami*

Students are able to sit the CILS exam (see qualifications, page 15) in the last week of the course.

Accommodation *Alloggio*

The cost of accommodation is included in the price of the course. This consists of a twin room in either Palazzo Feltrinelli, a local hotel or with an Italian family. Some of the rooms in Palazzo Feltrinelli have lake views. Students paying for the course, rather than scholarship winners, are given first choice of room.

Enrolment *Iscrizione*

An application form can be downloaded from the Internet or requested from the *segreteria* by post or email (gargano@unimi.it). The application must be received by March but as places are limited applying as early as November is advisable. The application requires a curriculum vita in Italian, proof of existing level of Italian (diploma, exam certificate, previous course attendance etc), a passport photograph and a photocopy of your passport.

Scholarships *Borse di studio*

There are 40 scholarships available which cover the cost of the course, board and lodging. Applications are judged on the basis of merit and reasons for studying Italian. The application should include a reference from the director of an Italian Cultural Institute or a language teacher. Successful candidates are informed after Easter. They are required to pay a €50 deposit to secure their place and this is refunded on arrival. Scholarships are not available for students over 40.

Trentino-Alto Adige

Trentino and Alto Adige are culturally distinct although they are joined in one region. Alto Adige was part of Austria until 1919 and the population is mostly of German descent. The area still calls itself Südtirol, German is spoken as often as Italian and all of the signs are in both languages. Trentino on the other hand has always retained its Italian identity. Despite the linguistic mix, the area makes a good base for those wanting access to the mountains, vineyards or nearby Lake Garda. We have chosen a school in Bolzano, which lies at the border between Trentino and Alto-Adige (page 210), and a school on Lake Garda (page 207).

Highlights of Trentino-Alto Adige *Da Non Perdere del Trentino-Atto Adige*

- the spectacular Dolomites, world-class walking and skiing

- the *'strada del vino'*, a wine lover's dream around the vineyards of Bolzano

- cross-country skiing in the Alpe di Siusi and Val Gardena

- the Tyrolean castles of Alto Adige

- the fifteenth century frescoes of Bressanone's cathedral.

Bolzano *Bozen*

Bolzano is in a valley of vineyards surrounded by snow-capped mountains. It is a pretty town with Gothic architecture and a population of 97,000. It is an ideal base for wine lovers, skiers, hikers, walkers or gourmets.

It was part of Austria before the First World War and there is still a strong Austrian influence with many people speaking German. There is a daily food market in the Piazza dell' Erbe which is a small scale version of the one in Padova. The cable cars run conveniently from the outskirts of the town straight to the mountains. There is one language school that runs part-time courses that can be supplemented with private lessons or combined with wine tasting, skiing or walking.

Alpha Beta Corsi di Lingua

Via Talvera 1/A
Bolzano 1–39100
Tel: (0471) 978600 Fax: (0471) 979940
Email info@alphabeta.it Website www.alphabeta.it (German and Italian only)
Self-access centre open Monday to Thursday from 16.00–19.00
This school offers **part-time courses** in Italian, English, German, Dutch, Spanish, French, Portuguese, Russian and Arabic. The brochure is in Italian and German but the secretary speaks English. The school opened in 1987 and is in a smart building in a quiet area of town. There is a **self-access centre** with multimedia facilities and a teacher to help. Group size is five to 12 people.

Courses and costs *Corsi e costi*
The standard **part-time** 80-hour course starts in October and has five months of teaching with a break of one month for Christmas. There are two sessions per week of two hours. This course costs €275. Shorter courses of five or seven weeks start in April, July and September. These consist of 15 two hour sessions either twice or three times per week and cost €120. The ten-week **Saturday course** has 40 hours of lessons starting in October. This costs €157. There is also a ten-week **conversation course** starting in October which meets once a week for 90 minutes. This costs €80. **Individual lessons** cost €30 for 45 minutes. All the courses have an end of course test and attendance certificate included in the price. There is no enrolment fee but the text books cost €26.

Accommodation *Alloggio*

The school does not have an accommodation service but the tourist information centre *Azienda di Soggiorno e Turismo* has a list of options.

Piazza Walther, 8

Tel: (0471) 30 70 00

Website www.bolzano-bozen.it

Open Monday to Friday 09.00–18.30 and Saturdays 09.00–12.30

Caffé Delle Lingue/Sprachcafe

Bar of Centro Giovani (papperlapapp), Piazza Duomo, 8

Information Viola Daubenspeck

Tel: (0471) 978 589 Email sprachcafe@papperla.net

This free informal club is organised by the Alpha Beta language school at 18.00 on the first Tuesday of each month. It is a meeting point to practise conversation in Italian, English, Dutch, Spanish or French in a local bar. Teachers attend to aid the process.

Friuli-Venezia-Giulia

This region in the far northeast corner of Italy is often overlooked by tourists. It is as if everyone has been sucked to the beach. The fabulous Carnic and Julian Alps bordering Austria and Slovenia offer trekking, mountain biking and bird watching opportunities. Towns such as Trieste and Udine hold treasures from successions of rulers and Aquileia, Carso and Collio districts produce some of the best white wine in Italy. The sandy beaches along the Adriatic coast near Venice are overdeveloped but are an irresistible draw to many. We have listed the University in Udine (page 212) and Linguaviva's residential junior summer school (page 214). The IRSE in Pordenone (page 14) offer scholarship courses in the summer.

Highlights of Friuli-Venezia-Giulia *Da non perdere del Friuli-Venezia-Giulia*

▶ walking, mountain biking or bird watching in the Carnic and Julian Alps

▶ visiting vineyards in Collio

▶ Illy coffee from its home town in Trieste

❯ the sweet San Daniele prosciutto

❯ the pretty town of Udine.

Udine

Udine is a pretty town with a population of 100,000. The surrounding flat agricultural plain is brightened by the Alps on the horizon. The town has several cafés, small markets and an air of quiet prosperity. The central square, Piazza della Libertà, has a series of fine Renaissance buildings surrounding a *campanile* topped by two Moorish bell strikers. The nearby *castello* sits on a hill commanding views of the town and countryside.

Udine University

Information for the summer courses:

Alessia Bruno (coordinator)
Università degli Studi di Udine
Centro Rapporti Internazionali
Via Palladio 8
I–33100 Udine
Tel: (0432) 556497 Fax: (0432) 556496
Website web.univd.it click on Rapportiinternationazionali, then Italian Summer Course.
Information for the non-summer courses:

Dottoressa Anna Olivo
CLAV Centro Linguistico Audiovisivi
Via Zanon 6
33100 Udine
Tel: (0432) 275570/74
Language centre and the self-access *laboratorio linguistico* open Monday to Friday 08.00–18.30

The University of Udine offers several Italian language courses for foreigners. There is a three-week intensive summer course in July and non-intensive three month courses throughout the year.

Courses and costs *Corsi e costi*

The three-week **summer intensive course** consists of four hours of teaching a day (20 hours a week) and costs €470. This includes a tour of the city, a guided visit to a local town, one meal a day from the University canteen (except on Sundays) and, for the intermediate and advanced students, six to eight hours of seminars. Students also have access to a small language laboratory. The **groups** have a maximum of 12 students.

The University also runs **non-intensive** three-month courses during the year. These consist of 50 hours of group teaching (approximately four hours a week) and self-access to the language laboratory. The course costs €247.90. The maximum group size is 28 students and there must be a minimum of 12 students for the courses to run.

Enrolment for the summer course *Iscrizione*

An application form can be downloaded from the Internet or requested from the Centro Rapporti Internazionali. Applications should be made at least one month in advance and requires a €200 deposit sent by bank transfer.

Enrolment for the non-intensive courses throughout the year *Iscrizione ai corsi non-intensivi per tutto l'anno*

Applications for the non-intensive three-month courses during the year can be obtained from Dr Anna Olivo at the CLAV address above.

Facilities

The CLAV building has a small self-access **language laboratory**. This includes computers, Internet access and audio and video cassettes. The building is a five-minute walk from the classrooms and is not air conditioned. The University **canteen** (*mensa*) serves lunch (*pranzo*) and dinner (*cena*) from Monday to Saturday costing €3.10 per meal.

Accommodation *Alloggio*

The University can help organise accommodation for students. The cost of a **single** room is approximately €220 for the length of the summer course. A double room costs about €180.

Scholarships *Borse di studio*

There are no scholarships available.

Linguaviva Summer School for Juniors in Lignano Sabbiadoro

Address of the course:

Soggiorno Onda Azzurra

Viale Centrale 29
I–33054 Lignano Sabbiadoro
Tel: (0431) 73481 Fax: (0431) 721566

Information about the course should be obtained from:

Linguaviva Head office

Via Fiume 17
I–50123 Firenze
Tel: (055) 294 359 or 055 280 016 Fax: (055) 283 667
Email info@linguaviva.it

Linguaviva runs a residential summer school for 10–16 year olds in Lignanano Sabbiadoro. This combines an Italian language course with a full programme of sport and recreation. It is held in the Villaggio Adriatico, a 'holiday village' on the Adriatic coast near Venice. This school also has Italian students of the same age learning English, giving a mix of nationalities and 'full immersion' in the Italian language. The courses run in the months of July and August each year and students can attend from two to eight weeks. There are an average of 50 students at the school at any one time. The package is fully inclusive and includes accommodation, food, lessons and all sporting, recreational activities and excursions.

The school *La scuola*

Onda Azzurra is a basic, plain, white concrete building set among pine trees a couple of hundred feet from the beach. There is a games room, classrooms, computer room with Internet access, a television room, a canteen and vending machines. Bedrooms are on the first floor and sleep three students with a private bathroom. Students are allocated rooms according to age and sex.

Language lessons *Lezioni di lingua*

There are three hours of language lessons a day including Saturday (18 hours a week). Each lesson lasts 45 minutes and there are up to five levels, determined by a small test at the beginning. Classes have a maximum of 12 students and are usually held outdoors under the pine trees. The lessons are carefully tailored to each group and are designed to be interactive and fun.

Sports and recreation *Sport e ricreazione*

There are a wide variety of supervised sports including tennis, football, volleyball, beach volleyball, swimming and rollerblading. The activities are grouped according to age. The school has its own private beach. Day trips are organised to nearby places of interest including Venice, Verona, Udine and Gardaland.

Costs *Costi*

A two-week course costs €1,110, three weeks €1,665 and four weeks €2,220. This includes accommodation, meals, teaching, sport, excursions, laundry service once a week and medical assistance from a doctor and nurse in the holiday village. A deposit of 30% is required and full payment of the course must be paid at least two weeks before the start. Refunds after the course has commenced are not available.

Veneto

The Veneto region in the northeast of Italy is mostly a flat, bleak landscape formed from the tail of the Po valley leading to Venice and the Adriatic Sea. Fortunately it is dotted with beautiful towns and monuments, world-class vineyards, international opera and fine *osteria*. The foothills of the Dolomite Mountains rise in the north and are easily accessible for week-end skiing or trekking. We have listed schools in Padova (page 220), Treviso (page 222), Verona (page 217) and Venice (page 223).

Highlights of Veneto *Da non perdere del Veneto*

▶ the Padova food market, one of the ultimate food experiences in Italy

▶ driving the hilly *Strada del Prosecco* near Valdobiaddene

❱ Treviso's clear Venetian canals

❱ Palladio's bridge, *Ponte degli Alpini*, in Bassano del Grappa and his nearby villas

❱ the summer opera festival in the first century Roman amphitheatre in Verona

❱ Giotto's frescoes in the Scrovegni Chapel in Padova

❱ the 16th century wooden anatomy theatre in Padova's University.

Summary table of language schools in Veneto: *Tavola sommario delle scuole di lingua*

School	Lingualt	Open Road	Bertrand Russell	Marco Polo	Istituto Venezia
Town	Verona	Padova	Padova	Treviso	Venice
Two weeks	€280	€225	€250	€320*	€290
Four weeks	€520	€450	€500	€540*	€540
Individual	€25	€24	€25	€25	€28
Enrolment	€45	€100	None	€24–48	None
Single room two weeks	€250	–	€150	€238	€300
Single room four weeks	€500	€370	€300	€392	€520
Maximum group size	8	10	10	6	12
Laboratory	No	No	No	No	No
Air conditioning	No	No	Yes	No	No
Discounts	Yes	No	Yes	Yes	Yes
Scholarships	Yes	No	Yes	Yes	Yes

* Three hours per day (15 hours per week)

Verona

This ancient university town sits on the bank of the River Adige near Lake Garda and the Lessini and Dolomite mountains. Its pedestrianised historic centre is built around a magnificent Roman amphitheatre, which houses the opera festival in July and August. The surrounding streets are paved with pink and white marble and are lined with cafés, exclusive shops, quiet piazzas, fountains and views of nearby hills. The Roman Theatre runs Shakespearian plays and a summer Jazz Festival and the prestigious wine fair, Vinitaly, brings together the world's top names in wine.

Lingualt

The Institute of Italian Language and Culture
Via Anfiteatro 10
Verona 37121
Tel: (045) 597 975 Fax: (045) 804 8728
Email info@linguait.it Website www.linguait.it
Segretaria open Monday to Friday from 09.00–12.00 and 16.00–18.00
This excellent small school is just behind the Roman amphitheatre on the first floor of a bright modern building. Via Anfiteatro is perpendicular to the back of the amphitheatre and is easily confused with Via Dietro Anfiteatro which runs parallel with the amphitheatre.

The school has a games room, an Internet point and a student common room with a small balcony. Here there are magazines, newspapers, a film library, tourist information leaflets, a vending machine and an Illy coffee maker. A welcoming tour of the city is given to all students and each week there is a free guided visit with the history of art teacher into the town. There are courses to suit everybody including an intensive weekend course, art, opera, Italian culture, wine, cooking and specialist courses. The group size is a maximum of 12.

Courses and costs *Corsi e costi*
The **standard** course of four hours teaching a day (20 hours a week) costs €280 for two weeks and €520 for four weeks. **Tandem courses** have two students per group with three hours teaching a day (15 hours a week) and cost €180 per week. **Intensive weekend courses** have 12 hours of lessons

over Saturday and Sunday and cost €144. **Individual** lessons are €25 per hour. There are non-intensive Italian **cultural** courses including history of art, literature, theatre, cinema, fashion and opera. These can be combined with a standard language course and consist of two 90-minute sessions per week. They cost €108 for a four-week course. **Specialist** language courses for professions consist of three hours teaching per week and cost €108 per month. Wine and cooking courses can be arranged on request. Weekend and day trips to nearby towns such as Venice, Padova, Vicenza, Parma, Modena and Treviso are charged for separately. The **enrolment** fee of €45 includes a student discount card.

Accommodation *Alloggio*
A single room in a shared apartment costs from €250 for two weeks or €500 for four weeks.

Scuola Media Statale Aosta

Via G. Trezzi 13
Tel: (045) 8002922
This secondary school offers *free* language lessons in the month of September, consisting of approximately three to four hours per week.

Verona Opera Festival

The Box Office
Via Dietro Anfiteatro 6a
Verona
Tel: (045) 8005151 Fax: (045) 801 3287
Website www.arena.it
Open during the opera season Monday to Friday 10.00–17.45, on performance days from 10.00–21.00, other months Monday to Friday 09.00–12.00, 15.15–17.45, Saturdays 09.00–12.00

Tickets can be bought online, by telephone or from the box office from as little as €14. The box office staff can give advice on performances and seats. The opera has an informal atmosphere in the cheap seats. People lounge on the warm stone steps lateral to the stage eating ice cream and take-away pizza.

Verona University summer course

Address for information:

ESU ARDSU di Verona
Servizi agli Studenti
Via dell'Artigliere 9
37129 Verona (VR)
Tel: (045) 8052861 Fax: (045) 8052840
Website www.esu.vr.it click on the 'Servizi allo Studente' picture, then on 'corsi di Lingua', then available in English under 'Summer course of Italian language and culture'.
Computer room (*aula informatica*) open Monday to Thursday 08.00–18.00 and Fridays 08.00–13.00

Halls of Residence
Residenza Millennium
Viale Venezia 89 (Porta Vescovo)
37131 Verona
Tel: (045) 520206

Courses and costs *Corsi e costi*
Verona University runs a one-month course in Italian language and culture every August. The course consists of 25 hours teaching a week divided into morning language lessons and afternoon cultural seminars. The cultural seminars can be substituted for further language teaching in the afternoon. The school also organises excursions and evening activities. Classes have a maximum of 15 students.

The course costs €500 which includes a welcome dinner, several excursions to local places of interest, materials for the course and an end of course dinner. The full package including accommodation, lunch and dinner costs €950 (see below).

Accommodation *Alloggio*
Accommodation can be arranged in the Residence Millennium for €250 per month. This is in a double room in a small shared apartment with other students and includes one change of sheets and towels per week. The residence was opened in 2000 and is a smart seven-storey apartment block with a reception and outdoor seating. It is set back from a busy main

road outside the eastern gate of *Porta Vescovo* a 30-minute walk from the centre. The apartments have balconies and the larger apartments have washing machines. It is also possible to book accommodation here independently of the University throughout the year.

Facilities
Students have access to the **computer room** (*aula informatica*) in the ESU building. The university **canteen** (*mensa*) costs €200 per month for lunch (*pranzo*) and dinner (*cena*) seven days a week. When the *mensa* is closed the University has arrangements with other local eateries.

Enrolment *Iscrizione*
Students should enrol at least 30 days in advance, as places are limited. The application form and bank details for the non-refundable deposit of €150 can be obtained from the website or from the *Servizi agli Studenti*. The application form should be sent with a copy of the receipt (*ricevuta*) for the deposit, a passport photo and a photocopy of your passport.

Scholarships *Borse di studio*
The University does not offer scholarships for the summer course.

Padova *Padua*

Padova is close to the Dolomites, Venice, Verona, the beaches of the Adriatic and nestled near some of the best vineyards in Italy. It has many famous buildings including the Scrovegni chapel with Giotto's remarkable frescoes and the second oldest university in Italy (1222). The daily food market is spread over two piazzas with a covered arcaded area in between for cheese, butchers, pasta and delicatessens. It is a food lovers' dream.

Bertrand Russell Scuola di Italiano

Via E. Filiberto 6
35122 Padova
Tel: (0039) 049 654 051 Fax: (0039) 049 875 4133
Email school@bertrand-russell.it Website www.bertrand-russell.it
Open Monday to Friday from September to May 09.00–20.00
Open Monday to Friday 09.00–13.00 June to August

This language school is centrally located, just off Piazza Garibaldi on the first floor of a shabby building. The classrooms come off a long narrow corridor, shared with a hairdressers and their towel-washing facilities. Class size is a maximum of ten students.

Courses and costs *Corsi e costi*
The **standard** course of four hours a day (20 hours per week) costs €250 for two weeks and €500 for four weeks. When a three-month course is booked and paid for in advance a fourth month is given free of charge. **Individual** lessons cost €25 an hour. There is a one-month course in August of 80 hours for preparation for the Italian University entrance exams. This course has a 100% success rate in the entrance exams and costs €650. There is no **enrolment** fee. Scholarships are available through Italian Cultural Institutes (see page 13).

Accommodation *Alloggio*
A single room with a family costs €150 for two weeks and €300 for four weeks.

Open Road Istituto Linguistico

Galleria degli Zabarella 3
35121 Padova
Tel: (049) 656880 Fax: (049) 656727
Email openroad@tin.it Website www.openroad.it
This language school was moving to its current location when we visited. It is on the second floor of a modern building in a small shopping arcade, Galleria Zaberilli. This is a good position in the centre of Padova. The school had been recently decorated with purple carpets and matching paint work and is light and airy. There is a small library and Internet access. The director is friendly but does not speak much English. The group size is small with a maximum of ten.

Courses and costs *Corsi e costi*
The **standard** course of four hours per day (20 hours per week) costs €225 for two weeks and €450 per month. **Individual** lessons cost €24 per hour. There is a (hefty) €100 **enrolment** fee.

Accommodation *Alloggio*

A single room with use of the kitchen costs €340 per month. A mini apartment costs €900 per month.

Treviso

Treviso is a beautiful small town 20km north of Venice. It is known as *Città d'aqua* (City of water) due to its pretty canals and fountains. The River Sile runs around the sixteenth century walls and flows rapidly through the town. This supplies a fantastic fish market on weekday mornings. Surprisingly, there are few tourists even at Christmas when the street decorations are stunning. There are many cafes, restaurants and wine bars and good nightlife.

Marco Polo

Centro di Lingua e Cultura Italiana

Viale Pasteur 25

31100 Treviso

Tel/Fax: (0039) 0422 321 984

Email info@marcopololinguae.it Website www.marcopololinguae.it

This small 'home tuition' school has been run by a husband and wife team, the Simionis, since 1996. It is located in a modern country house a 15-minute bus or bicycle ride from the centre. There are large windows with views of the garden and surrounding farmland and vineyards. The classrooms are upstairs but lessons are often held in the garden. There is a kitchen for making drinks and a large sitting room with sofas and a television for watching Italian videos. Students have access to the Treviso library and the school hires bicycles for the period of the course at €60 per month. The owners take great trouble with their students to ensure that they get the most out of their time in Italy. The maximum group size is six.

To find the school by car, follow the signs out of Treviso for the hospital. At the main roundabout turn right along Viale Pasteur, passing a factory on the right. The school is on the right-hand side of the road.

Courses and costs *Corsi e costi*

A **standard** course of three hours teaching a day (15 hours a week) costs €320 for two weeks and €540 for four weeks. A course of ten **individual** lessons costs €200 and can be used for preparation for the European Language Certificates of CILS or CELI. There are two residential summer courses in July for **teenagers** aged 14–18 and **children** aged 6–13. Both courses are two weeks and include 30 hours of language teaching, sports with Italian children, outings to Venice and other towns, residential accommodation in the campus and full board. There is an **enrolment** fee of between €24 and €48, depending on the course, which includes course books. The school can arrange workshops including art and Italian history, cooking and wine, painting, glass making and drawing. Scholarships are available through Italian Cultural Institutes (see page 13).

Accommodation *Alloggio*

A single room in a shared apartment costs €238 for two weeks and €392 for a month.

Venice *Venezia*

Proust said 'when I went to Venice, I discovered that my dream had become ... my address.' While gondolas glide tourists around the canals, the other Venetians are free for glass blowing, making lace and marbled paper or masks for the carnival. The Basilica di St Marco is the most famous of Venice's hundreds of churches. Its 10,500 square feet of mosaics took several hundred years to complete. The Rialto area has a morning market stacked high with fish, fruit and vegetables. During periods of high water (*acqua alta*) cafés resonate with stories of impending doom and concern over Venice sinking into the sea. At the moment Venice is thriving. Away from the main tourist routes it is easy to find a unique place to live and study. Each house in an area (*sestiere*) has its own number and street names are not always used, making navigating a challenge.

Istituto Venezia

Dorsoduro 3116/a
Campo Santa Margherita
Venezia 30123

Tel: (041) 522 4331 Fax: (041) 528 5628

Emergency accommodation Mobile: 347762 8361

Email veninst@tin.it Website www.istitutovenezia.com

Secretariat is open Monday to Thursday 08.45–17.00 and on Fridays 08.45–15.00

This school is on the first floor of a restored palazzo, near the pretty café-lined Campo Santa Margherita. St Mark's square and the hoards of tourists are a short *vaporetto* ride away. To find the school leave Campo Santa Margherita and walk along Rio Terà Canàl. The entrance is near the junction with Ramo Cappello, up a steep flight of steps lined with pots of geraniums. The *segretaria* is at the end of a long passageway, from which the whitewashed classrooms lead off.

There are extracurricular activities most afternoons and some weekend outings are included in the price. The school has free Internet access in the afternoon and students are given a discount card for local shops and restaurants. There is a collection of Italian videos that can be watched after classes. The maximum group size is 12. Scholarships are available through the Italian Cultural Institutes (see page 13).

Courses and costs *Corsi e costi*

The **standard** language course of four hours teaching a day (20 hours a week) costs €290 for two weeks and €540 for four weeks. Discounts are available for longer courses, eight weeks costs €940, 12 weeks costs €1,300 and each additional week is €80. There is a **super-intensive** option that has the same morning group classes with the addition of two hours in the afternoon in a smaller group of up to six students. This course costs €480 for two weeks and €900 for four weeks. **Individual** lessons cost €28 per hour and can be arranged to suit a student's interests and timetable. **Combi-courses** combine the intensive group lessons with afternoons of cooking, wine, watercolour painting, glass blowing (not practical), lace making, history of art or practical mask making. The glass, lace, watercolour and wine combi-courses cost €400 for two weeks. The combi-cooking costs €450, combi-history of art costs €480 and the combi-masks course costs €500. All prices are for two weeks and include materials except for the watercolour course where students bring their own paints. The combi-courses are only run when four of more students request them. There is no enrolment fee.

Accommodation *Alloggio*

A single room in a shared apartment costs €300 for two weeks and €520 for four weeks. All of the apartments are within a 25 minute walk of the school or a shorter *vaporetto* ride.

The excellent self-access language laboratory at the University of Venice (see below) costs €103 for 100 hours and can supplement a private language course.

University of Venice

Università Cà Foscari di Venezia

Centro Linguistico Interfacoltà CLI
Palazzo Bonvicini
Calle di Cà Bonvicini 2161 (which is off Calle Longa)
Santa Croce
30135 Venezia
Tel: (041) 234 9711 Fax: (041) 718 259
Email cli@unive.it Website www.unive.it/cli

Segretaria

(first floor) open Monday to Friday 09.00–12.00 and on Mondays, Wednesdays and Thursdays from 15.00–17.00

Self-access laboratory

(*laboratoio di auto apprendimento*) first and second floor, open Monday to Friday from 10.00–18.00. On Mondays, Tuesdays and Thursdays it stays open until 20.00.

The ESU Ente per il diritto allo studio

(Accommodation, Canteen and Canteen pass)
Palazzo Badoer, S. Polo 2480. Tel: (041) 721025/721988
Email segre@esuvenezia.it Website www.esuvenezia.it
Open Mondays and Thursdays 15.30–17.00 and Tuesdays, Wednesdays and Fridays 10.00–12.00

Badoer canteen

(*mensa*) on the first floor of the same Palazzo as the ESU office.
Rio Novo canteen (*mensa*) Dorsoduro, 3441. Tel: (041) 718 722
Open Monday to Friday 11.45–14.30

The University of Venice runs a series of non-intensive Italian language courses at its *Centro Linguistico Interfacoltà*.

Courses and costs *Corsi e costi*

The courses are primarily aimed at university exchange students but places are available for all foreigners if the courses are not oversubscribed. In practice about 1,700 people apply for 1,650 places. The courses consist of 50 hours of teaching and unlimited **self-access** to the language laboratory over a period of between nine to 12 weeks (four to six hours teaching a week). Courses start in October, January and April. The group size is approximately 20 students and the course costs €232.40. Students who are not able to get a place on the course can use the self-access language facilities (see below under facilities) for a bargain of €103 for 100 hours.

Applications should be made at least a month in advance at the above address with a passport and passport photo. Students with prior knowledge of Italian need to take an entrance test two weeks before the course starts. When the course is oversubscribed a computer randomly selects students and the results of this can be checked on the website a few days later. Students applying from abroad should write to cli@unive.it for further information.

Directions

The Venice postal addresses do not usually include the street name as there are many streets with the same name. To find the *Centro Linguistico Interfacoltà* look for Piazza S. Maria Mater Domini and the Bar da Fiore (which serves a good Illy coffee). Leaving the bar go straight ahead and to the right along the narrow Calle Longa. After a two-minute walk Calle di Cà Bonvicini leads off to the left. Calle di Cà Bonvicini is called Calle dell'Agnello on some maps. The Palazzo Bonvicini is wood panelled with whitewashed walls and stone floors. Many of the classrooms have frescoed ceilings and there is a panoramic view of Venice from the top floor.

Facilities

The self-access laboratory (*laboratorio di auto apprendimento*) always has someone available to help select suitable exercises in the different parts of the lab. *The sala di proiezione* is on the first floor and has a big screen for films. Free Italian films are shown on Wednesdays at 16.00. On the second floor, up a very steep flight of steps, is the *laboratorio audio* which has eight places for linguistic exercises such as pronunciation, listening and Italian for professional purposes. The *lab. satellitare* has 18 flat-screened computers for listening to CDs, watching DVDs, videos and satellite television. The *lab. multimediale* has 16 computers with CD-ROMs with language packages for Italian, French, Spanish, English and German. The library has books on grammar, dictionaries, novels and a small study area.

Accommodation and canteens *Alloggio e mense*

The ESU organises good value accommodation in the University halls of residence. The most central ones are the Domus Soccorso and the Ragusei Halls. A single room costs between €189 and €197 per month. When the halls are full the ESU can place students in other accommodation which costs between €200 and €350 per month.

There are two university canteens, the Badoer in the same palazzo as the ESU office and the Rio Novo in Dorsoduro. In both canteens meals costs €2.50–3.50 but Rio Novo has a nicer environment. For a canteen pass, students must take their enrolment document with a passport photo to the ESU office. To find the ESU Palazzo, go to Sestier de S. Polo and walk towards the canal Rio de S. Stin. Before the bridge turn right and after two minutes walk the ESU Palazzo Badoer is on the right on the corner of Calle del Magazen.

Scholarships *Borsi di Studio*

There are no scholarships available.

Emilia-Romagna

This region is famous for its food and the arts. The traditional specialities include the balsamic vinegars (*aceto balsamico*) of Modena, the hams (*prosciutto*) of Parma and parmesan cheese (*parmigiano*) all of which can be bought in the speciality shops of Bologna. Bologna has been an intellectual centre for centuries and has the oldest university in Italy. The Bolognian Teatro Comunale has regular concerts as well as an opera season. Rimini has great discos (*discoteche*) and long stretches of beach developments.

Highlights of Emilia-Romagna *Da non perdere dell' Emilia-Romagna*

▶ the Opera House in Bologna

▶ cycling in Ferrara in the historic centre with the locals

▶ discos on the beaches of Rimini

▶ the mosaics in Ravenna

▶ hams of Parma

▶ balsamic vinegars of Modena.

Bologna

Bologna is a beautiful medieval city of Etruscan origin. It is one of the gourmet centres of Italy with a food market to rival Padova's. There are long lines of stalls under the covered arcades; artichokes (*carciofi*) are stocked in six different types, Mamma, Romana, Violetta, Spinozi, Pugliesi, Riviera all of which are prepared in three different ways. Hams (*prosciutti*) from the heart of the Parma classification area hang from shop ceilings and tiny bottles of the exclusive, thick, intense balsalmic vinegar line the shelves. There is a thriving arts scene including the Teatro Comunale opera house, theatres and concerts. The International Contemporary Art Festival exhibits contemporary and nineteenth century art for a week each January (information in Italian on www.artfier.bolognafiere.it). Bologna lies on one of the key rail and road junctions between the north and south of Italy so is a good base from which to explore.

Cultura Italiana

Via Castiglione 4

I–40124 Bologna
Tel: 0516486453, 051228003, 051228011 Fax: 0516567720
Email info@culturaitaliana.it Website www.culturaitaliana.it
This school is on the first floor of a thirteenth century Gothic palazzo five minutes walk from Piazza Maggiore. Just before the entrance to the school

there is a large hallway with huge oil paintings. The school's hall feels rather small after this imposing entrance but the school has good facilities including a computer room, a reading room with large flat screen television and a small library. There is a range of standard and tailor-made courses. The six hours of extracurricular activities per week include seminars and days out. Each student is expected to do two hours homework per day. The maximum group size is 12.

Childcare

Childcare can be arranged either in the child's home or in a local childcare centre with other Italian children. Prices vary depending on the age of the child, where the child is to be looked after and whether meals are included. For a 5 year-old, for example, five days a week for four hours per day including lunch costs €320 per four weeks.

Courses and costs *Corsi e costi*

The **standard course** of four hours per day (20 hours per week) cost €323 for two weeks and €580 for four weeks. When a three-month course is booked there is a €124 discount. **Afternoon and evening classes** have two sessions per week of three hours and last between six and 12 weeks. **Individual lessons** cost €28 per hour or €698 for 30 hours. **Tailor-made courses** have four hours of group lessons and one individual lesson a day. There is a 10% discount on the course fees for people under 30 or over 60. There is no enrolment fee. Scholarships are available from the Italian Cultural Institutes (see page 13).

Certificates and qualifications *Certificati e titoli*

The school is a centre for the preparation for University of Siena CILS exams.

Accommodation *Alloggio*

A single room costs €108 per week in a shared apartment.

Società Dante Alighieri

Via de' Pignattari 1
Tel: (051) 226658 Mobile: 332642136
Secretariat open Tuesday to Friday 16.00–18.00

The Bologna branch of the Società Dante Alighieri runs good value, **part-time courses** from October to June. The school has an impressive location overlooking Bologna's main square, Piazza Maggiore. It is on the second floor of the Palazzo Notaio next door to the Basilica di San Petronio. The spacious, airy palazzo has wide marble stairs, terracotta floors and frescoed ceilings. The school has a single classroom with Gothic windows with views of the piazza. There is a small library but no *laboratorio linguistico*. The school is **closed in July and August** and there is no accommodation service.

Courses and costs *Corsi e costi*

The three-month **part-time** courses begin in October, January and April. Each course has a 90-minute session every Monday, Wednesday and Friday. The courses cost €80 for three months and there is no enrolment fee.

Bellaria-Igea Marina

This modern beach resort is 110km from Bologna and 15km from Rimini. It has a population of 15,000, which expands during the summer months with Italian families who flock to the sheltered beach and budget hotels. It is surrounded by modern developments with no architectural charm, which are largely closed from October to May. The major draw is an excellent language school that offers a range of courses including a course in Italian brail.

Demischool

Via Fratelli Cervi, 44
Bellaria-Igea Marina
Rimini 47814
Tel/Fax: (0541) 345271
Email info@demischool.com Website www.demischool.com
Open Monday to Friday 09.00–13.00

This delightful school is 400m from the sheltered beach in this modern seaside resort. The countryside surrounding the school is flat and developed. The school is on the first floor above a pizzeria on a road lined with beech trees. There is a kitchen in the school for making drinks and all courses include a **weekly cookery class**. There is a range of excellent value flexible courses to suit all tastes including ones for **children** and **courses in brail**. The directors take great trouble in making sure the students get the most out of their trip and they are passionate about teaching.

Courses and costs *Corsi e costi*

The **standard** course of four hours of teaching per day (20 hours a week) costs €230 for two weeks and €365 for four weeks. There is a two-hour per day **holiday course** costing €115 per week and an **intensive course** with 30 hours per week costing €200 per week. **Individual lessons** cost €16 per lesson. There is a €26 **enrolment** fee which includes the end of course attendance certificate. The **brail course** has two hours per day of group teaching and two hours of individual lessons specifically focused on brail. There is a 10% discount for two people who book together, for bookings made from January to March and in November and also for the second course attended at the school. There is an **essay competition** where the winner gets a 60% discount on a one-week course and the runner-up gets a 40% discount on a one-week course.

Accommodation *Alloggio*

A single room in a shared apartment costs from €16 per day depending on the season.

Tuscany *Toscana*

Tuscany lives up to its reputation as one of Italy's most beautiful regions. Florence, Siena, Pisa and Lucca contain some the world's most famous artistic treasures and Chianti's clipped and cultivated hills are a food and wine lover's heaven. Tuscany is not all Renaissance, wine, oil and tourists. The vast chestnut forests of Castentino in the northeast are one of Italy's most beautiful sights. It has ridges bordering Emilia-Romagna, high peaks and isolated monasteries. In the northwest, near Lucca, the Garfagnana and Apuan Alps are a near deserted wonderland for walking and wildlife. Off-season even Florence can be peaceful. On the west coast there are long stretches of sandy beaches in Viareggio, Cecina and Talamone, although these do not compare with the beaches elsewhere in Italy. We have chosen schools in Florence (page 31), Siena (page 65) and Lucca (page 233). Florence and Siena are covered in separate chapters as they both have a University for Foreigners.

Highlights of Tuscany *Da non perdere della Toscana*

▶ the view of Ponte Vechia from Ponte Trinità in Florence

▶ walking on top of the ancient city walls of Lucca

▶ pecorino cheese and lunch in Pienza

▶ walking in the chestnut forests of Castentino

▶ the bare-backed horse race *il Palio* in Siena

▶ Chianti wines and visiting their vineyards

▶ Florence's Uffizi gallery on the banks of the Rive Arno.

Lucca

This delightful Roman town in northern Tuscany was the birthplace of Puccini. This is marked annually with the Puccini Festival. The Renaissance era walls completely enclose the town excluding traffic. The locals take a daily walk (*passeggiata*) around the top of the wall (a 2.5 mile round trip) at sunset and admire the surrounding mountains, numerous towers, over 100 churches and coloured houses before pausing for an *aperitivo*. The tower Torre Guinigi has a miniature roof garden of young oak trees 145m above the town. The stripy marble Duomo is in the same style as the one in Florence. The town is surrounded by the Gufagnana Mountains and Apuana Alps so Lucca is a perfect base for walking, climbing, skiing and exploring Tuscany. Lucca's 100 churches have regular concerts listed in Italian on the website www.luccamusica.it. There is a monthly antiques market during the third weekend of each month in Piazza San Martino.

The Puccini Festival

This festival starts in mid-July and last five weeks. All the operas begin at 21.15 and tickets cost from €26. The website www.puccinifestival.it has the history and synopsis of all the operas and it is possible to buy tickets on line. Some of the performances take place in Torre del Lago a few miles away.

Centro Koinè

Via Mordini 60
Lucca 55100
Tel: (0583) 493040 Fax: (0583) 491689
Email koinelu@tin.it Website www.koinecenter.com

This school has a quiet position in the historic centre of the town. It is on the second floor with views over the rooftops of Lucca. The classrooms have high-beamed ceilings, whitewashed walls and stone floors. There is no *laboratorio linguisitico* but there are some books and films for loan. The maximum group size is 12.

Courses and costs *Corsi e costi*
The **standard language and culture course** of four weeks has 80 hours of language teaching and 14 hours of culture activities. The course is available from October to May each year and it is possible to attend for only two or three weeks. There are four hours of language lessons per day from Monday to Friday. The cultural programme changes monthly and includes guided visits to Lucca and local towns, the history of Italian cinema, excursions to local farms, parks, villas and garden architecture. Some of these trips (and all entrance tickets) are charged for separately. The course costs €360 for two weeks or €586 for four weeks. **Individual lessons** cost €31 each when booked in a course of ten hours over a week. There is no enrolment fee.

The **Tuscan countryside course** is an action packed two-week programme. It includes nine sessions of language teaching each of four hours, a weekend trip and tour to the Island of Capraia, a tour of Lucca and four afternoon trips. The afternoon trips include olive oil and wine tasting, the Park of San Rossore, Carrara and the marble quarries and the Le Pievi medieval settlement. There are also dinners in local restaurants. The cost of this two-week course is €880.

Accommodation *Alloggio*

The school organises accommodation in hotels, with Italian families and in shared or independent apartments. A single room in a shared apartment costs €260 for two weeks and €410 for four weeks. A single room and half-board with a family costs €390 for two weeks and €767 for four weeks.

Umbria

Henry James called Umbria 'the most beautiful garden in the world'. This spellbinding region has hills dotted with olive trees and fortified hill towns. There are mountains that take up entire visual fields with the colour of chestnut and oak woods. To the east the Apennine Mountains rise up in the Monti Sibillini bordering Le Marche. There is trekking, skiing and stunning wild flowers in spring. To the west more gentle hills roll away to the cultivated beauty of Tuscany. The region has some of Italy's finest works of art including Giotto's fresco cycle of the Life of St Francis (c.1290) in Assisi. Perugia has the renowned National Gallery of Umbria and also Etruscan remains in the Archaeological Museum. The hill towns of Spoletto, Gubbio, Montefalco and Orvieto are a succession of medieval beauty. The region's food includes black truffles, wild mushrooms, cured hams and sausages.

Perugia is the region's capital, near to Assisi and only 50km from our favourite small town in Italy, Spoleto. We have chosen schools in Perugia (page 89), Spoleto (page 236) and Orvieto (page 237).

Highlights of Umbria *Da non perdere dell'Umbria*

▶ living in Perugia

▶ Città di Castello white truffle fair (*Tuber Magnatum Pico*) first weekend in November

▶ walking, skiing and wild flowers in the Monti Sibillini mountains

▶ the small fortified medieval hilltop towns of Spello and Spoletto

▶ the views of 'green' Umbria from Perugia and Montefalco

❱ Gubbio's Candles (*Ceri*) Race on 15 May, the eve of St Ubaldo

❱ the Duomo in Spoleto and the opera, dance and art festival The Two Worlds

❱ the wines from around Orvieto and Montefalco.

Summary table of language schools in Umbria *Tavola: sommario delle scuole di lingua*

	University for Foreigners	ABC	Comitato	Istituto Europeo	Lingua Si
Town	Perugia	Perugia	Perugia	Spoleto	Ovieto
Two weeks	–	€235	€220	€300	€389
Four weeks	€233	€470	€440	€450	€629
Individual	–	€20	€30	€12	€31
Enrolment	–	None	€52	None	€46
Single room two weeks	–	€180–€200	€195	€250	€207–245
Single room four weeks	€290	€250–300	€335	€400	€310–365
Maximum group size	No Max.	10	12	4	8
Air conditioning	No	No	No	No	No
Laboratory	Yes for use in lessons only	No	No	No	No
Discounts	No	Yes	10% after 12 weeks	No	No
Scholarships	Yes apply to Prof. Winter in UK	No	Yes apply directly to the school	Yes apply directly to the school	Yes from Italian Cultural Institutes

Spoleto

The hill town of Spoleto is 400m above sea level and has a population of 38,000. There are stunning views from the footpath of the fourteenth century 80m long aqueduct (*Ponte delle Torri*). It spans a deep gorge over the River Tessino and brings water to the town. Walking from the fortress (*Rocca*) to the twelfth century Romanesque Duomo one sees the views over Umbria's green hills and then the long flight of steps down to the Duomo. In this Piazza, there are concerts during the Festival of the Two Worlds (*Festival dei Due Mondi*). The Festival was established by the composer Menotti in 1958 to promote cultural relations between Italy and America. It catapulted Spoleto into hosting a prestigious international music and arts festival. From the end of June there is a fortnight of operas, plays, classical and jazz concerts, cinema, dance and art exhibitions. Spoleto has not lost its charm despite its fame.

Festival of the Two Worlds *Festival dei Due Mondi*
The tickets cost from €5 to €200 and can be bought from the ticket office in Piazza della Libertà, 12. This is open Monday to Friday from 10.30–13.30 and 16.30–19.00. Tickets can be bought online and collected from the ticket office in or from the theatre before the performance (Email info@spoletofestival.it , Website www.spoletofestival.it).

Istituto Europeo Della Lingua Italiana

Piazza Garibaldi 8
Spoleto 06049
Tel/Fax: (0743) 47300
Email info@italian.org Website www.italian.org

This small school is just inside the city walls at the bottom of the old town. It is on the second floor, over a speciality baker, where the smell of fresh bread wafts through the open windows in summer. The traffic in Piazza Garibaldi does not detract from the views up to the *Rocca*. The school is newly opened with fresh paint work and modern fittings. The classrooms are light and airy with video facilities. There are a few books for loan but no library or *laboratorio linguistico*. Group size is a maximum of four students. The individual lessons are good value and there is no enrolment fee. Extra curricular activities are only arranged on request and the social opportunities are few due to the small numbers of students at the school.

Courses and costs *Corsi e costi*

The **standard group course** of four hours a day (20 hours a week) costs €300 for two weeks and €450 for four weeks. When less than three students are enrolled the number of lessons is reduced. **Individual lessons** cost €12 per hour and there is no enrolment fee. Scholarships are available by applying to the school's director, Carmelo Maneta.

Accommodation *Alloggio*

A single room in a shared apartment costs €250 for two weeks or €400 for four weeks. An independent apartment costs €500 for two people per month. During the Two Worlds Festival, the last week in June and the first week in July, prices of accommodation double and must be booked at least three months in advance.

Orvieto

Orvieto is a medieval walled town with a population of 20,000. There are 3,000 years of history concentrated into its small historic centre, including subterranean wells and tunnels and a magnificent thirteenth century Duomo. The town hosts the Winter Umbrian Jazz festival and is just 15 minutes from Lake Bolsena for cool summer swimming. The region is also known for its excellent white wines.

Lingua Sì

Via Soliana 2

Villa Mercede

05018 Orvieto

Tel: (0763) 393545

Email linguasi@tin.it Website www.linguasi.it

The school is only 20 metres from the thirteenth century Duomo. It is in a sixteenth century monastery overlooking the Umbrian countryside. There is a pretty garden, a tennis court and a five a side football pitch. The school has a small library, videos, Internet point, ping pong table, multimedia programmes and a mini-bar. There are extracurricular activities including a tour of the town, welcome and farewell dinner, Italian films, meals in local restaurants, wine tasting, seminars, excursions to local towns and concerts. Each student is paired with an Italian student for extra conversation practice. Once a month there is a student party (*festa*) where each student brings something that they have cooked from a recipe from their own country. The cost of the course includes a discount card that can be used in over 100 restaurants, museums, car rentals and shops. The class size is a maximum of eight.

Courses and costs *Corsi e costi*

All courses can be taken from one week to three months or longer; the longer the course, the better the value. The **standard course** of 20 hours per week costs €389 for two weeks and €629 for four weeks. There are **more intensive options** with 30 hours per week costing €660 for two weeks or €996 for four weeks. **Individual lessons** cost €31 each when booked in a course of ten lessons. The **business Italian** course is two hours per day and can be taken with one of the other language courses. It costs €430 per week. The **intensive Viva La Lingua course** includes eight and a half hours of one-to-one teaching, accommodation and meals with a teacher and costs €459 per day. The **senior citizen course** has four hours of lessons per day and costs €349 for one week. There are also **flexible courses** from one day to two or more weeks in cookery, art, archaeology, photography, music and wine. There is an enrolment fee of €46. Scholarships are available through the Italian Cultural Institutes (see page 13).

Accommodation *Alloggio*

The school's monastery has rooms for €23 to €28 per day. A single room in a shared apartment or with a family costs from €207 to €245 for two weeks and from €310–365 for four weeks.

Le Marche

Le Marche is nestled between the Apennines and the Adriatic. Its interior is a fairytale landscape. Steep hills are topped by fortified towns housing works of art amid spectacular Renaissance architecture. The Monti Sibillini in the west of the region are among the wildest mountains in Italy. Some of the villages in this park still become inaccessible in the winter months and it is home to numerous protected animals and plants, including wolves, wildcats, golden eagles and eagle owls. On the east coast there is an almost unbroken line of beaches, although these are often amid ugly modern developments. The region is famed for its spectacular fish lunches (*pranzi di pesche*). We have chosen schools in Urbino (page 240) and Belforte all'Isauro (page 241).

Highlights of Le Marche *Da non perdere delle Marche*

▶ Palazzo Ducale in Urbino, a Renaissance masterpiece

▶ the Monti Sibillini, some of Europe's wildest scenery for trekking and wildlife

▶ a day at the beach near the beautiful Conero Peninsula

▶ the fish feasts and fish stew (*brodetto*)

▶ the fairytale hilltop towns, separated by green wilderness

▶ Ascoli Piceno, one of the prettiest towns in the region.

Urbino

Urbino is one of Le Marche's most distinguished towns. Baldassare Castiglione described it as being built in the 'shape of a palace'. It is perched on a hill commanding views across the region and has a population of 15,000. The Palazzo Ducale, seen for miles around, is one of Italy's most beautiful Renaissance Palaces. It was built for the one-eyed, hook-nosed Federico Montefeltro, Duke of Urbino, in the fifteenth Century. His right eye was lost in a battle and the hook in his nose was fashioned in an early feat of plastic surgery so that he could glance to his blind side. The Ducal Palace houses the National Gallery of Le Marche and includes Raphael's *Portrait of a Lady*. The College of Doctors was founded by Duke Guidobaldo at the beginning of the sixteenth century and later became the University where the summer course is run.

Urbino University summer course

Information and location of the course:
Università degli Studi di Urbino
Via Saffi 2
1–61029 Urbino (PU)
Tel: (0722) 305250
Email italianoestivo@uniurb.it Website www.uniurb.it

The University of Urbino runs an excellent course in Italian language and culture every August lasting three weeks. This course includes language, literature, art, music, history of cinema and politics. The groups have a maximum of 20 students. It is a sociable course with an opening and closing party. The availability of University accommodation offsets the price of the course.

Course and costs *Corsi e costi*

The morning classes are for Italian language lessons in seven levels from complete beginners to advanced. For people doing intermediate Italian there is a seminar over the lunch break for analysing contemporary Italian literature. For those with a reasonable level of Italian, there are four afternoon classes each week in Italian culture. These classes include the history of Urbino, twentieth century Italy and Italian films. For those with a lower level of Italian, films are available using simpler language with an English introduction. At the weekends, there are trips to towns such as Spoleto, Assisi and Ravenna. Each Sunday there is a free guided walk of the city lasting two to three hours. The course costs €370 plus an €80 enrolment fee. Students must enrol at least two weeks before the start of the course. The University also offers a special course for tour operators.

Accommodation *Alloggio*

The University halls of residence have rooms with communal bathrooms and kitchens costing €160 for the duration of the course. This money must be added to the course fee in a single payment and sent with the enrolment form. This accommodation is a 20-minute walk from the town centre but there is a good bus service. There are also rooms available with families for between €200 and €300 per month.

Enrolment *Iscrizione*

The application form and the Italian test to decide the level of entrance on the course must arrive at the University at least two weeks before the start of the course. There is a maximum of 240 places. A photocopy of the payment for the fees and accommodation must be sent with the application form as well as a passport photo. Keep photocopies of all *documenti*. The letter of confirmation of acceptance on the course is needed at the start of the course.

When you arrive *Quando arrivi*

Accommodation is available from the Sunday before the course starts. Student ID cards (*tessera*) can be collected on the first Monday of the course, between 09.00 and 10.00, from the *Aula Magna* classroom in the Nuovo Magistero, Via Saffi 15. An acceptance letter and receipt of pre-payment is required. The *tessera* is used when entering the University buildings and the canteen (*mensa*), where meals cost €4. A welcome talk is given at 10.00 in the *Aula Magna* and the class programmes given out.

Belforte all'Isauro

Belforte all'Isauro is a tiny village of 700 inhabitants. It is in an isolated spot among the hills of Le Marche, close to the border with Tuscany. There are a couple of bars, a small supermarket, a few houses and nothing else.

Carmelo Maneta (also runs the school in Spoleto, see page 236)

Centro 'Giacomo Leopardi'
Via Castello 61020
Belforte all'Isauro (PS)
Tel: (0722) 726000 Fax: (0722) 726010
Email centroleopardi@wnt.it Website www.italian.org

This is possibly the only language school in Italy located in a castle. Belforte castle was built in the Middle Ages on the site of an ancient Lombard fort. It was restored in 1994 and is used as an Italian language and cultural centre. The castle is tall and narrow and sits at the top of the village, commanding impressive views across Le Marche. It lacks battle fortifications and looks more like an ancient manor house sturdily built to deter enemies rather than to fight them.

The school offers a package that includes the language course, accommodation and all excursions. Classes and accommodation are all within the castle, rather like a small house party. The classrooms are plainly decorated rooms with wood beam ceilings and metre-thick walls. The maximum class size is five but the courses run even when only one student is enrolled. Scholarships are available by applying to the director Carmelo Maneta (who also runs the school in Spoleto, page 236).

Courses and costs *Corsi e costi*

The **language course** consists of four hours teaching a day (20 hours a week) and costs €600 for two weeks and €900 for four weeks. This includes basic accommodation in the castle in a room shared with up to four other students and an extensive afternoon and evening programme. There are guided visits to nearby towns such as San Marino, Assisi, Gubbio, Perugia, Florence and Venice, speciality food tastings, cooking lessons and walks. The school will try to organise trips and events based around the students' interests. **Individual classes** cost €15 per hour. **Optional courses** can be organised in other areas such as music, painting, ceramics, sculpture, cooking (in a local restaurant) and fashion. These are priced depending on demand. Lunch and dinner are optional and cost €80 per week. There is no enrolment fee.

Accommodation *Alloggio*

The **standard** accommodation included in the package is basic. These rooms are within the castle and each sleeps four people with a private bathroom. **Single rooms** are available at a supplement of €10 a night. **Mini-apartments** are also available at a supplement of €20 a night. The apartments are separate from the main building and are dark and cramped. They have tiny kitchens with two electric hobs (no oven) and a mini bathroom.

Abruzzo

Abruzzo became a region distinct from Molise in 1963. It lies at the border between central and southern Italy and offers both spectacular mountains and pretty beach resorts. It is known as the 'region of parks' as almost a third of its territory is protected by three National Parks. These boast a variety of landscapes including the highest Apennine range contained entirely within Italy's borders, Monte Gran Sasso d'Italia and Caldernoe, which is Europe's most southern glacier. The protected southern stretch of rocky coast is famous for its *trabocchi*, ancient wooden fishing platforms. The wildlife and flowers are as impressive as the landscape. The parks have a number of rare animals including Marsica brown bears, Apennine wolves, golden eagles and otters. In spring it is covered in wild flowers and in autumn the colours are equally stunning. There are opportunities for skiing, trekking, mountain biking and exploring the coast. Nearby, Pescara has regular ferries to the Croatian islands for weekends away. A car would be useful as public transport is limited.

Highlights of Abruzzo *Da non perdere dell' Abruzzo*

◗ magnificent walks in the National Parks

◗ easy access to Rome

◗ wildlife and wild flowers

◗ southern Abruzzo coast with the *trabocchi* fishing platforms

◗ relatively unexplored by the English and Americans

◗ the town of L'Aquila and its Fontana delle 99 Cannelle (1292).

Lanciano

Lanciano is an ancient town near the Adriatic coast, in easy reach of the Abruzzo National Park. Although its outskirts are uninspiring, it has a pretty historic centre, which is easy to explore on foot. There are several beautiful churches including the thirteenth century Santa Maria Maggiore and the Duomo with its prominent bell tower. The town also hosts an annual international music festival.

Athena

International School of Italian Language
Via Luigi de Crecchio 45
66034 Lanciano (Chieti)

Tel: (0872) 42651 or (0872) 619074 Fax: (0872) 619615
Email info@athena-it.com Website www.athena-it.com
This small language school is on a main road five minutes walk from the
old centre of the town. It occupies the quiet back rooms of the third floor
and is decorated in a modern Italian style. Both classrooms have large
windows with small balconies. There is a selection of books for loan but
no other facilities. Courses and accommodation are carefully tailored to
the individual. The class size is limited to a maximum of eight students.

Courses and costs *Corsi e costi*

The **standard** language course has three hours of teaching a day (15 hours
a week) and costs €280 for two weeks and €480 for a month. The **enrolment** fee is €90 and does not include the accommodation booking service.
The course includes a guided tour of Lanciano and a musical evening with
'Italian friends'. The school can arrange individual courses for families
and **children** on request. **Individual** lessons cost €25 per hour.

Accommodation *Alloggi*

The school can arrange accommodation in Lanciano or in one of the
nearby hill towns on the coast which have good public transport with the
town. There is a fee of €20 for the service. A room in a shared apartment
costs €150–200 per week. A private mini apartment for two people costs
€800 per month.

Campania

Campania has more contrasts than any other region in Italy. One day may
be spent in the frenetic nucleus of Naples and the next sailing up on a
chairlift, in the silence and sea breezes to the top of Capri. The following
day may be on the dramatic Amalfi coast among sky, sea and rock and the
next visiting archaeological sights in Pompeii and Paestrum. The quiet
fishing villages further south feel like another world. The inland areas
remain remote and unvisited. Everywhere, however, you eat like a king:
sweet buffalo mozzarella bought straight from the dairy, soft wood-
smoked pizza from thick Neapolitan (*Napoletano*) ovens and super ripe
sun dried tomatoes from San Marzano. Nowhere else can you have five

different holidays in the space of two weeks. Our top choice of school is in Naples but there is also a school in Sorrento.

Highlights of Campania *Da non perdere della Campania*

◗ walking among earth, sky and rock on the Almalfi coast

◗ a night at the opera: Teatro di San Carlo in Naples is the oldest and biggest opera house in Italy

◗ pizza on the Parthenopean waterfront while the sun sets over Capri

◗ the archaeological frenzy of Pompeii, Herculaneum and the Temples of Paestum

◗ the Neapolitan *brasiliano*, a small sweet cocoa-topped cappuccino in a glass

◗ a weekend at the seaside in the village of Santa Maria Castellabate

◗ sipping *limoncello* among the citrus groves of the Sorrento peninsular

◗ the 'heroically cultivated' wines of Coata, especially from around Fuore

◗ buffalo milk ice cream from mozzarella farms in the south

◗ a trip to Anacapri to see the remarkable villa and gardens of San Michele

◗ a boat trip to Positano, the prettiest village on the Almalfi coast

◗ the garden of La Mortella at William Walton's house on the Island of Ischia.

Opening hours of the archeological sites *Orario d'apertura dei siti archeologici*

◗ **Pompeii** open daily 08.30–19.30 entrance fee €10

◗ **Paestum** open in winter 09.00–16.00 summer 09.00–19.30 entrance fee €6.50

◗ **Herculaneum** open daily 08.30–19.30 entrance fee €10.

Summary table of language schools in Campania *Tavola: sommario delle scuole di lingua*

School	Centro Italiano	Sorrento Lingue
Town	Naples	Sorrento
Two-week course	€270	€381
Four-week course	€485	€738
Individual lesson	€26	€30
Single room two weeks	€235	€400
Single room four weeks	€350	€800
Enrolment fee	None	€52
Maximum group	12	12
Air conditioning	No	Yes
Laboratory	No	No
Discounts	No	No
Scholarships	No	Yes

Naples *Napoli*

The Bay of Naples dotted with small islands is one of the most spectacular sites in the world. Naples rises up out of this bay with the active Mount Vesuvius close behind. It is 220 km south of Rome and has a dense population of over a million people, most of whom appear to be crammed into the Spanish Quarter. The city is built on a hill with the elegant Parthenopean waterfront lined with bars and pizzerias. According to UNESCO the centre, a short climb up from the sea, is one of the most architecturally varied in the world. Its large stone-paved Piazza Plebiscito houses the oldest and largest opera house in Italy, *Teatro San Carlo*. Most of the major designers have shops in Piazza Martiri and some of the best coffee anywhere in Italy can be found around the giant nineteenth century glass and steel shopping arcade. The central areas are easy to explore on foot and there is a funicular service that climbs the steepest of the hills.

Opera in Naples

Teatro di San Carlo
Box Office Via San Carlo 98f
Tel: (0039) 081 7972331 Fax: (0039) 081 400902

Email biglietteria@teatrosancarlo.it Website www.teatrosancarlo.it
Naples' opera house, Teatro di San Carlo (1737), is the oldest and biggest
in Italy. The opera season runs annually from February to November and
the cheapest ticket are €30. There are tours of the house in English or
Italian from Monday to Friday at 11.00.

Centro Italiano

Vico S. Maria dell'Aiuto 17
Napoli 80134
Tel: (081) 5524331 Fax: (081) 5523023
Email info@centroitaliano.it Website www.centroitaliano.it
This delightful school has the dual advantage of being good value and
well run. Like many places in Naples it is quite hard to find. It is in the
centre of the old city near the main port and the University. From Via
Montoliveto, turn into S. Maria La Nova and pass through a small square
which has a number 17 boarded up. Continue straight ahead into Vico S.
Maria dell'Aiuto. Number 17 is on your right and is easily recognised by
its large wooden arched door with a small entrance door within it (mind
your head!).

The school is painted in pastel shades and is decorated with photographs
of Naples. The classrooms are smart and there is Internet access. The maximum group size is 12.

Courses and costs *Corsi e costi*

There are courses from one week to three months or longer. The **standard**
course of four hours teaching a day (20 hours a week) costs €270 for two
weeks and €485 for four weeks. The price includes a guided tour of Naples
and its surroundings, a weekly Italian film and a fortnightly two-hour
seminar in Italian culture. Topics covered include Italian and Neapolitan
music, Italian cinema, Neapolitan theatre, regions of Italy, and the history
and traditions of Naples. There are **less intensive** 14-week courses from
November to February and from March to June. These consist of two
hours teaching three times a week and the same extra lessons in Italian
culture as in the standard course. The course costs €500 for 14 weeks.

The school runs two one-month courses in **Commercial Italian** (dates vary) which consist of two hours of teaching three times a week and cost €180. Topics covered include finance, tourism, business and commercial correspondence. Personalised **total immersion** courses are available for one or two students together. These courses have eight hours of lessons per day (40 hours per week) including lunch with a teacher. They cost €900 per week. **Individual lessons** cost €26 per hour or €42 for two hours. These can be arranged in the student's own home, in towns on the coast or on the Islands. The school will even book the student's hotel room. There are CILS **exam** preparation courses available on request.

The **colours and flavours of Naples** is a one-week course of language, practical cookery and Italian culture. This course is held in the afternoons and evenings and can be combined with a standard language course. It includes two practical cooking classes, one dinner in a local restaurant, three guided walks, a lecture on the tradition of the Neapolitan crib and a Saturday excursion. The course costs €300. There are other courses run by the school when more than four students request them. These include Italian cookery, Italian wine, artistic ceramics, the Neapolitan crib, nine-teenth century Italian literature, creative writing and archaeology. There is no extra enrolment fee.

Accommodation *Alloggio*
A single room in a shared apartment costs €235 for two weeks or €350 for four weeks.

Sorrento

Sorrento is a central port for boats to the Islands and the towns along the Almalfi coast and beyond. It is within easy reach of Pompeii, the temples of Paestum and Naples. The old town has winding streets, good food shops and a pretty marina. Despite the fact that there are more English voices and blue rinses than Blackpool, it is possible to find a bar where Italians drink their coffee. The town has a population of 20,000 and more than half as many hotel beds.

Sorrento Lingue

Via S. Francesco 8
Sorrento 80067 (Napoli)
Tel: (081) 807 5599 Fax: (081) 532 4140
Email administration@sorrentolingue.it Website www.sorrentolingue.it

This school is on the second floor of a rather run-down sixteenth century palazzo and is very expensive for the facilities on offer. There is no *laboratorio linguistico* or library. There is a roof terrace, however, with views over the town. Class sizes are limited to 12 and the school offers some extracurricular activities. The school has a number of affiliations with University courses and an internship programme. The school also has courses in English, German or French, making it easier to meet other Italians. Scholarships are available through the Italian Cultural Institutes (see page 13).

Courses and costs *Corsi e costi*
The **standard** course of four hours a day (20 hours per week) costs €381 for two weeks and €738 for four weeks. The **internship programme** allows students to continue learning Italian in a business environment. Internships can be in hotels, travel agencies, tour operators, gastronomy, teaching, arts and retail. The cost of **individual lessons** is €30 per hour. There is an enrolment fee of €52 which is valid for a year.

Accommodation *Alloggio*
Accommodation can be arranged in shared or private apartments, with Italian families or in local hotels. A single room in a shared apartment costs €400 for two weeks and €800 for four weeks.

Puglia

Puglia, the heel of southern Italy, has some of the most beautiful towns and architecture in Italy. Lecce is the most pure Baroque town in Italy (see page 169), Castel del Monte is one of the country's most beautiful castles and the Itria Valley is dotted with pretty *trulli*. The National Park of the Gargano has dense forests and mountains, as well as some of the region's best beaches, and opportunities for trekking and mountain biking. The rest of the region is famous for its food, wine, olive oil and long stretches of coast. Despite all of this it is less visited by the British than other parts of Italy and apart from July and August it is cheaper to live here than in the north. We have chosen schools in Lecce (page 175), Cisternino (page 252) and Otranto (page 253). Lecce is covered in a separate chapter as it has a University for Foreigners.

Highlights of Puglia *Da non perdere della Puglia*

▶ Lecce, the most pure Baroque town in Italy

▶ the *trulli* towns of the Itria valley

▶ Frederick II's *Castel del Monte*, the most beautiful castle in Italy

▶ the frenzied energy of Puglia's Pizzicato music and dance

▶ vineyard hopping through Puglian towns with names such a *Squinzano* and *Copertino*

▶ the Gargano National Park's magnificent Umbra Forest, mountains and beaches

▶ the hill town of Monte S. Angelo with an altitude of 843m.

▶ *orecchiette con cime di rape*, concave ears of pasta with beetroot tops, served with slow-cooked anchovies in olive oil.

▶ Otranto's Duomo with its huge mosaic floor depicting the Tree of Life.

Summary table of the language schools in Puglia *Tavola: sommario delle scuole di lingua*

School	University Of Lecce	Scuola D'Italiano	Porta d'Oriente	Centro Studi Hodegitria
Town	Lecce	Lecce	Otranto	Cisternino
Two weeks	€200	€300–450	€310	€240
Four weeks	€400	€600–700	€620	€480
Individual	€21	€25	€31	€24
Single room for two weeks	–	€110	€270+€26 for cleaning	€280
Single room for four weeks	€90 in halls of residence	€210	€537+€26	€560 for cleaning
Enrolment fee	None	None	€70	€16
Maximum group size	12	10	10	7
Air conditioning	Yes	No	Yes	No
Laboratory	Yes	No	Computers only	No
Discounts	No	No	5% after four weeks	Yes 10% after four weeks
Scholarship	Yes	No	Yes	Yes

Cisternino and the Trulli country

This small hill town is 400m above sea level midway between Lecce and Bari in the Valley of Itria. The old part of the town has narrow winding streets and attractive whitewashed houses. It has a population of 12,000 and is within easy reach of the beaches along the Adriatic Coast. The area is famous for its thousands of *trulli*. These ancient round houses have a characteristic shape similar to a whitewashed dovecot with a ball on top, not unlike an Alessi coffee pot. The biggest concentration of these buildings is in the nearby town of Alberobello, now a UNESCO World Heritage Site. They are mostly used by farmers but are also available for self-catering accommodation all over the area. There is even a *trullo* hotel.

Centro Studi Hodegitria

c/o via Vasco de Gama 6
72014 Cisternino (Br)
Puglia
Tel/Fax: (0039) 0804446110
Information by telephone Wednesdays and Thursdays between 16.00 and 18.30
Email hodegitria@bigfoot.com
Website http://utentilycos.it/hodegitria (If problems, run a Google search under Hodegitria)

This tiny school is housed in a small, modern, garage-like room in a residential area five minutes walk from the town centre. This room serves as a classroom and office. There are no other facilities.

Courses and costs *Corsi e costi*
The courses can be tailored to students' interests. The group size is small with a maximum of seven students. The **standard** course consists of three hours teaching a day (15 hours per week) and costs €240 for two weeks and €480 for four. **Individual** lessons cost €24 per hour or €130 for a course of ten. The school also runs cookery and art courses. At the end of each day on the cookery course students eat whatever they have cooked. There is an enrolment fee of €16. Scholarships are available on request from the school.

Accommodation *Alloggio*
It is possible to stay with a family, in an independent apartment or in a *trullo*. A single room in an apartment or with a family costs €140 per week. A *trullo* costs €160 per week. The town has many apartments to rent directly from the owners, which cost much less than booking through the language school.

Otranto

Otranto is a small medieval seaside town 40km southeast of Lecce. It is the most eastern town in Italy and has a population of 5,000. Before the Turkish invasion in 1480 it was one of the biggest and most important ports on the Salento peninsular. There is little evidence of that now except in its tiny historic centre. This has winding narrow streets and white-washed houses surrounding an eleventh century Duomo. The Duomo, which is the largest church in Puglia, has a beautiful three-nave interior with a huge mosaic floor depicting the Tree of Life. It also houses the bones (ossi) of the 800 Christian martyrs, slaughtered by the Turks when they refused to renounce their Christianity. The martyrs are remembered during a festival the *Festa dei Martiri d'Otranto* which is celebrated between 13–15 August. The town overlooks the pretty harbour and the sparkling waters of the Adriatic. The town is swamped by Italian holidaymakers in July and August and prices rise.

Scuola Porta D' Oriente

Corso Garibaldi 28
Otranto 73028
Tel/Fax: (0836) 801 964 or 3384562722
Email porta.doriente@libero.it Website www.porta-doriente.com
This small school is on a narrow, stone paved street, in the heart of the old town. It is 20m from the sea but faces inland without any views. From the front door there is a narrow staircase leading up to the school. Classrooms are air-conditioned and there is a small room with a computer and a selection of books for loan. The price of the courses includes a tour of the town, a guided visit to an underground Byzantine church and Italian video showings. There are also boat trips with fishermen, folk dancing classes, organised hikes and opportunities to work with local archaeologists. These are organised and charged for separately. Groups have a maximum of ten students.

Courses and costs *Corsi e costi*
The **standard** course of four hours a day (20 hours a week) costs €310 for two weeks and €620 for four weeks. These prices are high considering the facilities available. The **intensive-plus** course has five or six hours of lessons per day, consisting of the same lessons as the intensive course but with the addition of either one individual lesson per day or two extra lessons in a group per day. Also included are afternoon cultural classes in art, history, folklore, current affairs and politics. The intensive-plus course costs €660 for two weeks and €1,220 for four weeks.

There are a range of **specialist** one-week courses focusing on Italian art and architecture, literature, medicine, science or business. These courses consist of 20 hours of teaching (four hours a day) and cost €240. They can also be combined with the intensive or intensive-plus courses. The school runs an Italian language and culture course that consists of two hours of grammar and conversation and two hours of lessons on cinema, theatre, gastronomy, songs and fashion. These cost €350 for two weeks or €650 for four weeks. **Individual** lessons can be arranged to suit the student's timetable and interests and cost €31 per hour.

There is a one-week course for preparing for the CILS exams of the University of Siena (see page 69). This consists of 20 hours of teaching and costs €950 for the week!

The Italian cooking course is both practical and theoretical and takes place in the separate state-run cooking school of Otranto. The course is two days per week and costs €105 per week. After the class students have a lunch with the teachers and eat whatever they have cooked. The course is not available in the months of July, August and the first two weeks of September when the cooking school is closed. The school also runs a course for **children** costing €240 per week. There is a €70 **enrolment** fee which remains valid for one year.

Accommodation *Alloggio*

A single room in a shared apartment costs €270 for two weeks or €465 for four weeks. There is a €26 fee for final cleaning at the end of the stay. Prices include electricity and gas but heating and towels are extra. In July and August there is a surcharge of €70 and in September one of €20 per person per week.

To stay with a family costs €435 for two weeks or €870 for four weeks' half-board.

Calabria

Calabria forms the 'toe' of Italy next to the Straits of Messina and Sicily in its south and Campania and Basilica in its North. In the past it has been overshadowed by poverty and crime but now has much to offer the more independent traveller. There are two of Italy's most spectacular National Parks, the Aspromonte and the Sila Massif, providing opportunities for trekking, mountain biking and cross-country skiing. The pretty towns of Scilla and Tropea have the winning combination of white sand and turquoise sea and two of Italy's finest beaches. The region's food specialities include stuffed fresh anchovies (*alici ripiene*) and buckets of fish, citrus fruits and figs. We have listed language schools in Reggio di Calabria (covered in Chapter 8, page 154) and Tropea (page 256).

Highlights of Calabria *Da non perdere della Calabria*

▶ the wild and beautiful National Parks of Aspromonte and Sila Mastive

▶ cross-country skiing on the Sila Massif

▶ the seaside *passeggiata* in Reggio di Calabria which overlooks *Sicilia*

▶ white sandy beaches and turquoise waters in Scilla and Tropea

▶ the bargain University for Foreigners in Reggio di Calabria

▶ fish feasts and red onion (*cipolla rossa*) extravaganzas in Tropea.

Summary table of language schools in Calabria Tavola: *sommario delle scuole di lingua*

School	Università per Stranieri	Caffè Italiano Club
Town	Reggio di Calabria	Tropea
Two-week course	–	€345
Four-week course	€105	€650
Individual lesson	–	€32
Single room two weeks	–	€275
Single room four weeks	€195	€495
Enrolment fee	€52	€100
Maximum group	15	6
Air conditioning	No	No
Laboratory	Computers only	No
Discounts	No	Yes
Scholarships	Yes, apply directly	Yes, from Italian Cultural Institutes

Tropea

Tropea is a small medieval seaside town with a population of 7,000. It is an ideal place for beach lovers. It sits on a 42 metre high rock which commands views down to the long sandy beach and clear blue waters. The streets leading down to the sea are packed with cafés and pizza restaurants. There are numerous sports available including horse riding, diving, mountain biking, sailing, surfing, tennis, trekking and volleyball. Despite the Italian and German tourists, the small centre maintains its old charm with its narrow winding streets and secluded piazzas. On every corner there are shops selling bunches of the famous Tropean red onions (*cipolle rosse di Tropea*), pots of stuffed peppers (*peperoni ripiene*) and sun dried tomatoes. The town is not far from the Aspromonte National Park for superb trekking, walking and wildlife.

Caffè Italiano Club

Largo Antonio Pandullo 5
89861 Tropea
Tel/Fax: (0963) 603284
Website www.caffeitalianoclub.net
This well marketed school is located in an attractive house in a small shady courtyard in the heart of Tropea. There are creepers growing up the front wall and small terraces for outside teaching. There is a small computer room on the ground floor with Internet access and CD-ROMS for studying after classes. Group size is a maximum of six students.

Courses and costs *Corsi e costi*
The **standard** course of four hours teaching per day (20 hours a week) costs €345 for two weeks and €650 for four weeks. There is an **intensive** course, which consists of the standard course plus two hours private tuition three times a week. This costs €690 for two weeks and €1,215 for four weeks. For students with some knowledge of Italian there is a **conversation class** of two hours teaching per day. The conversations are based around art, culture and politics. The course costs €233 for two weeks or €345 for four weeks. **Individual** lessons cost €320 for ten hours, **two-to-one lessons**, with two students and one teacher, cost €195 per person for

ten hours. The school can arrange a preparatory course for the CILS examinations of the University of Siena (see page 69) consisting of one hour of individual teaching after classes each day. There is a range of extracurricular activities including a welcome drink and video evening. The school has mountain bikes and a motorboat for hire.

There is a €100 **enrolment** fee which includes *either* transfer to and from the airport or train station *or* two excursions. It also includes a course text book, club card for discounts in the town, a welcome cocktail, guided tour of Tropea, a weekly documentary video about Calabria and an Italian film.

Accommodation *Alloggio*
Like many language schools the cost of accommodation is high if you book through the school. A single room in a shared apartment costs €190 per person for one week, €275 for two weeks or €495 for a month. Prices for a double room in a shared apartment start at €155 per person per week. An apartment for two people for a month would cost €1,040 which is double what it would cost to book locally (see below). There is also a surcharge of €40 per person per week for the month of July and €90 surcharge for August.

Other accommodation *Altri alloggi*
The TIC has information in English about reasonably priced rooms and apartments for rent. Students make the reservation directly with the owner of the accommodation.
Piazza Ercole Tel: (0963) 61 475
Open daily September to June 09.00–12.00 and 16.00–19.30
July daily 09.00–13.00 and 17.00–21.00 August daily 09.00–13.00 17.00–22.00

Hotel Terrazzo sul Mare
Via Croce
Tel/Fax: (0963) 61020
This hotel has rooms with private bathroom, balcony and sea view. A double room with breakfast costs €60 per night. There is a steep path down to the beach and a shady terrace with a bar.

Restaurants and bars *Ristoranti e bar*

Bar and Pasticceria Gelateria 'Il Gioiello'

Santa Domenica di Ridadi (near Tropea)

Tel: (0963) 669277

This family run *gelateria* and *pasticceria* is in the main square of Santa Domenica di Ridadi near Tropea. It is well worth the trip over there to sample one of their sweetmeats. The owner, Giuseppe Mazzitelli, is a master pastry maker. His chocolate éclairs are the best in Italy, and his son's handmade ice creams are exceptional. In the front of house, his wife and daughter are on hand to give expert assistance.

Osteria del Pescatore

Via del Monte 7

Tropea

Tel: (0963) 603 018/603477

This small family run osteria is the place to sample Calabria's food. The chef is the wife of the owner and from an old Tropean fishing family, hence the name of the Osteria. Their daily changing menus include *nduja*, an ultimate (*ottimo*) home made spreadable spicy salami, herb stuffed anchovies, pasta with seafood and fish which is *freschissimo*.

Sicily *Sicilia*

Sicily is the largest island in the Mediterranean, on which many writers and artists have been inspired. In Homer's novel *The Odyssey* Ulysses fought the Cyclops at Mount Etna. Goethe wrote 'without Sicily, Italy leaves no image in the soul: it is the key to everything.' It is on the crossroads between Africa and Europe and has a unique blend of cultures and landscape. There are some of the most important ruins of the ancient Greek world, diverse architectural styles, beautiful beaches, hiking and some of the best food markets in Italy.

Highlights of Sicily *Da non perdere della Sicilia*

▶ the magnificent Greek ruins

▶ Mount Etna (3,350m), Europe's largest and most active volcano

- the sea around Taormina and Siracusa

- Palermo's Vucciria daily food market

- Stromboli, a small volcanic island used in the film *The Postman* (Il Postino)

- *Midnight in Sicily* by Peter Robb, a superb book about the mafia and Italian food

- *The Leopard* by Giuseppe Tomasi di Lampedusa, Sicily's most famous novel.

Siracusa *Syracuse*

Syracusa is the most important classical Greek city outside Athens. The island of Ortigia was the self-contained centre of the ancient city, now jointed to the mainland by a bridge. Its beautiful churches, monuments and narrow café-lined streets make it one of the highlights of Sicily.

Mediterranean Centre for Arts and Sciences Palazzo Ardizzone

Via Roma 124
96100 Siracusa
Tel: (0931) 449262 Fax: (0931) 449259
Website www.studyabroad-sicily.com

This school is a mini American university offering a full spectrum of courses including Italian language courses. The majority of the students are 18–22 year old Americans. It has a beautiful location on the Island of Ortigia. The centre's palazzo is newly renovated with large light classrooms, a multimedia room with computers, audio and video facilities, a common room and a shady courtyard. The school is affiliated with the University of Catania's Architecture Department and students also have access to these facilities, providing an opportunity to meet other Italian students. The Centre has an organised welcome package where students are collected from the airport, taken to their accommodation and given a tour of the town. On the first night there is welcome dinner and students are given an information pack on Syracuse and its province. There is a full programme of extracurricular activities including guided visits to classical sites, archaeological digs and excursions to the trails of Homer's *Odyssey*.

Courses and costs *Corsi e costi.*

Italian language group courses run throughout the year when there are five students enrolled. The maximum group size is 15. The **standard** course of four hours teaching a day (20 hours per week) costs $265 for two weeks and $560 for four weeks. A **less intensive** course of two hours teaching a day (ten hours per week) costs $140 for two weeks or $280 for a month. The school can also arrange a more **intensive** course of six hours teaching a day (30 hours a week) which costs $210 for the first week and $190/week thereafter.

The price includes tuition, Fairfield University transcript, orientation, excursions, full-time student advisor, Italian health insurance and airport transport.

The core academic programme comprises the arts, sciences and humanities and is taught in English by university lecturers from around Europe and the US. These courses are aimed at American university students but are open to anyone.

Accommodation *Alloggio*

The school can arrange accommodation for students for a non-refundable fee of $100. A single room in a small apartment costs $500 to $600 per month and a shared room $400 to $500 per month. A returnable deposit is required of $300.

Taormina

Taormina, on the east coast of Sicily, is 250m above the sea on Mount Tauro. From its Greek theatre, cafés and bars, there are views of nearby Mount Etna and the sparkling waters of the Mazzarò beach. It is a pretty resort town and also boasts one of the best private language schools in Italy, Babilonia.

Babilonia Italian Language School

Centro di Lingua e Cultura Italiana
Via del Ginnasio 20
98039 Taormina
Sicilia
Tel: (0039) 094223441
Email info@babilonia.it Website www.babilonia.it

Although expensive, Babilonia sets the gold standard for private language schools. It is located in a meticulously renovated and beautifully designed palazzo near the public gardens in the heart of Taormina. The classrooms are simple, bright and well equipped. There is a stunning roof terrace with views down to the sea and across to Mount Etna. This is equipped with trendy chairs and tables under white shades and is attached to a library/coffee room with an Illy coffee machine and free Internet access. The owner and his team have thought about everything. There is also a well-organised series of excursions, extra curricular activities and cultural courses.

Courses and costs *Corsi e costi*
A **standard** course of four hours teaching a day (20 hours a week) costs €370 for two weeks and €721 for four. The **standard plus** course includes one hour of individual lessons per day and costs €700 for two weeks or €1,365 for four. The **intensive** course consists of six hours teaching a day (30 hours a week) and costs €680 for two weeks or €1,326 for four. There is a **less intensive** course consisting of two hours teaching a day and costing €230 for two weeks and €448 for four weeks. **Individual** lessons cost €35 per hour and two-to-one lessons cost €27.50 per hour per person. **Non-language courses** including cooking, arts and crafts, adventure sports, hiking and golf can be combined with any of the above courses. There is a €50 **enrolment** fee.

Accommodation *Alloggio*
The school will arrange accommodation in the centre of Taoromina. A single room in a shared apartment costs €126 per week. All of the properties are regularly checked to make sure they are up to standard.

Sardinia *Sardegna*

Sardinia is a different place to study with beautiful beaches, stunning mountains, food, wine and prehistoric *nuraghe*. It is the second largest island in the Mediterranean and sits far out to the west of the mainland, below Corsica. Unlike Sicily, it feels like an island cut off from Italy. People speak the *'sardo'* dialect as well as Italian and often wear the traditional dress. The Barbagia (Barbarian) region in the interior remains an untouched wilderness of mountains, populated by shepherds, goats and cheese makers. Many of the rural villages are frozen in time, isolated by the landscape. The coastline has been changed by the outside world but the waters and beaches are still among the finest in Italy and renowned for their emerald sparkle. The towns of Cagliari and Sassai are lively and interesting.

There are other factors to take into consideration when planning a trip here. Firstly a car is important for those wanting to explore the island as public transport is limited. Secondly the short tourist season (Easter until the end of October) leaves many facilities closed for much of the year. Finally, the language school we have listed is expensive for the facilities it offers.

Highlights of Sardinia *Da non perdere della Sardegna*

▶ trekking in the Barbagia with one of the many local guides to keep you on the path

▶ the emerald sea, beautiful beaches and scuba diving

▶ pony trekking

▶ the prehistoric *nuralghe*

▶ free and rock climbing around the limestone cliffs on the coast

▶ pecorino cheese at its pinnacle of perfection

▶ *pane carasau* bakers, making the famous thin crispy bread of the shepherds

▶ a late night pick-up of amaretto biscuits dipped into caramel coloured Mirto liquor.

Posada

Posada is a tiny hillside village on the eastern coast a mile from the beach. It is also within striking distance of the Barbagia area of mountains. The old town clings to the side of the hill and has just a handful of houses, a couple of bars and a hotel. Its narrow cobbled streets wind their way up to a twelfth century tower with views of the surrounding countryside. The modern new town lies below.

Sun Studies

Piazza Rockefeller
Posada (NU) 08020
Tel: (0362) 501 727
Email info@sunstudies.com Website www.sunstudies.com

This Milan-based company runs courses in Posada from May to September each year. The school is in an uninspiring, modern two-storey building on the main square in the new part of the town. In addition to the standard lessons, there are language courses combined with **diving** and **sailing**. The school is expensive with limited facilities but the group size is limited to a maximum of six students.

Courses and costs *Corsi e costi*
The **standard** course of four hours teaching a day (20 hours per week) costs €440 for two weeks or €880 for four weeks. The **language and diving** course consists of 20 hours of language lessons and three dives with a local Padi diving school each week. The **language and sailing** course includes a 20-hour sailing course in seven metre Nytec boats at a local club. Both of these cost €400 per week. The **language and cooking** course has 20 hours of language lessons and ten hours of practical cooking per week. The cookery classes are led by Bruno Murrighile, a local chef, and the course costs €520 per week. **Individual** classes cost €27 each when booked in a course of 20 hours. There is no enrolment fee.

Accommodation *Alloggio*
The cost of a single room in a shared apartment varies with the time of year. In July it costs €220 per week, in August €270 and from September to June the cost is €200 per week. It would be cheaper to book accommodation locally.

Glossary

At the market *Al mercato*

Dairy products *Latticini*

Butter *Burro*
Milk *Latte*
Parmesan cheese *Parmigiano*
Sheeps' milk cheese *Pecorino*

Fish *Pesce*

Amphibian with an ugly head used for making stock (*brodo*) *Coda di pescatrice*
Bass *Persico*
Calamari *Calamari*
Clams *Vongole*
Cuttlefish *Seppie*
Langoustines *Pannocchie*
Muscles *Cozze*
Prawns *Gamberi*
Sole *Sogliole*
Squid *Totani*
Trout *Trote*
Tuna *Tonno*
For other types of fish see page 180

Fruit *Frutta*

Apples *Mele*
Bananas *Banane*
Grapefruits *Pompelmi*
Grapes *Uva*
Oranges *Arance*

Pears *Pere*
Tangerines *Mandarini*

Groceries *Alimentari*

Coffee *Caffé*
Egg *Uova*
Flour *Farina*
Oil *Olio*
Sugar *Zucchero*
Tea *Tè*
Vinegar *Aceto*
Yeast *Lievito*

Herbs *Erbe aromatiche*

Basil *Basilico*
Bay *Alloro*
Chillies *Peperoncino/piccanti*
Oregano *Origano*
Parsley *Prezzemolo*
Sage *Salvia*
Tyme *Timo*

Household cleaning *Prodotti per la pulizia della casa*

Fabric softener *Ammorbidente*
Floor cleaner *Detersivo per pavimenti*
Hand soap *Sapone per le mani*
Rubber gloves *Guanti di gomma*
Soap powder for clothes washing machine *Sapone in polvere per lavatrice*
Soap powder for washing up machine *Sapone in polvere per lavastoviglie*
Washing up liquid *Detersivo liquido per stoviglie*
Washing up sponge *Spugna per piatti e stoviglie*

Meat *Carne*

Bacon *Pancetta*
Beaf *Manzo*
Chicken *Pollo*
Lamb *Agnello*
Pork cheek muscle *Barbozzo* for making *spaghetti alla carbonara*
Veal *Vitello*

Spices *Spezie*

Black pepper *Pepe nero*
Cinnamon *Cannella*
Cloves *Chiodi di garofano*
Ginger *Zenzero*
Nutmeg *Noce moscata*
Salt *Sale*

Terms *Termini*

A bag *Un sacchetto*
Gram *Grammo*
Kilo *Chilo*
Piece *Pezzo*
Slice *Fetta*

Toiletries *Articoli da toletta*

Dental floss *Filo interdentale*
Electric razor *Rasoio elettrico*
Moisturiser *Crema idratante*
Mouthwash *Colluttorio*
Razor *Rasoio*
Shaving brush *Pennello da barba*
Shaving cream *Crema da barba*
Shaving foam *Spuma da barba*

Sun protection cream *Crema solare protettiva*

Toothbrush *Spazzolino da denti*

Toothpaste *Dentifricio*

Tampons *Tamponi/Assorbenti*

Vegetables *Vedura*

Artichokes *Carciofi*

Aubergine *Melanzane*

Beetroot *Bieta / barbabietola*

Cabbage *Cavolo verza*

Cabbage with long leaves which is almost black *Cavolo nero*

Carrots *Carote*

Cauliflower *Cavolfiore*

Celery *Sedano* (*sellero a Perugia*)

Chicory *Radicchio*

Courgettes *Zucchini*

Cucumber *Cetrioli*

Fennel *Finnoccio*

Garlic *Aglio*

Looks like large, tough old celery but tastes like artichokes *Cardi/gobbi*!

Mixed salad *Misticanza*

Mushroom often bought dried *Porcini cep o boletus*

Onions *Cipolle*

Peppers *Peperoni*

Pumpkin *Zucca gialla*

Radishes *Ravanelli*

Tomatoes *Pomodori*

Turnips *Rape*

Turnips grown around Lake Tresimino *Rapi del lago*

At the Language School *Alla Scuola di Lingua*

Student identity card showing course and payment details *Tessera*

Documents eg passport, driving licence *Documenti*

At the Post Office *Alla Posta*

Padded envelope *Busta imbottita*
Postal order *Vaglia Postale*
Postcards *Cartoline*
Stamps for priority mail *Francobolli per posta prioritaria*
Writing paper *Carta da lettere*

Useful Books

Bringing Italy Home, Ursula Ferrigno (Mitchell Beazley, 2001). A seasonal guide to Italian cooking with interesting descriptions of ingredients and tempting photographs.

English Yellow Pages is an annual directory of English speaking professionals, businesses, organisations and services in Italy. It covers Rome, Florence, Milan, Naples, Genoa and Bologna. Email: eyp@isinet.it Website: www.mondo@b.it/eyp

Grandi Giardini Italiani, Judith Wade (Rizzoli Libri Illustrati, 2002). In Italian with pictures and addresses. Website: ww.grandigiardini.it. This beautiful coffee table book discusses and photographs some of Italy's best gardens.

Italian Bed and Breakfast, Touring Club Italiano (TCI) (editor) ISBN 8836529011. This annual publication, also available in Italian, lists bed and breakfasts in every region of Italy. The accommodation is usually good value (about €30 per person per night).

Italian for Adults, C. Duff (Hodder and Stoughton Educational, 1974). This is a small book that is easy and fun to work through.

Italian Wines, Gambero Rosso® Slow Food Editore. Italian or English. The ultimate annual wine guide to Italy. Leave the rest at home.

Let's Go Italy (Macmillan). Published annually. This is one of the best up-to-date comprehensive guides to Italy.

Osterie D'Italia, Slow Food Editore. In Italian. This annual publication is a must for anyone interested in eating well in Italy. It covers every region, listing slow food *osteria* for delicious seasonal, regional cooking. It is useful even if you don't speak Italian. It can be ordered from the slow food website: www.slowfood.com

The *Food of Italy*, Sophie Braimbridge et al (Murdoch Books, 2000). A big, brilliant guide to Italian food with superb recipes and excellent food photography.

Umbria, Ian Campbell Ross (Penguin, 1996). An interesting, comprehensive guide to Umbria's history, architecture and landscape.

Walking and Eating in Tuscany and Umbria, James Lasdun and Pia Davis (Penguin, 1997). This is one of the best walking guides to Italy and a great way to plan interesting weekends away.

World Food Italy, Matthew Evans, Gabriella Cossi, Peter D'Onghia (Lonely Planet, 2000). A superb little guide to the food of Italy, covering regional specialities, highlights and recipes with wonderful photos.

Index
Indice

If you want to know how...

■ To buy a home in the sun, and let it out

■ To move overseas, and work well with the people who live there

■ To get the job you want, in the career you like

■ To plan a wedding, and make the Best Man's speech

■ To build your own home, or manage a conversion

■ To buy and sell houses, and make money from doing so

■ To gain new skills and learning, at a later time in life

■ To empower yourself, and improve your lifestyle

■ To start your own business, and run it profitably

■ To prepare for your retirement, and generate a pension

■ To improve your English, or write a PhD

■ To be a more effective manager, and a good communicator

■ To write a book and get it published

If you want to know how to do all these things and much, much more...

howtobooks

Practical books that inspire

If you want to know how ... to learn another language

"Gill James has published several collections of teaching materials, which emphasise the students' control of their own language learning. In the course of offering private tuition she discovered ways, outlined in her book, of making the learning of language easier.

"If only I had known all this sooner! When I first started on my own language learning for instance, or when I first started teaching others. We would have attained our goals more rapidly. I hope this book will offer you a short cut."

Gill James

The Complete Guide to Learning a Language
How to learn a language with the least amount of difficulty and the most amount of fun
Gill James

"Language expert James injects the learning process with a mega-dose of fun, giving us this book filled with tips and tactics to pluck up our courage and get us mingling with the natives in no time at all." – *The Good Book Guide*

ISBN 1 85703 903 3

If you want to know how ... to go and live in Italy

"The Italian lifestyle, the wealth of culture and the excellent food attract more people every year, whether it is to start a new life or to take an extended holiday. Those travelling with children will appreciate just how much the Italians love *bambini*, while any foreigner is generally made to feel welcome as Italians are immensely proud of their country and enjoy sharing it with visitors. *Going to Live in Italy* aims to help visitors experience the real Italy and is ideal for those who want to venture off the beaten track and do things the Italian way. Good luck!"

Amanda Hinton

Going to Live in Italy
Your practical guide to life and work in Italy
Amanda Hinton

"This is a guide to all aspects of doing business, studying, living and working in Italy. It is packed with information such as what documents you need, what to take and how to get there. It also explains how the health, welfare and education systems work." – *Daily Mirror*

ISBN 1 85703 855 X

If you want to know how ... to buy a property in Italy

"Buying a property in Italy is neither more nor less difficult than in the UK, but the system is different, and therefore it is best to be well informed before making any decisions. At the same time as adjusting to a new system, you will also be changing your lifestyle. You will find that the better informed you are the easier it will be. This book prepares you for setting up home in Italy, I hope you will find [it] a useful reference guide, both before you leave and after you arrive in Italy." *Auguri!*

Amanda Hinton

Buying a Property in Italy
An insider guide to finding a home in the sun
Amanda Hinton

"An up-to-date and expert guide, from someone who has done it herself, taking you through the whole process of setting up home in Italy." – *Sunday Telegraph*

ISBN 1 85703 891 6

If you want to know how ... to plan your gap year

"The world, and the world of travel, is changing continually. While travellers should be aware of the impact of recent events, it is important for people to continue to seek out new experiences and different cultures and ways of life. Achieving a better understanding of communities around the world is an important way for everyone to break down barriers and misconceptions. *Planning Your Gap Year* covers the areas of travel, work, and study and it also includes information about how the internet can be used to great advantage when you are planning your gap year."

Nick Vandome

Planning Your Gap Year
Hundreds of opportunities for employment, study, volunteer work and independent travel
Nick Vandome

"A magnificent reference tool...it's strength is its honesty - it strives to unravel the pros and the cons and it dispels the myth of the open road." – *The Guardian*

"Practical advice on planning, how to utilise the internet for preparation and details of more than 220 organisations worldwide." – *Evening Standard*

"Should be required reading... unlike most reference books this one should be read right through." – *SLJ*

ISBN 1 85703 879

How To Books are available through all good bookshops, or you can order direct from us through Grantham Book Services.

Tel: +44 (0)1476 541080
Fax: +44 (0)1476 541061
Email: orders@gbs.tbs-ltd.co.uk

Or via our website

www.howtobooks.co.uk

To order via any of these methods please quote the title(s) of the book(s) and your credit card number together with its expiry date.

For further information about our books and catalogue, please contact:

How To Books
3 Newtec Place
Magdalen Road
Oxford OX4 1RE

Visit our web site at

www.howtobooks.co.uk

Or you can contact us by email at info@howtobooks.co.uk